Betty Crocker

CHRISTMAS
COOKBOOK

WILEY

Wiley Publishing, Inc.

LIBRARY OF CONGRESS CATALOGING-IN-PUBLICATION DATA IS AVALIABLE UPON REQUEST

ISBN 978-0-470-87403-5

MANUFACTURED IN THE UNITED STATES OF AMERICA

10 9 8 7 6 5 4 3

Second Edition

General Mills

Director, Book and Online Publishing: Kim Walter
Manager, Cookbook Publishing: Lois Tlusty
Editor: Lori Fox
Recipe Development and Testing: Betty Crocker Kitchens
Photography: General Mills Photography Studios and Image Library
Photographer: Val Bourassa
Food Stylists: Carol Grones and Amy Peterson
Craft Stylist: Janice R. Matter

Wiley Publishing, Inc.

Publisher: Natalie Chapman
Executive Editor: Anne Ficklen
Editor: Kristi Hart
Production Editor: Ava Wilder
Cover Design: Suzanne Sunwoo
Photography Art Direction: Janet Skalicky
Photo Lab: Clint Lahnen
Manufacturing Manager: Kevin Watt

Interior Design and Layout: Vertigo Design, NYC

The Betty Crocker Kitchens seal guarantees success in your kitchen. Every recipe has been tested in America's Most Trusted Kitchens™ to meet our high standards of reliability, easy preparation and great taste.

FIND MORE GREAT IDEAS AND SHOP
FOR NAME-BRAND HOUSEWARES AT

BettyCrocker.com

Dear Friends,

Christmas is a memory-filled, festive time of year and often very hectic! The decorations, the shopping, the get-togethers and special events can make planning and doing everything seem just a bit stressful and not as joyful as you would like these special moments to be.

Let Betty Crocker grant your Christmas wish for a smoother holiday season. Set the scene for success with Betty's holiday survival tips and countdown calendar and find inspiration in the delicious recipes and heartwarming ideas so you can glide through the season like Santa's sleigh.

So, let this book help you give yourself the best present ever—a very Merry Christmas! And remember, the best gift of the season is a smile.

Warmly,

Betty Crocker

contents

249

17

137

holiday survival guide

The holidays are a season of great expectation, filled with family, friends and fun. Along with the fun, we tend to have lots of things to do, like shopping, socializing, decorating, baking and cooking. It can seem there are more things to do than time to do them! We all tend to recycle our habits, even those causing stress. Think of this as a final postscript: Nobody ever says they wished to have spent more time at the office, cleaning house or cooking from dawn to dusk. At how many holidays did you finally sit down for dinner and realize, "Hey, I didn't really get to talk to anyone and I'm exhausted!" So, change direction—stepping away from stress creators and stepping toward stress busters is easier than you think! Here are some suggestions:

- Look for the good in situations. If you've always hated loading the dishwasher or washing dishes, think of it as a relaxing time for yourself (because most likely everyone else left the kitchen to avoid getting stuck with the job!). Now you can stretch that valuable "time-out" as long as you'd like!

- If everyone will be in the family room and dining room, let go of cleaning every room. It's good enough as is; the house doesn't have to pass the perfectly clean, "white glove" inspection.

- Didn't deck the house from stem to stern with holiday decorations? Nobody is checking, and no one will even notice. Instead, concentrate on the areas that give you joy, those that will delight you day and night. Oh, and then there is the food. Ask people to bring something to share, like an appetizer, bread, salad or dessert—or all of these!

- Instead of wrapping all your gifts, use holiday gift bags and colorful tissue paper. The neat thing is that the recipient can reuse the gift bag.

- For the foods you're providing, mix it up between homemade and store-bought or restaurant favorites. Folks care about the effort overall and being together, not whether your rolls or pies were made from scratch.

- Have a cookie exchange with six or eight friends or family members. That way, you need to bake only one kind of cookie but you'll end up with up six to eight different kinds to store and serve!

So let go a little, relax, enjoy, revel in the day and feel the stress slip away. Above all, remember that the best holiday gifts are your presence and a smile!

holiday countdown calendar

The secret to a memorable, relaxed and enjoyable holiday season is to break up what seem to be overwhelming projects into smaller doable tasks. This calendar will help you get started.

The Best Holiday Gift Is a Smile

1 Get into a positive state of mind for the upcoming season. Feel comfortable saying no. Enjoy the moments of life!

2 Make a list of what you need for the holidays: gifts, cards, groceries for your menus, etc.

3 Put up the tree and decorate it while playing holiday music or a favorite holiday movie.

4 Mail gifts and cards now to guarantee arrival by the 25th. Hint, the post office isn't as busy now—shorter lines!

5 Start decorating the house—a bit here, a bit there, instead of at once. Or have a party and let everyone pitch in. Order pizza or Chinese take-out, so it's stress-free.

6

7 Volunteer! Introduce kids to the warm, fuzzy feeling of giving to others. Even simple gestures count, like shoveling snow from a neighbor's driveway or inviting someone spending the holidays alone to your home for dinner.

8 Create a holiday goodies day for baking cookies and making candies and such. Play music; make it fun!

9

10 Clear space in the freezer for make-ahead foods and sweet treats. Have plenty of containers with lids on hand.

11

12 Create an area in the home as the "gift-wrapping station," complete with gift wrap and bags, scissors, tape, ribbon and name tags, and scope out those great hiding places!

13 For more great ideas, visit BettyCrocker.com

14 Host a "tour of Christmas lights" party. Hire a bus or limousine or just form a caravan to enjoy the outdoor lights. Afterwards, have everyone over for dessert, milk and coffee.

15

16 Happy Hanukkah! Remember your Jewish friends and family today.

17

18 Plan a "my family" day or night of activities.

19

20 Set the table and get out all of the serving pieces you will be using—one less thing to worry about the night before or the day of Christmas Eve or Christmas Day.

21 If you bought a frozen turkey, put it in the fridge (in a baking pan with sides so it doesn't leak) to thaw safely and completely. Birds over 20 lbs may need 5 days to thaw in the fridge.

22 Tidy up the house. If pressed for time, clean just the rooms everyone will see or use and let the rest go.

23 Buy the most perishable groceries like berries, deli orders and bakery breads so they're as fresh as possible. Double-check your menu, too, to make sure you have everything you need.

24 Follow family tradition, such as going to your place of worship, or create new traditions, such as volunteering with charities and community organizations serving hot holiday meals to those in need.

25 Relax and enjoy. Merry Christmas!

26 Celebrate Kwanzaa.

27

28 Think post-holiday sales! Prices for gift wrap, cards and decorations are a huge bargain now.

29

30 Don't throw out the tree. Instead prop it up outside and decorate with suet feeders, hanging seed cakes and scraps of bread for our bird friends.

31

14

21

GLORIOUS APPETIZERS
and HOLIDAY CHEER

BEER-CHEESE DIP

prep 15 min *total time* 2 hr 15 min
makes 20 servings (2 tablespoons dip and 3 vegetable pieces each)

1 loaf (1 lb) prepared cheese product, cut into cubes
1/2 cup regular or nonalcoholic beer
1/2 to 1 teaspoon red pepper sauce
Assorted fresh vegetables

1. In 3-quart saucepan, heat cheese and beer over medium heat, stirring constantly, until cheese is melted and mixture is smooth. Stir in pepper sauce.

2. Pour cheese mixture into fondue pot or 1- to 2 1/2-quart slow cooker on Low heat setting. Dip will hold up to 2 hours in slow cooker. Serve with vegetables.

1 SERVING: Calories 100 (Calories from Fat 60); Total Fat 7g (Saturated Fat 4.5g; Trans Fat 0g); Cholesterol 20mg; Sodium 340mg; Total Carbohydrate 2g (Dietary Fiber 0g; Sugars 0g); Protein 6g; % DAILY VALUE: Vitamin A 8%; Vitamin C 30%; Calcium 10%; Iron 0%; EXCHANGES: 1/2 Vegetable, 1/2 Medium-Fat Meat, 1 Fat; CARBOHYDRATE CHOICES: 0

holiday inspiration

Make festive vegetable cutouts! Using small cookie cutters, cut shapes out of bell peppers or sliced jicama, zucchini and cucumbers. Red and green tortilla chips also make tasty dippers.

PIZZA DIP

prep 15 min *total time* 15 min
makes 16 servings (2 tablespoons dip and 5 chips each)

1 package (8 oz) cream cheese, softened
1/2 cup pizza sauce
2 cloves garlic, finely chopped
1/2 cup chopped pepperoni
1 can (2.25 oz) sliced ripe olives, drained
1/3 cup finely diced red bell pepper
5 medium green onions, sliced (1/3 cup)
1/2 cup shredded mozzarella cheese (2 oz)
1/4 cup shredded fresh basil leaves
Colored tortilla chips or French baguette bread slices

1. In small bowl, mix cream cheese, pizza sauce and garlic. On 12- or 13-inch round ovenproof serving plate, spread mixture in thin layer. Top with pepperoni, olives, bell pepper and onions. Sprinkle with mozzarella cheese.

2. Set oven control to broil. Broil with top about 4 inches from heat 1 to 2 minutes or until mozzarella cheese is melted. Sprinkle with basil. Serve immediately with tortilla chips.

1 SERVING: Calories 140 (Calories from Fat 90); Total Fat 10g (Saturated Fat 4.5g; Trans Fat 0g); Cholesterol 20mg; Sodium 240mg; Total Carbohydrate 8g (Dietary Fiber 0g; Sugars 1g); Protein 4g; % DAILY VALUE: Vitamin A 10%; Vitamin C 6%; Calcium 6%; Iron 4%; EXCHANGES: 1/2 Starch, 1/2 Medium-Fat Meat, 1 1/2 Fat; CARBOHYDRATE CHOICES: 1/2

TROPICAL PIZZA DIP Substitute chopped cooked ham for the pepperoni and 1 can (8 oz) crushed pineapple (drained) for the olives; omit the basil.

make-ahead magic

To make ahead, assemble this dip on a pretty ovenproof platter up to 1 day before serving; cover tightly with plastic wrap and store in the refrigerator. Broil as directed.

Pizza Dip

ITALIAN SAUTÉED OLIVES

prep 15 min *total time* 15 min

makes 20 servings (6 olives each)

2 tablespoons olive or vegetable oil
2 tablespoons chopped fresh parsley
1 medium green onion, chopped (1 tablespoon)
1 teaspoon crushed red pepper flakes
2 cloves garlic, finely chopped
1 cup Kalamata olives (8 oz), drained, pitted
1 cup Greek green olives (8 oz), drained, pitted
1 cup Gaeta olives (8 oz), drained, pitted

1. In 10-inch skillet, heat oil over medium heat. Cook parsley, onion, red pepper and garlic in oil about 4 minutes, stirring frequently, until garlic just begins to become golden brown.

2. Stir in olives. Cover; cook about 5 minutes, stirring occasionally, until olives are tender and skins begin to wrinkle.

1 SERVING: Calories 45 (Calories from Fat 35); Total Fat 4g (Saturated Fat 0.5g; Trans Fat 0g); Cholesterol 0mg; Sodium 210mg; Total Carbohydrate 2g (Dietary Fiber 0g; Sugars 0g); Protein 0g; % DAILY VALUE: Vitamin A 2%; Vitamin C 0%; Calcium 2%; Iron 4%; EXCHANGES: 1 Fat; CARBOHYDRATE CHOICES: 0

holiday inspiration

Create an easy yet impressive appetizer platter by pairing the olives with a sliced baguette loaf and wedges of cheese like Asiago, Parmesan, manchego, Gouda, blue and Brie.

CREAMY PESTO DIP

prep 5 min *total time* 5 min

makes 10 servings (2 tablespoons dip and 4 vegetable pieces each)

1 container (8 oz) sour cream
1/4 cup basil pesto
Chopped tomato, if desired
Assorted fresh vegetables

1. In small bowl, mix sour cream and pesto until well blended. Sprinkle with tomato.

2. Serve dip with vegetables.

1 SERVING: Calories 90 (Calories from Fat 70); Total Fat 8g (Saturated Fat 3.5g; Trans Fat 0g); Cholesterol 15mg; Sodium 75mg; Total Carbohydrate 4g (Dietary Fiber 1g; Sugars 2g); Protein 2g; % DAILY VALUE: Vitamin A 45%; Vitamin C 30%; Calcium 6%; Iron 2%; EXCHANGES: 1 Vegetable, 1 1/2 Fat; CARBOHYDRATE CHOICES: 0

new twist

- Christmas red and green can grace your appetizer table, too! Use sun-dried tomato or roasted red pepper pesto for a red dip—for a crowd make one batch red and the other green.

- It's nice to be able to offer a few less-indulgent appetizers to guests. To cut the fat in this marvelous dip, substitute fat-free sour cream for regular sour cream.

SHRIMP NACHO BITES

prep 15 min   *total time* 15 min   *makes* 24 nachos
see photo on page 8, top

24 large corn tortilla chips
1/2 cup black bean dip (from 9-oz can)
1/4 cup chunky-style salsa
24 cooked peeled deveined medium shrimp (about 3/4 lb)
1 avocado, pitted, peeled and cut into 24 slices
1/2 cup shredded Colby-Monterey Jack cheese (2 oz)
24 fresh cilantro leaves, if desired

1. Top each tortilla chip with about 1 teaspoon bean dip, 1/2 teaspoon salsa, 1 shrimp, 1 avocado slice and about 1 teaspoon cheese. Place on cookie sheet.

2. Set oven control to broil. Broil with tops about 5 inches from heat 2 to 3 minutes or just until cheese is melted. Garnish with cilantro leaves. Serve immediately.

1 NACHO: Calories 50 (Calories from Fat 30); Total Fat 3g (Saturated Fat 1g; Trans Fat 0g); Cholesterol 30mg; Sodium 105mg; Total Carbohydrate 2g (Dietary Fiber 0g; Sugars 0g); Protein 4g; **% DAILY VALUE:** Vitamin A 2%; Vitamin C 0%; Calcium 2%; Iron 4%; **EXCHANGES:** 1/2 Very Lean Meat, 1/2 Fat; **CARBOHYDRATE CHOICES:** 0

new twist

Mix it up! Instead of topping all the tortilla chips with shrimp, top half of them with a piece of lump crabmeat, imitation crabmeat or imitation lobster.

GORGONZOLA *and* TOASTED WALNUT SPREAD

prep 10 min   *total time* 10 min
makes 16 servings (2 tablespoons spread and 2 bread or fruit slices each)

1 cup crumbled Gorgonzola cheese (4 oz)
1 package (8 oz) cream cheese, softened
3 tablespoons half-and-half
1/4 teaspoon freshly ground pepper
1/2 cup chopped walnuts, toasted (page 110)
1 tablespoon chopped fresh parsley
French bread slices
Apple and pear slices

1. Reserve 1 tablespoon of the Gorgonzola cheese for garnish. In food processor, place cream cheese, remaining Gorgonzola cheese, half-and-half and pepper. Cover; process just until blended.

2. Reserve 1 tablespoon of the walnuts for garnish. Stir remaining walnuts into cheese mixture. Spoon into shallow serving plate. Sprinkle with reserved Gorgonzola cheese, walnuts and the parsley. Serve with bread and apple slices.

1 SERVING: Calories 200 (Calories from Fat 100); Total Fat 11g (Saturated Fat 5g; Trans Fat 0g); Cholesterol 25mg; Sodium 350mg; Total Carbohydrate 19g (Dietary Fiber 1g; Sugars 2g); Protein 6g; **% DAILY VALUE:** Vitamin A 6%; Vitamin C 0%; Calcium 8%; Iron 8%; **EXCHANGES:** 1/2 Starch, 1/2 Other Carbohydrate, 1/2 Medium-Fat Meat, 2 Fat; **CARBOHYDRATE CHOICES:** 1

holiday inspiration

Even a simple spread can look smashing with a
simple little technique. Spoon the spread into a
shallow bowl or dish with at least a 1-inch rim.
Brush the rim lightly with water, then immediately
sprinkle the rim with chopped fresh parsley. The
parsley sticks to the water—it's so easy and pretty.

FRUIT BRUSCHETTA

prep 15 min   *total time* 15 min   *makes* 28 bruschetta

1 package (10.75 oz) frozen pound cake loaf, cut into fourteen 1/2-inch slices

2/3 cup soft cream cheese with strawberries, raspberries or pineapple

1 can (11 oz) mandarin orange segments, well drained

56 bite-size pieces assorted fresh fruit (kiwifruit, strawberry, raspberry, pear, apple)

Chocolate-flavor syrup, if desired

Toasted coconut or sliced almonds, if desired

1. Set oven control to broil. Place cake slices on rack in broiler pan. Broil with tops 4 to 5 inches from heat 3 to 5 minutes, turning once, until light golden brown.

2. Spread each cake slice with about 2 teaspoons cream cheese. Cut slices diagonally in half to make 28 pieces. Top with orange segments and desired fruit. Drizzle with syrup; sprinkle with coconut.

1 BRUSCHETTA: Calories 90 (Calories from Fat 45); Total Fat 5g (Saturated Fat 2.5g; Trans Fat 0g); Cholesterol 15mg; Sodium 30mg; Total Carbohydrate 11g (Dietary Fiber 1g; Sugars 7g); Protein 1g; % DAILY VALUE: Vitamin A 4%; Vitamin C 25%; Calcium 0%; Iron 0%; EXCHANGES: 1/2 Other Carbohydrate, 1 Fat; CARBOHYDRATE CHOICES: 1

new twist

Make it merrier with extra flavor—try drizzling the fruit with strawberry-flavored pancake syrup or caramel topping instead of the chocolate syrup.

make-ahead magic

To make ahead, toast the pound cake up to a day earlier. Assemble the bruschetta up to 4 hours before your party, then lightly cover and refrigerate until serving time.

Betty Crocker Christmas Cookbook

a toast to beverages

Usher in the tidings of the season and be full of good cheer! Holiday entertaining and beverages go hand in hand. Whether you're serving wine, cocktails, beer, coffee or hot chocolate, here are some easy ways to jazz them up.

stock the bar

You don't need to have one of everything to have a well-stocked bar. Start with a few wines and liquors that you and your friends really like, then build from there. Buy small bottles of before- and after-dinner drinks because smaller amounts of these are usually used. Have a supply of nonalcoholic beverages on hand, too.

- WATER AND SODA POP The most basic bar can be just an assortment of plain and flavored sparkling water and diet and regular soda pop.

- BEER regular and light

- WINE AND CHAMPAGNE red and white wine and champagne (dry and sweet styles)

- LIQUOR bourbon, gin, rum, Scotch, tequila, vermouth (sweet and dry), vodka, whiskey

- MIXERS bloody Mary mix (or tomato juice), club soda, fruit juice (cranberry, grapefruit, orange), ginger ale, grenadine, margarita mix, soda (regular and diet colas and lemon-lime), sweetened lime juice, tonic water (regular and diet)

- BEFORE- AND AFTER-DINNER DRINKS brandy, liqueurs (chocolate, coffee, creme de menthe, Irish cream, orange, raspberry)

- GARNISHES celery stalks (with leaves), fresh fruit, lemons and limes, maraschino cherries, mint leaves, olives, pickle spears, salt, sugar (regular and colored). For hot sweetened drinks, try cocoa, cinnamon sticks, chocolate (chopped, curls, grated, mini chips), chocolate-covered coffee beans, candy sprinkles, ice-cream toppings, ground spices (apple pie spice, cinnamon, nutmeg, pumpkin pie spice), toasted coconut, whipped cream (aerosol type) or frozen whipped topping.

- GIZMOS AND GADGETS blender, bottle opener, coasters, cocktail napkins, corkscrew, ice, ice bucket, ice tongs, pitcher, shaker cocktail strainer (wire strainer), jigger (shot glass), muddler (for crushing mint in Mojitos, for example), stirring sticks, straws

raise your wine glass

Wine is a year-round favorite. Enjoy it served as is, or "doctor it" a bit.

- Try homemade wine coolers! Mix equal parts of white or light red wine, like rosé, and fruit juice and a shot of fruit-flavored liqueur if you like.

- For wine spritzers, mix 2 cups chilled dry white wine or nonalcoholic wine, 1 cup chilled cranberry-apple juice drink and 1 cup chilled sparkling water. Serve over ice. Garnish with fresh fruit or mint leaves. Makes 6 servings (about 2/3 cup each).

- For mulled wine, add honey and whole spices such as cinnamon, cardamom and cloves to red wine, then heat slowly. Or, look for mulling spices in large specialty kitchen and cookware stores.

spirited mixed drinks

- Make spiked gelatin "poppers!" Make any 4-serving-size box of flavored gelatin using 1 cup boiling water. Once gelatin dissolves, stir in 3/4 cup rum, brandy, vodka, gin or champagne. Pour into ice-cube trays; refrigerate until set. Remove from the trays to serve.

- Go classic! A traditional dry martini is 1 1/2 to 2 ounces of gin and 2 teaspoons of dry vermouth. Vodka can be substituted for gin. Shake or stir with ice; strain. Garnish with an olive.

- Go Manhattan style! Mix 2 ounces rye or bourbon whiskey, 1 ounce sweet vermouth and a dash of bitters. A "perfect" Manhattan is equal parts sweet and dry vermouth, and a "dry" uses just dry vermouth. Garnish with a maraschino cherry.

pour a frothy one

If you've never thought of adding a new twist to your favorite brew, you're in for a tasty surprise!

- Put beer mugs in the freezer—for a frosty mug.

- To a tall glass of beer, add a shot of amaretto, gin, rum, vodka or whiskey.

- Spike a full glass of beer with a shot of sweetened lime juice.

- Mix equal parts of chilled beer and either chilled bloody Mary mix or tomato juice, champagne, ginger ale, lemonade or lemon-lime soda.

drink dazzlers for beer

- Use celery stalks, cucumber sticks, pickle spears or sprigs of fresh dill weed as stirrers.

- Add lime, orange or lemon wedges to glasses.

hot and cozy drinks

Tradition, comfort. What better words to describe a mug of hot chocolate or coffee? Explore your options with these ideas:

- To coffee or hot chocolate, stir in about 1 tablespoon chocolate syrup, liqueur, flavored coffee syrup, caramel topping or a scoop of ice cream.

- Add pieces of vanilla bean, a cardamom pod or cinnamon stick to a pot or cups of coffee or hot chocolate for a spicy flavor and aroma.

hot and cozy drink dazzlers

- Use a cinnamon stick or peppermint stick as a stirrer.

- Top with whipped cream, and garnish with chocolate-covered coffee beans, grated chocolate, chopped nuts, mini chocolate chips, toasted coconut or crushed candies or cookies. Or drizzle with ice cream topping.

drink dazzlers for mixed drinks

- Rub rims of glasses with the cut side of a lime or lemon and then dip into salt or sugar. Try using a colored sugar—see Rainbow Dust on page 292, or use purchased colored sugars.

- Make ice cubes out of juices for a flavor and color duo.

- Use fresh berries, cherries, citrus twists, kiwifruit slices or melon wedges. Cut a small slit and hook the fruit on the glass rim, or thread fruit on decorative toothpicks and rest it in the glass.

"Cran-tinis"

"CRAN-TINIS"

prep 5 min *total time* 5 min
makes 4 servings (about 1/2 cup each)

1 cup cranberry juice (8 oz)
1/2 cup citrus vodka or plain vodka (4 oz)
1/4 cup Triple Sec or orange juice (2 oz)
1 teaspoon fresh lime juice
Fresh cranberries, if desired
Lime slices, if desired

1. Fill martini shaker or 3-cup covered container half full with ice. Add all ingredients except cranberries and lime slices; cover and shake.

2. Pour into martini or tall stemmed glasses, straining the ice. Garnish glasses with fresh cranberries and lime slices on picks.

1 SERVING: Calories 45 (Calories from Fat 0); Total Fat 0g (Saturated Fat 0g; Trans Fat 0g); Cholesterol 0mg; Sodium 0mg; Total Carbohydrate 11g (Dietary Fiber 0g; Sugars 10g); Protein 0g; % DAILY VALUE: Vitamin A 0%; Vitamin C 35%; Calcium 0%; Iron 0%; EXCHANGES: 1/2 Fruit, 1/2 Fat; CARBOHYDRATE CHOICES: 1

holiday inspiration

- Pretty in pink describes the beautiful blushing hue of this very hip version of the classic martini. Cran-tinis are sweeter than regular martinis so true martini drinkers may want to cut the cranberry juice in half. For a slightly less potent drink, serve Cran-tinis on the rocks and add a splash of sparkling water.

- Garnish each drink by skewering fresh cranberries on a toothpick and placing the skewer and a strip of lime peel in the bottom of each glass.

FROSTY CITRUS PUNCH

prep 10 min *total time* 10 min
makes 15 servings (about 1/2 cup each)
see photo on page 8, bottom

1 can (12 oz) frozen limeade or lemonade concentrate, thawed
3 cups cold water
2 cans (12 oz each) lemon-lime soda pop, chilled
1/2 pint (1 cup) lime or lemon sherbet, softened

1. In large pitcher, mix limeade concentrate and water.

2. Just before serving, stir in soda pop. Pour into punch bowl. Float scoops of sherbet on top.

1 SERVING: Calories 80 (Calories from Fat 0); Total Fat 0g (Saturated Fat 0g; Trans Fat 0g); Cholesterol 0mg; Sodium 10mg; Total Carbohydrate 19g (Dietary Fiber 0g; Sugars 17g); Protein 0g; % DAILY VALUE: Vitamin A 0%; Vitamin C 6%; Calcium 0%; Iron 0%; EXCHANGES: 1 Fruit, 1/2 Other Carbohydrate; CARBOHYDRATE CHOICES: 1

holiday inspiration

Light the way with luminarias! Here's how:

- Purchase luminaria bags at a party store. Fill with about 3 inches of sand or kitty litter. Place a 1-pint canning jar into the sand and add a votive candle. Place outside. Light luminarias right before the guests arrive.

- Fill a 7-inch balloon with water until 6 inches in diameter; tie end. Place filled balloon in a plastic container of similar size for support. Freeze at least 12 hours or until ice is about 1/2 inch thick around inside of balloon. Remove balloon from around ice ball. Chisel opening in top of ball; drain water. Place outside, insert a votive candle and light candle. If you'd like a colored luminaria, add a few drops of food color to the water.

- Or for a super-simple idea, use a 1-liter soda pop bottle to make holes in the snow along a driveway or walkway. Fill holes with candles for a glowing path of light.

QUICK CRANBERRY PUNCH

prep 5 min *total time* 5 min
makes 24 servings (about 3/4 cup each)

1 can (12 oz) frozen lemonade concentrate, thawed
1 1/2 cups cold water
1 bottle (64 oz) cranberry juice cocktail, chilled
4 cans (12 oz each) ginger ale, chilled
Ice ring (see holiday inspirations, at right) or ice

1. In pitcher, mix lemonade concentrate and water.

2. Just before serving, pour lemonade into large punch bowl. Stir in cranberry juice cocktail and ginger ale. Add ice ring.

1 SERVING: Calories 100 (Calories from Fat 0); Total Fat 0g (Saturated Fat 0g; Trans Fat 0g); Cholesterol 0mg; Sodium 10mg; Total Carbohydrate 24g (Dietary Fiber 0g; Sugars 22g); Protein 0g; % DAILY VALUE: Vitamin A 0%; Vitamin C 35%; Calcium 0%; Iron 0%; EXCHANGES: 1 Fruit, 1/2 Other Carbohydrate; CARBOHYDRATE CHOICES: 1 1/2

new twist

Add a touch of "glam" to holiday drinks with these festive add-ons:

- Garnish glass rims with a slice of starfruit.
- Freeze fresh mint leaves and cranberries in water in ice-cube trays and use instead of regular ice cubes.
- Make ice cubes with some of your punch recipe or use just juice instead of water. When the juice cubes melt, the punch won't be diluted.

holiday inspiration

Make a frosty ice ring by filling a ring mold or fluted tube cake pan with crushed ice (the mold needs to be smaller than your punch bowl). Cut fruit like lemons, limes, oranges and starfruit into 1/4-inch slices; arrange in the ice so the fruit sticks up above the top of the mold. Or cut citrus peel into star shapes, using tiny cookie cutters. Freeze the mold 15 minutes, then slowly add cold water, some of the punch or fruit juice to fill the mold. Freeze overnight or until solid. When you're ready to serve the punch, run hot water over bottom of the mold to loosen the ice ring. Remove the ice ring and float it in the punch. Or with the same technique, use muffin cups to make floating ice disks, which take less time to freeze.

MERRY MIMOSAS

prep 5 min *total time* 5 min

makes 12 servings (about 2/3 cup each)

2 cups chilled orange juice

2 cups chilled cranberry juice cocktail

1 bottle (1 liter) dry champagne or sparkling wine, chilled

1. In 1 1/2-quart pitcher, mix orange juice and cranberry juice cocktail.

2. Pour champagne into glasses until half full. Fill glasses with juice mixture.

1 SERVING: Calories 45 (Calories from Fat 0); Total Fat 0g (Saturated Fat 0g; Trans Fat 0g); Cholesterol 0mg; Sodium 5mg; Total Carbohydrate 11g (Dietary Fiber 0g; Sugars 10g); Protein 0g; % DAILY VALUE: Vitamin A 0%; Vitamin C 40%; Calcium 0%; Iron 2%; EXCHANGES: 1/2 Fruit, 1/2 Fat; CARBOHYDRATE CHOICES: 1

holiday inspiration

What would a brunch be without those delightful mimosa cocktails? For the best flavor, serve them icy cold. You can even use frosty glasses. Place glasses on a tray and freeze 1 hour or more until serving time; remove from the freezer just before serving.

CARIBBEAN CHICKEN WINGS

prep 10 min *total time* 1 hr 10 min *makes* 24 drummettes

1/2 cup pineapple juice

1/2 cup ketchup

1/4 cup packed brown sugar

1/4 cup teriyaki marinade and sauce
   (from 10-oz bottle)

1/4 cup honey

2 cloves garlic, finely chopped

2 lb chicken wing drummettes (about 24)

1. Heat oven to 350°F. Line 13 × 9–inch pan with foil.

2. In 1-quart saucepan, heat all ingredients except chicken to boiling, stirring occasionally. Place chicken in pan; pour sauce over chicken.

3. Bake uncovered about 1 hour, turning chicken 2 or 3 times, until juice of chicken is clear when thickest part is cut to bone (180°F).

4. Spray inside of 3 1/2-quart slow cooker with cooking spray. Place chicken in slow cooker. Cover; keep warm on Low heat setting.

1 DRUMMETTE: Calories 70 (Calories from Fat 25); Total Fat 3g (Saturated Fat 1g; Trans Fat 0g); Cholesterol 10mg; Sodium 190mg; Total Carbohydrate 8g (Dietary Fiber 0g; Sugars 7g); Protein 4g; % DAILY VALUE: Vitamin A 0%; Vitamin C 0%; Calcium 0%; Iron 0%; EXCHANGES: 1/2 Other Carbohydrate, 1/2 Medium-Fat Meat; CARBOHYDRATE CHOICES: 1/2

make-ahead magic

To make ahead, prepare and bake these drummettes up to 24 hours before serving. Cover with foil and refrigerate, then reheat them in the oven.

ROAST BEEF BRUSCHETTA

prep 20 min *total time* 30 min *makes* 30 bruschetta

1 loaf (1 lb) French baguette bread, cut into thirty
   1/4-inch slices

2 tablespoons olive or vegetable oil

1/2 cup chive-and-onion cream cheese spread
   (from 8-oz container)

1/2 lb thinly sliced deli roast beef

1/4 teaspoon coarsely ground pepper

4 plum (Roma) tomatoes, thinly sliced

8 medium green onions, sliced (1/2 cup)

1. Heat oven to 375°F. Brush both sides of bread slices with oil. Place on ungreased cookie sheet. Bake about 5 minutes or until crisp. Cool 5 minutes.

2. Spread cream cheese over each slice. Top with beef; sprinkle with pepper. Top with tomato slice and green onions.

1 BRUSCHETTA: Calories 70 (Calories from Fat 25); Total Fat 3g (Saturated Fat 1g; Trans Fat 0g); Cholesterol 5mg; Sodium 200mg; Total Carbohydrate 9g (Dietary Fiber 0g; Sugars 0g); Protein 3g; % DAILY VALUE: Vitamin A 4%; Vitamin C 6%; Calcium 0%; Iron 4%; EXCHANGES: 1/2 Starch, 1/2 Fat; CARBOHYDRATE CHOICES: 1/2

new twist

Think bruschetta bar! Lox, deli pastrami or deli smoked turkey or chicken breast can be used instead of the deli roast beef—even hummus for meatless fans.

GORGONZOLA *and* ROSEMARY CREAM PUFFS

prep 15 min *total time* 45 min *makes* 25 puffs

1/2 cup water
1/4 cup butter or margarine
1/2 cup all-purpose flour
1/4 teaspoon salt
1/4 teaspoon dried rosemary leaves, crushed
1/8 teaspoon coarsely ground pepper
2 eggs
1 cup crumbled Gorgonzola cheese (4 oz)
2 tablespoons chopped pistachio nuts

1. Heat oven to 425°F. Spray large cookie sheet with cooking spray.

2. In 3-quart saucepan, heat water and butter to boiling over medium heat. Add flour, salt, rosemary and pepper all at once; stir constantly 30 to 60 seconds or until mixture forms ball. Remove from heat. Add eggs, one at a time, beating with electric mixer on medium speed until mixture is well blended.

3. Drop mixture by heaping teaspoonfuls about 2 inches apart onto cookie sheet. Bake 15 to 20 minutes or until golden brown. Cool 5 minutes.

4. Gently press center of each puff with tip of spoon to make slight indentation. Sprinkle with cheese and nuts. Bake 2 to 4 minutes or until cheese is melted. Serve warm.

1 PUFF: Calories 50 (Calories from Fat 35); Total Fat 4g (Saturated Fat 2g; Trans Fat 0g); Cholesterol 25mg; Sodium 105mg; Total Carbohydrate 2g (Dietary Fiber 0g; Sugars 0g); Protein 2g; **% DAILY VALUE:** Vitamin A 2%; Vitamin C 0%; Calcium 2%; Iron 0%; **EXCHANGES:** 1 Fat; **CARBOHYDRATE CHOICES:** 0

make-ahead magic

To make ahead, prepare cream puff dough as directed, except drop mixture by heaping teaspoonfuls onto cookie sheet covered with waxed paper. Freeze until firm. Place drops of dough in airtight container or resealable food-storage plastic bag. To bake, place frozen dough on cookie sheet and continue as directed.

holiday inspiration

Searching for a few last-minute appetizers to round out your platter? Give these a whirl:

- Wrap small slices of honeydew melon or cantaloupe with thinly sliced smoked turkey. Or wrap pear slices with prosciutto or thinly sliced deli ham.

- Heat a round of Brie cheese at 350°F for 8 to 10 minutes or until cheese is soft and partially melted. Top with 1/4 cup whole berry cranberry sauce or red or green pepper jelly.

- Arrange slices of fresh mozzarella cheese and ripe tomatoes in a circle; sprinkle with chopped fresh basil leaves and drizzle with olive oil.

MAKE-AHEAD ITALIAN MEATBALLS

prep 15 min   *total time* 1 hr 10 min

makes 30 appetizer meatballs

1 lb lean (at least 80%) ground beef
1 medium onion, chopped (1/2 cup)
1/3 cup dry bread crumbs (any flavor)
1/4 cup milk
1 egg
1 teaspoon salt
1/8 teaspoon pepper
1 cup chili sauce
1/2 cup cold water
1 1/4 cups tomato pasta sauce (any variety)
1 teaspoon yellow mustard

1. Heat oven to 400°F. In large bowl, mix beef, onion, bread crumbs, milk, egg, salt and pepper. Shape mixture into thirty 1-inch balls. Place in ungreased 13 × 9–inch pan.

2. Bake uncovered about 15 minutes or until no longer pink in center. (To serve immediately, continue as directed in Step 4—except decrease simmer time to 15 minutes.)

3. Place meatballs on ungreased cookie sheet. Freeze uncovered about 20 minutes or until firm. Place partially frozen meatballs in heavy food-storage plastic bag or freezer container. Seal, label and freeze no longer than 3 months.

4. About 25 minutes before serving, in 2-quart saucepan, mix chili sauce, water, pasta sauce and mustard. Add meatballs. Heat to boiling, stirring occasionally; reduce heat. Cover; simmer about 20 minutes or until meatballs are hot.

1 MEATBALL: Calories 60 (Calories from Fat 20); Total Fat 2.5g (Saturated Fat 1g; Trans Fat 0g); Cholesterol 15mg; Sodium 270mg; Total Carbohydrate 5g (Dietary Fiber 0g; Sugars 2g); Protein 3g; % DAILY VALUE: Vitamin A 4%; Vitamin C 2%; Calcium 0%; Iron 2%; EXCHANGES: 1/2 Starch, 1/2 Fat; CARBOHYDRATE CHOICES: 1/2

holiday inspiration

In addition to appetizers, these easy-to-make meatballs are great to keep on hand for last-minute dinner creations. Tossed with pasta or baked into a casserole are just two of the possibilities!

PESTO PINWHEELS

prep 20 min   *total time* 30 min   *makes* 40 pinwheels

1 package (17.3 oz) frozen puff pastry sheets, thawed
1 cup basil pesto
1 egg, slightly beaten

1. Heat oven to 400°F. On very lightly floured surface, roll each sheet of puff pastry into 14 × 10–inch rectangle.

2. Spread 1/2 cup of the pesto evenly over each rectangle to within 1/2 inch of long sides. Starting at 10-inch side, loosely fold each pastry sheet into roll; brush edge of roll with egg, then pinch into roll to seal.

3. Cut each roll into 1/2-inch slices, using sharp knife. Place on ungreased cookie sheet. Bake 8 to 10 minutes or until golden brown. Serve warm.

1 PINWHEEL: Calories 100 (Calories from Fat 70); Total Fat 8g (Saturated Fat 2.5g; Trans Fat 0g); Cholesterol 20mg; Sodium 85mg; Total Carbohydrate 6g (Dietary Fiber 0g; Sugars 0g); Protein 2g; % DAILY VALUE: Vitamin A 0%; Vitamin C 0%; Calcium 2%; Iron 4%; EXCHANGES: 1/2 Starch, 1 1/2 Fat; CARBOHYDRATE CHOICES: 1/2

holiday inspiration

Finding it hard to squeeze in time to make both Christmas Eve and Christmas Day dinners? Go for all appetizers instead of the traditional sit-down holiday dinner. Here is a fun "red and green" themed appetizer menu:

- Bloody Mary Shrimp Cocktail (page 28)
- Brie in Puff Pastry with Cranberry Sauce (page 42)
- Bruschetta Romana (page 43)
- Creamy Pesto Dip (page 13)
- Herb-Coated Mini Cheese Balls (page 48)
- Italian Nachos (page 37)
- Pesto Pinwheels (above)

BLOODY MARY SHRIMP COCKTAIL

prep 30 min *total time* 2 hrs 40 min
makes about 50 shrimp (with 2 teaspoons sauce each)

1 1/2 lb cooked peeled deveined medium shrimp
    (46 to 52), thawed if frozen
1/2 cup tomato juice
1/4 cup vodka, if desired
1/2 teaspoon red pepper sauce
1/2 teaspoon sugar
1/2 teaspoon celery salt
2 tablespoons chopped fresh parsley
1 cup cocktail sauce
1/4 cup finely chopped green olives

1. In 11 × 7–inch glass or plastic dish, arrange shrimp in single layer.

2. In 1-quart saucepan, heat tomato juice, vodka and pepper sauce to boiling over medium-high heat. Stir in sugar; reduce heat. Simmer uncovered 5 minutes, stirring occasionally. Stir in celery salt and parsley; pour over shrimp. Cover; refrigerate 2 to 3 hours. Don't marinate longer than 3 hours because the tomato juice will make the shrimp tough.

3. Mix cocktail sauce and olives; pour into small serving bowl. Remove shrimp from marinade with slotted spoon; arrange on serving platter. Serve shrimp with sauce and toothpicks.

1 SHRIMP: Calories 20 (Calories from Fat 0); Total Fat 0g (Saturated Fat 0g; Trans Fat 0g); Cholesterol 25mg; Sodium 130mg; Total Carbohydrate 2g (Dietary Fiber 0g; Sugars 1g); Protein 3g; % DAILY VALUE: Vitamin A 2%; Vitamin C 2%; Calcium 0%; Iron 2%; EXCHANGES: 1/2 Very Lean Meat; CARBOHYDRATE CHOICES: 0

holiday inspiration

Break out of the serving platter rut and arrange the shrimp in an oversized martini glass (about 12 to 14 inches in diameter). Pour cocktail sauce mixture over shrimp, and garnish like a Bloody Mary with a skewer of olives, a large lime wedge and a celery stick.

Betty Crocker Christmas Cookbook

ROASTED CARROT *and* HERB SPREAD

prep 10 min *total time* 55 min

makes 20 servings (2 tablespoons spread and 3 bread slices each)

2 lb ready-to-eat baby-cut carrots

1 large dark-orange sweet potato, peeled, cut into 1-inch pieces

1 medium onion, cut into 8 wedges, separated

1/4 cup olive or vegetable oil

2 tablespoons chopped fresh or 1 teaspoon dried thyme leaves

2 cloves garlic, finely chopped

3/4 teaspoon salt

1/4 teaspoon freshly ground pepper

French baguette bread slices or crackers

1. Heat oven to 350°F. Spray 15 × 10 × 1–inch pan with cooking spray. Place carrots, sweet potato and onion in pan. Drizzle with oil. Sprinkle with thyme, garlic, salt and pepper. Stir to coat.

2. Bake uncovered 35 to 45 minutes, stirring occasionally, until vegetables are tender.

3. Place vegetable mixture in food processor. Cover; process until blended. Spoon into serving bowl. Serve warm, or cover and refrigerate until serving time. Serve with bread slices.

1 SERVING: Calories 310 (Calories from Fat 60); Total Fat 6g (Saturated Fat 1g; Trans Fat 0.5g); Cholesterol 0mg; Sodium 670mg; Total Carbohydrate 55g (Dietary Fiber 4g; Sugars 4g); Protein 9g; % DAILY VALUE: Vitamin A 190%; Vitamin C 6%; Calcium 10%; Iron 20%; EXCHANGES: 3 Starch, 1 Vegetable, 1 Fat; CARBOHYDRATE CHOICES: 3 1/2

make-ahead magic

To make ahead, prepare this unique root vegetable dip up to 2 days before your party. Cover and refrigerate until serving. If you prefer it warm, reheat in the microwave oven.

SAVORY PECANS

prep 5 min *total time* 15 min
makes 16 servings (2 tablespoons each)

2 cups pecan halves
2 medium green onions, chopped (2 tablespoons)
2 tablespoons butter or margarine, melted
1 tablespoon soy sauce
1/4 teaspoon ground red pepper (cayenne)

1. Heat oven to 300°F. In small bowl, mix all ingredients. In ungreased 15 × 10 × 1–inch pan, spread pecans in single layer.

2. Bake uncovered about 10 minutes or until pecans are toasted. Serve warm, or cool completely. Store in airtight container at room temperature up to 3 weeks.

1 SERVING: Calories 110 (Calories from Fat 90); Total Fat 10g (Saturated Fat 1.5g; Trans Fat 0g); Cholesterol 0mg; Sodium 65mg; Total Carbohydrate 2g (Dietary Fiber 1g; Sugars 0g); Protein 1g; % DAILY VALUE: Vitamin A 0%; Vitamin C 0%; Calcium 0%; Iron 2%; EXCHANGES: 2 Fat; CARBOHYDRATE CHOICES: 0

CHINESE-SPICED PECANS Omit ground red pepper. Stir in 2 teaspoons five-spice powder and 1/2 teaspoon ground ginger.

TEX-MEX PECANS Omit soy sauce and ground red pepper. Stir in 1 tablespoon Worcestershire sauce, 2 teaspoons chili powder, 1/4 teaspoon garlic salt and 1/4 teaspoon onion powder.

holiday inspiration

Variety is the spice of life! Try walnut halves or peanuts instead of the pecans. Or to really wow everyone, use whole macadamia nuts (hint—club stores often sell these for a song, but in larger amounts, so split the container with friends).

CRANBERRY-ORANGE SLUSH COCKTAIL

prep 10 min *total time* 8 hrs 10 min
makes 30 servings (about 1/2 cup each)

4 cups (32 oz) cranberry juice cocktail
2 cups brandy
1 can (12 oz) frozen cranberry juice concentrate, thawed
1 can (12 oz) frozen orange juice concentrate, thawed
2 bottles (1 liter each) lemon-lime soda pop or sparkling water
Lime slices, if desired

1. In large container, mix all ingredients except soda pop and lime slices. Divide among pint containers. Cover; freeze at least 8 hours or until slushy.

2. For each serving, stir equal amounts of slush mixture and soda pop in glass. Garnish with lime slices.

1 SERVING: Calories 90 (Calories from Fat 0); Total Fat 0g (Saturated Fat 0g; Trans Fat 0g); Cholesterol 0mg; Sodium 10mg; Total Carbohydrate 22g (Dietary Fiber 0g; Sugars 21g); Protein 0g; % DAILY VALUE: Vitamin A 0%; Vitamin C 50%; Calcium 0%; Iron 0%; EXCHANGES: 1 Fruit, 1/2 Other Carbohydrate; CARBOHYDRATE CHOICES: 1 1/2

make-ahead magic

Prepare as directed and freeze up to 2 months ahead of time; the mixture will stay slushy until you're ready to serve it. For crowd-size amounts, freeze in large containers like ice-cream buckets.

HOT and SPICY PEANUTS

prep 10 min *total time* 10 min
makes 16 servings (2 tablespoons each)

2 teaspoons vegetable oil
2 cups unsalted dry-roasted peanuts
2 teaspoons chili powder
1/4 teaspoon ground red pepper (cayenne)
1/2 to 3/4 teaspoon garlic salt

1. In 8-inch skillet, heat oil over medium heat. Stir in peanuts, chili powder and red pepper. Cook over medium heat about 2 minutes, stirring occasionally, until peanuts are warm; drain on paper towels.

2. Sprinkle garlic salt over peanuts; toss. Cool completely. Store in tightly covered container at room temperature.

1 SERVING: Calories 120 (Calories from Fat 90); Total Fat 10g (Saturated Fat 1.5g; Trans Fat 0g); Cholesterol 0mg; Sodium 35mg; Total Carbohydrate 4g (Dietary Fiber 1g; Sugars 0g); Protein 5g; % DAILY VALUE: Vitamin A 2%; Vitamin C 0%; Calcium 0%; Iron 2%; EXCHANGES: 1 Medium-Fat Meat, 1 Fat; CARBOHYDRATE CHOICES: 0

new twist

Customize your munchies! Mix the spiced peanuts with small corn chips or cheese curls for a great snack mix.

OLIVE APPETIZER TREE

prep 55 min *total time* 55 min
makes 30 servings (3 pieces each)

1 bottle (10 oz) small pimiento-stuffed olives
1 bottle (10 oz) large pimiento-stuffed olives
6 oz pitted Kalamata or ripe olives
1 block (1 lb) Colby cheese
1 package (125-count) round toothpicks
1 cone shape (9 inches tall) green or white floral foam
Rosemary sprigs, if desired

1. Drain olives. Cut block of cheese horizontally into 2 pieces, each about 1/2 inch thick. Cut cheese with 1-inch star-shape canapé or cookie cutter. Cover cheese stars with plastic wrap.

2. Break toothpicks in half as needed. Starting at bottom of cone, insert toothpicks in random order until they stay securely in place. Push each olive onto toothpick half. When placing olives around the tree, vary the olive sizes and leave spaces for the cheese stars. For stability of the tree, place most of the larger olives near the bottom.

3. Push each cheese star onto toothpick half; insert into cone among the olives. Top tree with a cheese star that has been inserted horizontally on toothpick between points of star. Insert rosemary sprigs randomly among olives and cheese. Serve immediately or cover loosely and refrigerate no longer than 8 hours before serving.

1 SERVING: Calories 80 (Calories from Fat 60); Total Fat 7g (Saturated Fat 3g; Trans Fat 0g); Cholesterol 15mg; Sodium 350mg; Total Carbohydrate 1g (Dietary Fiber 0g; Sugars 0g); Protein 3g; % DAILY VALUE: Vitamin A 4%; Vitamin C 0%; Calcium 10%; Iron 0%; EXCHANGES: 1/2 Medium-Fat Meat, 1 Fat; CARBOHYDRATE CHOICES: 0

holiday inspiration

Sometimes not everything goes as perfectly as planned, and that's okay. Before guests arrive, tell yourself to stay laid-back and at ease—no matter what happens. If you're relaxed, your guests will be too and they won't notice those little glitches!

make-ahead magic

A cup of warm cheer is just minutes away! For individual servings, freeze 2 tablespoons batter in each section of ice-cube trays; when frozen, place cubes in freezer bag. That's convenience.

holiday inspiration

With everyone dressed in their best holiday attire, juggling plates of food and drinks can be difficult, so you'll want to avoid congestion. To minimize the chances of people bumping into one another, put drinks on one table and appetizers on another. If using disposable dishes, put wastebaskets throughout the house. Or if using regular dishes and glasses, put trays throughout the house and have someone frequently empty them of dirty dishes.

HOT BUTTERED RUM

prep 15 min *total time* 15 min

makes about 3 cups batter (enough for 24 servings, about 3/4 cup each)

Hot Buttered Rum Batter

1 cup butter or margarine, softened

1 cup plus 2 tablespoons packed brown sugar

1 cup whipping (heavy) cream

2 cups powdered sugar

1/4 teaspoon ground nutmeg

1/8 teaspoon ground cloves

1/8 teaspoon ground cinnamon

For each serving

2 tablespoons rum

1/2 cup boiling water

Ground nutmeg

White chocolate curls, if desired

1. In medium bowl, beat butter and brown sugar with electric mixer on medium speed about 5 minutes or until light and fluffy. Beat in whipping cream and powdered sugar alternately on low speed until smooth. Stir in nutmeg, cloves and cinnamon. Use immediately, or spoon into 1-quart freezer container. Cover, label and freeze up to 3 months.

2. For each serving, place rum and 2 tablespoons Hot Buttered Rum Batter in mug. Stir in boiling water. Sprinkle with nutmeg and white chocolate curls.

1 SERVING: Calories 180 (Calories from Fat 100); Total Fat 11g (Saturated Fat 6g; Trans Fat 0.5g); Cholesterol 30mg; Sodium 60mg; Total Carbohydrate 20g (Dietary Fiber 0g; Sugars 20g); Protein 0g; % DAILY VALUE: Vitamin A 8%; Vitamin C 0%; Calcium 2%; Iron 0%; EXCHANGES: 1 1/2 Other Carbohydrate, 2 Fat; CARBOHYDRATE CHOICES: 1

HOT SPICED WINE

prep 15 min *total time* 30 min
makes 10 servings (about 3/4 cup each)

1 cup packed brown sugar

2 1/2 cups orange juice

1 cup water

Peel of 2 oranges, cut into 1/4-inch strips

6 whole cloves

3 whole allspice

1 four-inch stick cinnamon

1 bottle (750 milliliters) dry red wine or nonalcoholic
  red wine

Orange slices, if desired

Additional whole cloves, if desired

1. In 4-quart Dutch oven, heat all ingredients except wine, orange slices and additional cloves to boiling, stirring occasionally; reduce heat. Simmer uncovered 15 minutes.

2. Remove orange peel and spices. Stir in wine. Heat just until hot (do not boil). Serve hot in mugs or heatproof glasses. Garnish each serving with orange slice studded with additional whole cloves.

1 SERVING: Calories 120 (Calories from Fat 0); Total Fat 0g (Saturated Fat 0g; Trans Fat 0g); Cholesterol 0mg; Sodium 15mg; Total Carbohydrate 29g (Dietary Fiber 0g; Sugars 27g); Protein 0g; % DAILY VALUE: Vitamin A 0%; Vitamin C 20%; Calcium 4%; Iron 6%; EXCHANGES: 1 Fruit, 1 Other Carbohydrate; CARBOHYDRATE CHOICES: 2

make-ahead magic

To make ahead, cover and refrigerate spiced wine up to 1 week before serving. Just reheat until hot (do not boil) before serving.

COSMO SLUSH

prep 10 min *total time* 8 hrs 10 min
makes 14 servings (about 1/2 cup each)

6 oz frozen (thawed) limeade concentrate
  (from 12-oz can)

3 tablespoons powdered sugar

2 cups citrus-flavored vodka or orange juice

1 cup orange-flavored liqueur or orange juice

4 cups 100% cranberry juice blend

1. In blender, place limeade concentrate and powdered sugar. Cover; blend on high speed until well mixed. Add vodka and orange liqueur. Cover; blend until well mixed.

2. In 13 × 9–inch (3-quart) glass baking dish, stir limeade mixture and cranberry juice until well mixed.

3. Cover; freeze at least 8 hours until slushy. Stir before serving.

1 SERVING: Calories 100 (Calories from Fat 0); Total Fat 0g (Saturated Fat 0g; Trans Fat 0g); Cholesterol 0mg; Sodium 0mg; Total Carbohydrate 24g (Dietary Fiber 0g; Sugars 22g); Protein 0g; % DAILY VALUE: Vitamin A 0%; Vitamin C 15%; Calcium 0%; Iron 0%; EXCHANGES: 1 Fruit, 1/2 Other Carbohydrate; CARBOHYDRATE CHOICES: 1 1/2

holiday inspiration

Add a little pizzazz! Serve this version of the trendy Cosmopolitan martini in martini glasses or other glasses with sloped sides. Put a strip of orange peel in the bottom of each glass.

holiday inspiration

Instant flavor is just a spray away. Look for olive oil cooking spray for added flavor! Crunched for time? Instead of toasting the baguette slices, try pita bread chips or bagel chips and continue as directed in Step 2 after heating your oven.

ITALIAN NACHOS

prep 20 min *total time* 35 min *makes* 28 nachos

28 slices (1/4 inch thick) baguette French bread
(from 12-oz loaf, 2 to 2 1/2 inches in diameter)

Olive oil cooking spray

1/2 lb bulk hot Italian sausage

2/3 cup Alfredo pasta sauce

1 teaspoon Italian seasoning

1 large tomato, seeded, chopped (1 cup)

1 can (2.25 oz) sliced ripe olives, drained

1 1/2 cups shredded mozzarella cheese (6 oz)

Chopped fresh parsley, if desired

1. Heat oven to 400°F. Line large cookie sheet
with foil. On cookie sheet, arrange bread slices
with sides touching. Spray tops of bread slices
lightly with cooking spray. Bake 6 to 8 minutes or
until light golden brown.

2. Meanwhile, in 10-inch skillet, cook sausage
over medium-high heat 5 to 7 minutes, stirring
occasionally and breaking into small pieces, until
no longer pink; drain. Stir in Alfredo sauce and
Italian seasoning.

3. Spoon sausage mixture evenly over bread
slices. Sprinkle evenly with tomato, olives and
cheese. Bake about 6 minutes or until cheese is
melted. Sprinkle with parsley. Serve hot.

1 NACHO: Calories 80 (Calories from Fat 45); Total Fat 5g (Saturated Fat
2.5g; Trans Fat 0g); Cholesterol 15mg; Sodium 160mg; Total
Carbohydrate 3g (Dietary Fiber 0g; Sugars 0g); Protein 4g; % DAILY
VALUE: Vitamin A 4%; Vitamin C 0%; Calcium 6%; Iron 2%; EXCHANGES:
1/2 High-Fat Meat, 1/2 Fat; CARBOHYDRATE CHOICES: 0

HOT CRAB DIP

prep 15 min *total time* 35 min

makes 20 servings (2 tablespoons dip and 4 crackers
each)

1 package (8 oz) cream cheese, softened

1/4 cup grated Parmesan cheese

1/4 cup mayonnaise or salad dressing

1/4 cup dry white wine or apple juice

2 teaspoons sugar

1 teaspoon ground mustard

4 medium green onions, thinly sliced (1/4 cup)

1 clove garlic, finely chopped

1 can (6 oz) crabmeat, drained, cartilage removed
and flaked*

1/3 cup sliced almonds

Assorted crackers or fresh vegetables

1. Heat oven to 375°F. In medium bowl, mix all
ingredients except crabmeat, almonds and crackers until well blended. Stir in crabmeat.

2. In ungreased 9-inch glass pie plate or shallow
1-quart casserole, spread crabmeat mixture.
Sprinkle with almonds.

3. Bake uncovered 15 to 20 minutes or until hot
and bubbly. Serve with crackers.

*6 oz imitation crabmeat, coarsely chopped, can be substi-
tuted for the canned crabmeat.

1 SERVING: Calories 150 (Calories from Fat 100); Total Fat 11g (Saturated
Fat 4g; Trans Fat 1g); Cholesterol 20mg; Sodium 200mg; Total
Carbohydrate 8g (Dietary Fiber 0g; Sugars 2g); Protein 4g; % DAILY
VALUE: Vitamin A 4%; Vitamin C 0%; Calcium 4%; Iron 4%; EXCHANGES:
1/2 Starch, 1/2 Lean Meat, 2 Fat; CARBOHYDRATE CHOICES: 1/2

new twist

Lighten up this all-time favorite! For 1 gram of fat
and 20 calories per serving, use fat-free cream
cheese and fat-free mayonnaise. Skip the almonds.

BAKED COCONUT SHRIMP

prep 30 min *total time* 45 min *makes* about 40 shrimp (with about 1 teaspoon sauce each)

Apricot Sauce

3/4 cup apricot preserves

1 tablespoon lime juice

1/2 teaspoon ground mustard

Shrimp

1/4 cup all-purpose flour

2 tablespoons packed brown sugar

1/4 teaspoon salt

Dash of ground red pepper (cayenne)

1 egg

1 tablespoon lime juice

1 cup shredded coconut

1 lb uncooked peeled deveined extra-large shrimp (16 to 20), thawed if frozen, tail shells removed

2 tablespoons butter or margarine, melted

1. In 1-quart saucepan, mix all sauce ingredients. Cook over low heat, stirring occasionally, just until preserves are melted. Set aside.

2. Heat oven to 425°F. Spray rack in broiler pan with cooking spray.

3. In shallow bowl, stir flour, brown sugar, salt and red pepper until well mixed. In another shallow bowl, beat egg and lime juice with fork. In third shallow bowl, place coconut.

4. Coat each shrimp with flour mixture. Dip shrimp into egg mixture. Coat with coconut. Place on rack in broiler pan; drizzle with butter. Bake 9 to 11 minutes or until shrimp are pink and coating is beginning to brown. Serve with sauce.

1 SHRIMP: Calories 50 (Calories from Fat 15); Total Fat 1.5g (Saturated Fat 1g; Trans Fat 0g); Cholesterol 25mg; Sodium 45mg; Total Carbohydrate 7g (Dietary Fiber 0g; Sugars 4g); Protein 2g; **% DAILY VALUE:** Vitamin A 0%; Vitamin C 0%; Calcium 0%; Iron 2%; **EXCHANGES:** 1/2 Other Carbohydrate, 1/2 Lean Meat; **CARBOHYDRATE CHOICES:** 1/2

make-ahead magic

To make ahead, prepare the shrimp and sauce up to 2 hours before serving. Refrigerate covered, and bake just before serving.

CRAB CAKES

prep 25 min *total time* 25 min *makes* 6 crab cakes

1/3 cup mayonnaise or salad dressing

1 egg

1 1/4 cups soft bread crumbs (about 2 slices bread)

1 teaspoon ground mustard

1/4 teaspoon salt

1/4 teaspoon ground red pepper (cayenne), if desired

1/8 teaspoon pepper

2 medium green onions, chopped (2 tablespoons)

3 cans (6 oz each) crabmeat, well drained, cartilage removed and flaked*

1/4 cup dry bread crumbs

2 tablespoons vegetable oil

1. In medium bowl, mix mayonnaise and egg with wire whisk. Stir in remaining ingredients except dry bread crumbs and oil. Shape mixture into 6 patties, about 3 inches in diameter (mixture will be moist). Coat each patty with dry bread crumbs.

2. In 12-inch nonstick skillet, heat oil over medium heat. Cook patties in oil about 10 minutes, gently turning once, until golden brown and hot in center. Reduce heat if crab cakes become brown too quickly.

*3/4 lb cooked crabmeat, flaked, can be substituted for the canned crabmeat.

1 CRAB CAKE: Calories 320 (Calories from Fat 160); Total Fat 17g (Saturated Fat 3g; Trans Fat 0g); Cholesterol 105mg; Sodium 650mg; Total Carbohydrate 20g (Dietary Fiber 0g; Sugars 2g); Protein 19g; **% DAILY VALUE:** Vitamin A 4%; Vitamin C 2%; Calcium 15%; Iron 15%; **EXCHANGES:** 1 1/2 Starch, 2 Medium-Fat Meat, 1 Fat; **CARBOHYDRATE CHOICES:** 1

holiday inspiration

Crab cakes are a real treat and they're wonderful served as a main course—allow two per person. Tartar sauce tastes great on crab cakes and is found in the store with the other condiments. Most brands of tartar sauce are thick like mayonnaise; to make it thinner and give it a homemade touch, thin it with whipping cream until it's the consistency you like.

holiday inspiration

Crispy, crunchy and flaky on the outside and full of traditional egg roll flavor on the inside. And the best thing is—they're fat-free! Serve them with a purchased sweet-and-sour sauce or Apricot Sauce (page 38).

EASY PHYLLO EGG ROLLS

prep 30 min   *total time* 50 min   *makes* 18 egg rolls

1 lb ground turkey breast
4 cups coleslaw mix (from 1-lb bag)
3 tablespoons soy sauce
1 teaspoon grated gingerroot
1/2 teaspoon five-spice powder
1 small onion, chopped (1/4 cup)
2 cloves garlic, finely chopped
18 frozen (thawed) phyllo sheets (18 × 14 inches)
Cooking spray

1. Heat oven to 350°F. In 10-inch skillet, cook turkey over medium-high heat, stirring occasionally, until no longer pink; drain. Stir in remaining ingredients except phyllo and cooking spray. Cook 2 to 3 minutes, stirring occasionally, until coleslaw mix is wilted.

2. Cover phyllo sheets with plastic wrap, then with damp towel to keep them from drying out. Place 1 phyllo sheet on cutting board; spray with cooking spray. Repeat with 2 more phyllo sheets to make stack of 3 sheets. Cut stack of phyllo crosswise into thirds to make 3 rectangles, about 14 × 6 inches.

3. Place 1/4 cup turkey mixture on short end of each rectangle; roll up, folding in edges of phyllo. Place roll, seam side down, on ungreased cookie sheet. Repeat with remaining phyllo and turkey mixture. Spray rolls with cooking spray. Bake 15 to 20 minutes or until light golden brown. Serve warm.

1 EGG ROLL: Calories 100 (Calories from Fat 0); Total Fat 0g (Saturated Fat 0g; Trans Fat 0g); Cholesterol 15mg; Sodium 240mg; Total Carbohydrate 15g (Dietary Fiber 1g; Sugars 1g); Protein 8g; **% DAILY VALUE:** Vitamin A 10%; Vitamin C 6%; Calcium 0%; Iron 6%; **EXCHANGES:** 1 Starch, 1/2 Very Lean Meat; **CARBOHYDRATE CHOICES:** 1

ASIAGO CHEESE *and* ARTICHOKE DIP

prep 15 min   *total time* 30 min

makes 16 servings (2 tablespoons dip and 2 breadsticks each)

1 package (8 oz) fat-free cream cheese
1/2 cup fat-free sour cream
2 tablespoons fat-free half-and-half or evaporated fat-free milk
1/4 teaspoon salt
3/4 cup shredded Asiago cheese (3 oz)
1 can (14 oz) artichoke hearts, drained, chopped
4 medium green onions, chopped (1/4 cup)
2 tablespoons chopped fresh parsley
Crisp breadsticks or crackers

1. Heat oven to 350°F. In medium bowl, beat cream cheese with electric mixer on medium speed until smooth. Beat in sour cream, half-and-half and salt. Stir in Asiago cheese, artichoke hearts and onions. Spoon into 1-quart casserole or small ovenproof serving dish.

2. Bake uncovered 10 to 15 minutes or until hot and cheese is melted. Remove from oven; stir. Sprinkle with parsley. Serve with breadsticks.

1 SERVING: Calories 100 (Calories from Fat 30); Total Fat 3.5g (Saturated Fat 1.5g; Trans Fat 0g); Cholesterol 10mg; Sodium 310mg; Total Carbohydrate 12g (Dietary Fiber 2g; Sugars 2g); Protein 6g; **% DAILY VALUE:** Vitamin A 8%; Vitamin C 2%; Calcium 10%; Iron 4%; **EXCHANGES:** 1/2 Starch, 1/2 Vegetable, 1/2 High-Fat Meat; **CARBOHYDRATE CHOICES:** 1

MICROWAVE DIRECTIONS Use microwavable casserole or dish. Microwave uncovered on High 1 to 2 minutes, stirring every 30 seconds.

holiday inspiration

Explore a new taste. Asiago is a semifirm Italian cheese that is rich and nutty. Full of flavor, a little of this cheese goes a long way! Enjoy crisp breadsticks, raw veggies or baked pita or tortilla chips with this tasty, low-fat Asiago dip.

BRIE in PUFF PASTRY with CRANBERRY SAUCE

prep 30 min *total time* 1 hr 25 min

makes 12 servings (with 3 crackers each)

Cranberry Sauce

1 cup fresh cranberries

6 tablespoons packed brown sugar

1 tablespoon orange juice

1/2 teaspoon grated orange peel

Brie in Pastry

1 tablespoon butter or margarine

1/3 cup sliced almonds

1 frozen puff pastry sheet (from 17.3-oz package), thawed

1 round (14 to 15 oz) Brie cheese

1 egg, beaten

Assorted crackers or sliced fresh fruit

1. In 1-quart saucepan, stir cranberries, brown sugar and orange juice until well mixed. Heat to boiling, stirring frequently; reduce heat. Simmer uncovered 15 to 20 minutes, stirring frequently, until mixture thickens and cranberries are tender. Stir in orange peel; remove from heat.

2. In 8-inch skillet, melt butter over medium heat. Cook almonds in butter, stirring frequently, until golden brown; remove from heat.

3. Heat oven to 400°F. Spray cookie sheet with cooking spray. On lightly floured surface, roll pastry into 16 × 9–inch rectangle; cut out one 8 1/2-inch circle and one 7-inch circle.

4. Place cheese round on center of large circle. Spoon cranberry sauce and almonds over cheese. Bring pastry up and press around side of cheese. Brush top edge of pastry with egg. Place 7-inch circle on top, pressing around edge to seal. Brush top and side of pastry with egg. Cut decorations from remaining pastry and arrange on top; brush with egg. Place on cookie sheet.

5. Bake 20 to 25 minutes or until golden brown. Cool on cookie sheet on wire rack 30 minutes before serving. Serve with crackers.

1 SERVING: Calories 320 (Calories from Fat 190); Total Fat 21g (Saturated Fat 9g; Trans Fat 1.5g); Cholesterol 75mg; Sodium 340mg; Total Carbohydrate 22g (Dietary Fiber 1g; Sugars 8g); Protein 10g; % DAILY VALUE: Vitamin A 6%; Vitamin C 0%; Calcium 8%; Iron 8%; EXCHANGES: 1 Starch, 1/2 Other Carbohydrate, 1 Medium-Fat Meat, 3 Fat; CARBOHYDRATE CHOICES: 1 1/2

holiday inspiration

Handy little shortcuts give you more time to spend with family and friends so go ahead and skip making the Cranberry Sauce—buy a can of whole berry cranberry sauce instead.

BRUSCHETTA ROMANA

prep 15 min *total time* 25 min *makes* 12 bruschetta

1 jar (7 oz) roasted red bell peppers, drained, cut into
  1/2-inch strips
1 or 2 medium cloves garlic, finely chopped
2 tablespoons chopped fresh parsley or 1 teaspoon
  parsley flakes
2 tablespoons shredded Parmesan cheese
1 tablespoon olive or vegetable oil
1/4 teaspoon salt
1/4 teaspoon pepper
12 French baguette bread slices, each 1/2 inch thick

1. Heat oven to 450°F. In small bowl, mix all
ingredients except bread slices.

2. Place bread slices on ungreased cookie sheet.
Spoon bell pepper mixture onto bread. Bake 6 to 8
minutes or until edges are golden brown.

1 BRUSCHETTA: Calories 100 (Calories from Fat 25); Total Fat 2.5g
(Saturated Fat 0.5g; Trans Fat 0g); Cholesterol 0mg; Sodium 260mg;
Total Carbohydrate 17g (Dietary Fiber 1g; Sugars 0g); Protein 3g;
% DAILY VALUE: Vitamin A 15%; Vitamin C 20%; Calcium 4%; Iron 6%;
EXCHANGES: 1 Starch, 1/2 Fat; CARBOHYDRATE CHOICES: 1

holiday inspiration

Take an Italian flavor adventure by serving several
of these tempting little toasts. Bruschetta means
"toasted" in Italian, and these small open-faced
sandwiches remain a popular restaurant favorite.

PESTO-BRIE BRUSCHETTA Spread each bread slice with 1 tablespoon basil pesto. Top with thinly sliced unpeeled red apple and thinly sliced Brie cheese. Bake as directed.

PORTABELLA-PARMESAN BRUSCHETTA In 10-inch skillet, heat 2 tablespoons olive oil over medium heat. Add 2 cloves garlic, finely chopped, and 2 packages (12 oz each) portabella mushrooms, chopped. Cook about 10 minutes, stirring occasionally, until light brown. Stir in 1/4 teaspoon salt and 1/8 teaspoon pepper. Spoon mushroom mixture onto bread slices; sprinkle with 1 cup shredded Parm-esan cheese (4 oz). Bake as directed.

STAR BRUSCHETTA Cut bread slices with star-shape cookie cutter. Mix 1 1/2 cups drained, chopped oil-packed sun-dried tomatoes, 3 tablespoons olive oil and 2 cloves garlic, finely chopped. Spread each star with 1 tablespoon mixture. Bake as directed. Garnish each star with rosemary sprig if desired.

CINNAMON CIDER

prep 10 min *total time* 35 min
makes 32 servings (about 1/2 cup each)

1 gallon apple cider
2/3 cup sugar
2 teaspoons whole allspice
2 teaspoons whole cloves
2 cinnamon sticks, 3 inches long
2 oranges, studded with cloves

1. In 4-quart Dutch oven, heat all ingredients except oranges to boiling; reduce heat. Cover; simmer 20 minutes.

2. Strain punch through sieve or colander. Pour into small heatproof punch bowl. Float oranges in bowl. Serve hot.

1 SERVING: Calories 80 (Calories from Fat 0); Total Fat 0g (Saturated Fat 0g; Trans Fat 0g); Cholesterol 0mg; Sodium 0mg; Total Carbohydrate 19g (Dietary Fiber 0g; Sugars 16g); Protein 0g; **% DAILY VALUE:** Vitamin A 0%; Vitamin C 0%; Calcium 0%; Iron 2%; **EXCHANGES:** 1 Fruit, 1/2 Other Carbohydrate; **CARBOHYDRATE CHOICES:** 1

HOT CINNAMON CIDER FLOATS Make cider as directed—except omit oranges with cloves. Place a scoop of cinnamon or vanilla ice cream in large serving mugs; add hot cider and garnish with additional cinnamon sticks if desired.

holiday inspiration

- Pull out the slow cooker to help you with the holidays. When serving hot cider at a holiday buffet, pour heated cider into slow cooker set on Low, and let guests help themselves.

- If you prefer to keep the hot cider in the kitchen, keep the cider in an attractive saucepan right on the stove over low heat. Invite guests into the kitchen to ladle it into their own mugs.

- You can make a glass punch bowl safer for hot beverages by tempering it first. Start by filling it with hot water; let stand 30 minutes. Pour out water, and slowly add hot punch.

HOLIDAY EGGNOG

prep 10 min *total time* 30 min
makes 6 servings (about 3/4 cup each)

3 eggs, slightly beaten
1/3 cup granulated sugar
Dash salt
2 1/2 cups milk
1 teaspoon vanilla
1/2 cup rum, if desired
1 cup whipping (heavy) cream
1 tablespoon packed brown sugar
Ground nutmeg

1. In heavy 2-quart saucepan, mix eggs, granulated sugar and salt. Gradually stir in milk. Cook over low heat 15 to 20 minutes, stirring constantly, just until mixture coats a metal spoon; remove from heat. Stir in vanilla and rum. Keep warm.

2. Just before serving, in chilled small bowl, beat whipping cream and brown sugar with electric mixer on high speed until stiff. Gently stir 1 cup of the whipped cream into eggnog mixture.

3. Pour eggnog into small heatproof punch bowl. Drop remaining whipped cream into 4 or 5 mounds onto eggnog. Sprinkle nutmeg on whipped cream mounds. Serve immediately. Cover and refrigerate any remaining eggnog up to 2 days.

1 SERVING: Calories 260 (Calories from Fat 150); Total Fat 17g (Saturated Fat 10g; Trans Fat 0g); Cholesterol 160mg; Sodium 135mg; Total Carbohydrate 20g (Dietary Fiber 0g; Sugars 20g); Protein 7g; % DAILY VALUE: Vitamin A 15%; Vitamin C 0%; Calcium 15%; Iron 2%; EXCHANGES: 1 Other Carbohydrate, 1/2 Milk, 1/2 Medium-Fat Meat, 2 Fat; CARBOHYDRATE CHOICES: 1

HOT CAPPUCCINO EGGNOG Substitute coffee liqueur for the rum and add 1 cup hot espresso coffee.

new twist

Love the flavor of eggnog but not the calories? Substitute 2 eggs plus 2 egg whites for the 3 eggs and 2 1/4 cups fat-free (skim) milk for the milk. Instead of the beaten whipping cream and brown sugar, use 2 cups frozen (thawed) fat-free whipped topping.

holiday inspiration

The holidays give us permission to splurge on simple pleasures, such as a cup of creamy, heartwarming cheer. So go ahead and take an extra sip of simple indulgence.

- Freeze small dollops of whipped cream by scooping them onto a foil-lined cookie sheet and freezing until firm. Keep them handy in a resealable plastic freezer bag, freezing up to 2 months. Place one dollop on each drink just before serving, and sprinkle lightly with ground cinnamon or nutmeg.

- Put plain or chocolate-dipped pirouette cookies in a pretty serving piece for guests to use as edible stirring spoons.

- Don't have time to make your own eggnog? Dress up purchased eggnog instead. Pour eggnog into a punch bowl, scoop dollops of cinnamon or French vanilla ice cream over the nog and sprinkle with ground nutmeg.

GINGER SHRIMP KABOBS

prep 40 min *total time* 1 hr 40 min *makes* 12 kabobs

12 uncooked large shrimp in shells
1 tablespoon grated gingerroot
2 tablespoons lime juice
2 teaspoons soy sauce
1 teaspoon dark sesame oil
1/4 teaspoon crushed red pepper flakes
3 cloves garlic, finely chopped
2 medium bell peppers
12 small whole mushrooms
6 green onions, cut into 1-inch pieces

1. Peel shrimp. (If shrimp are frozen, do not thaw; peel in cold water.) Make a shallow cut lengthwise down back of each shrimp; wash out vein.

2. In glass or plastic dish, mix gingerroot, lime juice, soy sauce, sesame oil, red pepper and garlic. Stir in shrimp until well coated. Cover; refrigerate 1 hour.

3. Cut bell peppers with small star-shaped cookie cutter, or cut into 1-inch squares.

4. Set oven control to broil. Remove shrimp from marinade; reserve marinade. On each of twelve 6-inch skewers, alternately thread bell pepper star, mushroom, shrimp and onion pieces. Brush lightly with marinade. Place on rack in broiler pan.

5. Broil with tops about 4 inches from heat about 6 minutes, turning once, until shrimp are pink and vegetables are crisp-tender. Discard remaining marinade.

1 KABOB: Calories 25 (Calories from Fat 0); Total Fat 0.5g (Saturated Fat 0g; Trans Fat 0g); Cholesterol 10mg; Sodium 65mg; Total Carbohydrate 3g (Dietary Fiber 0g; Sugars 0g); Protein 2g; % DAILY VALUE: Vitamin A 2%; Vitamin C 15%; Calcium 0%; Iron 2%; EXCHANGES: 1/2 Very Lean Meat; CARBOHYDRATE CHOICES: 0

make-ahead magic

To make ahead, cover and refrigerate the kabobs up to 24 hours, broil just before guests arrive.

holiday inspiration

For a large group of guests who may not know one another, provide name tags. Have each guest add an interesting tidbit, like their favorite movie, under their name. They'll be great conversation icebreakers!

FESTIVE CHEESE PLATTER

prep 25 min *total time* 25 min
makes 16 servings

16 slices (1 oz each) assorted cheeses (such as Cheddar, Colby–Monterey Jack, pepper Jack and Swiss)
1/2 cup salted roasted whole almonds
16 crackers

1. Cut cheese with 2-inch tree, Santa, snowman, star or other cookie cutter in holiday shape. Leftover pieces of cheese can be used in other recipes like nachos, macaroni and cheese or omelets.

2. On medium platter, arrange cheese, overlapping shapes slightly. Sprinkle with almonds. Serve with crackers.

1 SERVING: Calories 160 (Calories from Fat 120); Total Fat 13g (Saturated Fat 6g; Trans Fat 0g); Cholesterol 30mg; Sodium 220mg; Total Carbohydrate 3g (Dietary Fiber 0g; Sugars 0g); Protein 8g; % DAILY VALUE: Vitamin A 6%; Vitamin C 0%; Calcium 15%; Iron 2%; EXCHANGES: 1 Vegetable, 1 High-Fat Meat, 1 Fat; CARBOHYDRATE CHOICES: 0

FESTIVE FRUIT AND CHEESE PLATTER Omit purchased sliced cheese. Cut two 8-oz blocks assorted cheeses (such as Cheddar, Colby-Monterey Jack or Swiss) crosswise into 1/4-inch-thick slices; place on platter. Arrange 1 pint (2 cups) small whole strawberries, 1 cup each whole green and red grapes, 1 medium unpeeled apple, sliced, and 1 medium unpeeled pear, sliced, on platter with cheese. Brush apple and pear slices with lemon or orange juice to prevent them from turning brown. 18 to 20 servings.

TEX-MEX CHEESE PLATTER Omit purchased sliced cheese. Cut two 8-oz blocks assorted cheeses (such as Cheddar, Colby–Monterey Jack or pepper Jack) into 1-inch cubes; place on platter. Arrange 1 cup each whole ripe olives and pimiento-stuffed olives on platter with cheese. Drizzle lightly with salsa, and garnish with fresh cilantro leaves. 18 to 20 servings.

Top to bottom: Festive Fruit and Cheese Platter, Tex-Mex Cheese Platter and Festive Cheese Platter

HERB-COATED MINI CHEESE BALLS

prep 30 min   *total time* 1 hr 30 min
makes 24 servings (1 cheese ball and 1 bagel chip each)

4 oz cream cheese (half of 8-oz package), softened
1/2 cup crumbled feta cheese (4 oz)*
1/2 teaspoon coarse ground pepper
1/4 cup finely chopped fresh parsley
3 tablespoons finely chopped fresh basil leaves
1 tablespoon finely chopped fresh rosemary leaves
1 teaspoon grated lemon peel
24 plain mini bagel chips (1 1/4 inch)

1. In small bowl, mix cheeses and 1/4 teaspoon of the pepper, using fork or back of spoon to mash feta, until well blended. Cover; refrigerate 45 to 60 minutes or until firm enough to shape into balls.

2. In small shallow bowl, mix parsley, basil, rosemary, lemon peel and remaining 1/4 teaspoon pepper. Shape cheese mixture into 1-inch balls (about 1 teaspoon cheese mixture for each ball); roll in parsley mixture to coat (some cheese will show through herbs).

3. To serve immediately, place each ball on a bagel chip. To make ahead, do not place cheese balls on bagel chips; cover with plastic wrap and refrigerate until ready to serve but no longer than 24 hours. Just before serving, place each ball on a bagel chip.

*Chèvre (goat) cheese or blue cheese can be substituted for the feta cheese, but the mixture will be softer.

1 SERVING: Calories 35 (Calories from Fat 25); Total Fat 3g (Saturated Fat 2g; Trans Fat 0g); Cholesterol 10mg; Sodium 75mg; Total Carbohydrate 1g (Dietary Fiber 0g; Sugars 0g); Protein 1g; % DAILY VALUE: Vitamin A 4%; Vitamin C 0%; Calcium 2%; Iron 0%; EXCHANGES: 1/2 Fat; CARBOHYDRATE CHOICES: 0

holiday inspiration

Good things come in small bites! Insert decorative plastic picks or wooden picks into these cool, flavor-packed cheese balls, and mingle with assorted olives on a flat or very shallow platter. Garnish with sprigs of fresh herbs.

SAUSAGE-CHEESE BALLS

prep 20 min   *total time* 45 min
makes about 8 1/2 dozen cheese balls

3 cups Original Bisquick® mix
1 lb bulk pork sausage
4 cups shredded Cheddar cheese (1 lb)
1/2 cup grated Parmesan cheese
1/2 cup milk
1/2 teaspoon dried rosemary leaves, crushed
1 1/2 teaspoons chopped fresh parsley or
    1/2 teaspoon parsley flakes

1. Heat oven to 350°F. Lightly spray 15 × 10 × 1-inch pan with cooking spray.

2. In large bowl, stir all ingredients until well mixed (you may need to use your hands). Shape mixture into 1-inch balls. Place in pan.

3. Bake uncovered 20 to 25 minutes or until brown. Immediately remove from pan. Serve warm.

1 CHEESE BALL: Calories 40 (Calories from Fat 25); Total Fat 3g (Saturated Fat 1.5g; Trans Fat 0g); Cholesterol 5mg; Sodium 115mg; Total Carbohydrate 2g (Dietary Fiber 0g; Sugars 0g); Protein 2g; % DAILY VALUE: Vitamin A 0%; Vitamin C 0%; Calcium 4%; Iron 0%; EXCHANGES: 1/2 High-Fat Meat; CARBOHYDRATE CHOICES: 0

HOLIDAY HAM BALLS Substitute 1 1/2 cups finely chopped fully cooked ham for the sausage. Use 2 tablespoons parsley flakes and 2/3 cup milk. Omit rosemary. Mix and bake as directed.

make-ahead magic

These tasty nibbles are one of Betty Crocker's most requested recipes, and they can be prepared up to 1 day ahead of time. Cover and refrigerate; bake as directed. Or cover and freeze unbaked balls up to 1 month. Bake frozen balls 25 to 30 minutes or until brown.

Top to bottom: Sausage-Cheese Balls
and Herb-Coated Mini Cheese Balls

POACHED SALMON APPETIZER

prep 35 min *total time* 3 hrs 5 min

makes 8 servings (with 2 bread slices each)

Salmon

4 cups water

3 or 4 slices lemon, cut in half

3 or 4 slices onion, cut in half

1/4 cup small sprigs parsley

1/2 teaspoon salt

1/4 teaspoon coarsely ground pepper

1 salmon fillet (1 lb)

1/4 teaspoon salt

Topping

1/4 cup chopped fresh parsley

2 tablespoons finely chopped red onion

2 teaspoons capers

1 teaspoon grated lemon peel

Honey Mustard Sauce

2 tablespoons lemon juice

1 tablespoon honey

1 tablespoon Dijon mustard

1 tablespoon olive or vegetable oil

Accompaniment

Cocktail bread slices or crackers, if desired

1. In 10- or 12-inch skillet, heat water, lemon slices, onion slices, parsley sprigs, 1/2 teaspoon salt and the pepper to boiling; boil 3 minutes. Reduce heat to medium-low. Add salmon, skin side down. Cover; cook 5 to 6 minutes or until salmon flakes easily with fork. Remove salmon from liquid in skillet; discard liquid. Let salmon stand up to 30 minutes to cool. Cover; refrigerate at least 2 hours but no longer than 24 hours.

2. In small bowl, mix all topping ingredients until well blended.

3. In small bowl, mix all sauce ingredients until well blended.

4. To serve, carefully remove skin from salmon; place salmon on serving plate. Sprinkle with 1/4 teaspoon salt. Drizzle sauce over top; sprinkle with topping. Serve with bread slices.

1 SERVING: Calories 100 (Calories from Fat 40); Total Fat 4.5g (Saturated Fat 1g; Trans Fat 0g); Cholesterol 30mg; Sodium 240mg; Total Carbohydrate 3g (Dietary Fiber 0g; Sugars 2g); Protein 10g; **% DAILY VALUE:** Vitamin A 4%; Vitamin C 4%; Calcium 0%; Iron 2%; **EXCHANGES:** 1 1/2 Lean Meat; **CARBOHYDRATE CHOICES:** 0

make-ahead magic

The Honey Mustard Sauce can be made up to 1 day ahead of time. Cover and refrigerate until serving time. If you need an extra shortcut, pick up a jar of honey mustard sauce at the store.

SLOW COOKER NACHO BEAN DIP

prep 20 min *total time* 4 hrs 20 min

makes 72 servings (2 tablespoons dip and 6 small or 3 large tortilla chips each)

2 cans (16 oz each) refried beans

2 cans (15 oz each) black beans, drained, rinsed

1 can (4.5 oz) chopped green chiles, undrained

1 package (1.25 oz) 40%-less-sodium taco seasoning mix

2 loaves (1 lb each) Mexican prepared cheese product with jalapeño peppers, cut into cubes

1 cup finely shredded Mexican cheese blend (4 oz)

Tortilla chips

1. In 3 1/2- to 4-quart slow cooker, mix all ingredients except shredded cheese blend and tortilla chips.

2. Cover; cook on Low heat setting 3 to 4 hours, stirring after 2 hours, until cheese is melted.

3. Scrape down side of slow cooker with rubber spatula to help prevent edge of dip from scorching. Sprinkle with shredded cheese blend. Serve with tortilla chips. Dip will hold on Low heat setting up to 2 hours.

1 SERVING: Calories 80 (Calories from Fat 30); Total Fat 3g (Saturated Fat 1g; Trans Fat 0g); Cholesterol 5mg; Sodium 190mg; Total Carbohydrate 9g (Dietary Fiber 2g; Sugars 0g); Protein 4g; % DAILY VALUE: Vitamin A 2%; Vitamin C 0%; Calcium 6%; Iron 4%; EXCHANGES: 1/2 Starch, 1/2 High-Fat Meat; CARBOHYDRATE CHOICES: 1/2

holiday inspiration

This dip definitely serves a crowd! If you're serving just a few, use the leftovers to make a filling for wraps, burritos and enchiladas, or serve it over baked potatoes. You can't beat cooking once and eating twice!

SLOW COOKER CREAMY BEEF DIP

prep 20 min *total time* 2 hrs 20 min

makes 26 servings (2 tablespoons dip and 2 bread slices each)

2 packages (8 oz each) cream cheese, cut into pieces, softened

2 packages (2.25 oz each) dried beef, chopped (1 1/4 cups)

1 cup shredded Swiss cheese (4 oz)

1/3 cup sliced green onions (about 5 medium)

3/4 teaspoon ground mustard

1/2 cup beer or reduced-sodium beef broth

About 1 1/4 lb sliced pumpernickel cocktail bread

1. In medium bowl, mix all ingredients except bread. Spoon into 2- to 3-quart slow cooker.

2. Cover; cook on Low heat setting 1 to 2 hours, stirring occasionally, until mixture is melted and hot. Dip will hold on Low heat setting up to 2 hours. Serve with bread.

1 SERVING: Calories 140 (Calories from Fat 70); Total Fat 8g (Saturated Fat 5g; Trans Fat 0g); Cholesterol 25mg; Sodium 380mg; Total Carbohydrate 11g (Dietary Fiber 1g; Sugars 1g); Protein 6g; % DAILY VALUE: Vitamin A 6%; Vitamin C 0%; Calcium 8%; Iron 6%; EXCHANGES: 1/2 Starch, 1/2 High-Fat Meat, 1 Fat; CARBOHYDRATE CHOICES: 1

holiday inspiration

Jazz up this sensational dip by sprinkling the top with more sliced green onions or a mixture of chopped green onions and red bell peppers for a classic color combo and great taste.

the MAIN EVENT

make-ahead magic

To make ahead, prepare through Step 2, then cover and refrigerate up to 12 hours. Bake as directed.

holiday inspiration

For a lovely brunch, serve with warm cornbread with honey butter and a fruit salad of orange and grapefruit sections along with mango pieces. Sprinkle the salad with pomegranate seeds. By the way, if you can't find a 12-oz package of sausage, use the 16 oz size.

Tex-Mex Sausage and Egg Bake

TEX-MEX SAUSAGE *and* EGG BAKE

prep 20 min *total time* 1 hr 30 min *makes* 10 servings

12 oz bulk spicy pork sausage

5 cups frozen southern-style hash brown potatoes (from 32-oz bag)

1 can (4.5 oz) chopped green chiles, undrained

3 cups shredded Colby-Monterey Jack cheese (12 oz)

6 eggs

1 1/2 cups milk

1/4 teaspoon salt

1 cup chunky-style salsa

Sour cream, if desired

1. Heat oven to 350°F. Spray 13 × 9-inch (3-quart) glass baking dish with cooking spray. In 10-inch skillet, cook sausage over medium heat 8 to 10 minutes, stirring occasionally, until no longer pink. Drain on paper towel.

2. Spread frozen potatoes in baking dish. Sprinkle with sausage, green chiles and 1 1/2 cups of the cheese. In medium bowl, beat eggs, milk and salt with fork or wire whisk until well blended. Pour over potato mixture. Sprinkle with remaining 1 1/2 cups cheese.

3. Bake uncovered 50 to 60 minutes or until knife inserted near center comes out clean. Let stand 10 minutes before serving. Cut into squares. Serve with salsa and sour cream.

1 SERVING: Calories 350 (Calories from Fat 180); Total Fat 20g (Saturated Fat 10g; Trans Fat 0g); Cholesterol 175mg; Sodium 770mg; Total Carbohydrate 26g (Dietary Fiber 2g; Sugars 4g); Protein 18g; % DAILY VALUE: Vitamin A 15%; Vitamin C 10%; Calcium 30%; Iron 8%; EXCHANGES: 1 1/2 Starch, 1 Vegetable, 1 1/2 Medium-Fat Meat, 2 Fat; CARBOHYDRATE CHOICES: 2

HASH BROWN POTATO BRUNCH BAKE

prep 15 min *total time* 1 hr 5 min *makes* 8 servings

1 can (10 3/4 oz) condensed cream of mushroom soup

1 can (10 3/4 oz) condensed cream of chicken soup

1 container (8 oz) sour cream

1/2 cup milk

1/4 teaspoon pepper

1 bag (30 oz) frozen shredded hash brown potatoes, partially thawed

8 medium green onions, sliced (1/2 cup)

1 cup shredded Cheddar cheese (4 oz)

1. Heat oven to 350°F. Spray 13 × 9-inch (3-quart) glass baking dish with cooking spray.

2. In very large bowl, mix soups, sour cream, milk and pepper. Stir in potatoes and onions. Spoon into baking dish.

3. Bake uncovered 30 minutes. Sprinkle with cheese. Bake 15 to 20 minutes longer or until golden brown on top and bubbly around edges.

1 SERVING: Calories 330 (Calories from Fat 140); Total Fat 15g (Saturated Fat 8g; Trans Fat 0g); Cholesterol 40mg; Sodium 680mg; Total Carbohydrate 39g (Dietary Fiber 4g; Sugars 4g); Protein 9g; % DAILY VALUE: Vitamin A 15%; Vitamin C 10%; Calcium 15%; Iron 6%; EXCHANGES: 2 1/2 Starch, 3 Fat; CARBOHYDRATE CHOICES: 2 1/2

HASH BROWN HAM AND POTATO BRUNCH BAKE
Stir in 2 cups diced fully cooked ham with the potatoes in Step 2.

make-ahead magic

To make ahead, assemble the recipe in the baking dish; cover and refrigerate up to 12 hours. Bake uncovered at 350°F for 40 minutes. Sprinkle with cheese, then bake 15 to 20 minutes longer as directed.

HAM and CHEDDAR STRATA

prep 15 min *total time* 1 hr 35 min *makes* 8 servings

12 slices bread
2 cups cut-up fully cooked ham (about 10 oz)
2 cups shredded Cheddar cheese (8 oz)
8 medium green onions, sliced (1/2 cup)
6 eggs
2 cups milk
1 teaspoon ground mustard
1/4 teaspoon red pepper sauce
Paprika

1. Heat oven to 300°F. Spray 13 × 9–inch (3-quart) glass baking dish with cooking spray.

2. Trim crusts from bread. Arrange 6 slices bread in baking dish. Layer ham, cheese and onions on bread in dish. Cut remaining bread slices diagonally in half; arrange on onions.

3. In medium bowl, beat eggs, milk, mustard and pepper sauce with fork or wire whisk; pour evenly over bread. Sprinkle with paprika.

4. Bake uncovered 1 hour to 1 hour 10 minutes or until center is set and bread is golden brown. Let stand 10 minutes before serving.

1 SERVING: Calories 370 (Calories from Fat 170); Total Fat 19g (Saturated Fat 9g; Trans Fat 0.5g); Cholesterol 215mg; Sodium 990mg; Total Carbohydrate 24g (Dietary Fiber 1g; Sugars 5g); Protein 25g; % DAILY VALUE: Vitamin A 20%; Vitamin C 2%; Calcium 30%; Iron 15%; EXCHANGES: 1 Starch, 1/2 Other Carbohydrate, 3 Medium-Fat Meat, 1/2 Fat; CARBOHYDRATE CHOICES: 1 1/2

make-ahead magic

To make ahead, follow the directions through Step 3, then cover and refrigerate up to 24 hours. Bake as directed.

BRUNCH OVEN OMELET

prep 10 min *total time* 45 min *makes* 12 servings

1/4 cup butter or margarine
18 eggs
1 cup sour cream
1 cup milk
2 teaspoons salt
4 medium green onions, chopped (1/4 cup)
Chopped fresh parsley

1. Heat oven to 325°F. In 13 × 9–inch (3-quart) glass baking dish, melt butter in oven; tilt dish to coat bottom.

2. In large bowl, beat eggs, sour cream, milk and salt with fork or wire whisk until blended. Stir in onions. Pour into baking dish.

3. Bake uncovered about 35 minutes or until eggs are set but moist. Sprinkle with parsley.

1 SERVING: Calories 200 (Calories from Fat 140); Total Fat 16g (Saturated Fat 7g; Trans Fat 0g); Cholesterol 340mg; Sodium 530mg; Total Carbohydrate 3g (Dietary Fiber 0g; Sugars 3g); Protein 11g; % DAILY VALUE: Vitamin A 15%; Vitamin C 0%; Calcium 8%; Iron 6%; EXCHANGES: 1 1/2 Medium-Fat Meat, 2 Fat; CARBOHYDRATE CHOICES: 0

MAPLE-GLAZED BACON AND CHEDDAR BRUNCH OVEN OMELET Cut 1 lb Canadian-style bacon into 24 (1/8-inch) slices. Reassemble slices of bacon on sheet of heavy-duty foil. Pour 1/4 cup maple-flavored syrup over bacon. Wrap and bake with omelet in oven. Sprinkle each serving of the omelet with shredded Cheddar cheese and then the parsley; serve with bacon.

MEDITERRANEAN BRUNCH OVEN OMELET Serve with a mixture of drained artichoke heart quarters or undrained marinated artichoke hearts (either warmed if desired), chopped red and orange bell peppers and sliced ripe olives or Kalamata olives. Omit the parsley and garnish with sprigs of fresh oregano.

Brunch Oven Omelet

BACON *and* SWISS QUICHE

prep 25 min *total time* 2 hrs 5 min *makes* 6 servings

Pastry

1 cup all-purpose flour

1/2 teaspoon salt

1/3 cup plus 1 tablespoon shortening

2 to 3 tablespoons cold water

Quiche

8 slices bacon, crisply cooked, crumbled

1 cup shredded Swiss cheese (4 oz)

1/3 cup finely chopped onion

4 eggs

2 cups whipping (heavy) cream or half-and-half

1/4 teaspoon salt

1/4 teaspoon pepper

1/8 teaspoon ground red pepper (cayenne)

Additional crisply cooked crumbled bacon, if desired

1. In medium bowl, mix flour and 1/2 teaspoon salt. Cut in shortening, using pastry blender (or pulling 2 table knives through ingredients in opposite directions), until particles are size of small peas. Sprinkle with cold water, 1 tablespoon at a time, tossing with fork until all flour is moistened and pastry almost leaves side of bowl (1 to 2 teaspoons more water can be added if necessary).

2. Gather pastry into a ball. Shape into flattened round on lightly floured surface. Wrap flattened round of pastry in plastic wrap and refrigerate about 45 minutes or until dough is firm and cold, yet pliable. This allows the shortening to become slightly firm, which helps make the baked pastry more flaky. If refrigerated longer, let pastry soften slightly before rolling.

3. Heat oven to 425°F. Roll pastry on lightly floured surface, using floured rolling pin, into circle 2 inches larger than upside-down 9-inch quiche dish or glass pie plate. Fold pastry into fourths; place in quiche dish or pie plate. Unfold and ease into dish, pressing firmly against bottom and side.

4. Sprinkle bacon, cheese and onion in pastry-lined quiche dish. In large bowl, beat eggs slightly with fork or wire whisk. Beat in remaining ingredients. Pour into quiche dish.

5. Bake 15 minutes. Reduce oven temperature to 300°F. Bake about 30 minutes longer or until knife inserted in center comes out clean. Sprinkle with additional bacon. Let stand 10 minutes before serving.

1 SERVING: Calories 620 (Calories from Fat 470); Total Fat 52g (Saturated Fat 25g; Trans Fat 3g); Cholesterol 255mg; Sodium 580mg; Total Carbohydrate 20g (Dietary Fiber 0g; Sugars 3g); Protein 17g; **% DAILY VALUE:** Vitamin A 25%; Vitamin C 0%; Calcium 25%; Iron 10% **EXCHANGES:** 1 1/2 Starch, 2 High-Fat Meat, 7 Fat; **CARBOHYDRATE CHOICES:** 1

SEAFOOD QUICHE Substitute 1 cup chopped cooked crabmeat (pat dry), shrimp, seafood sticks (imitation crabmeat) or salmon for the bacon, use green onions and increase salt to 1/2 teaspoon.

holiday inspiration

Divine, divine and divine—this will be the best quiche you've ever tasted! The filling is like liquid satin—it's just so rich and creamy, not at all "eggy tasting," like many recipes can be. To save time, go ahead and use a purchased refrigerated pie crust instead of making it from scratch.

SOUR CREAM–BLUEBERRY PANCAKES

prep 15 min   *total time* 15 min   *makes* 15 pancakes

2 cups Original Bisquick mix
1 cup sour cream
1/2 cup milk
2 eggs
1 cup fresh or frozen (thawed and drained) blueberries
Maple syrup, if desired

1. Heat griddle to 375°F or heat skillet over medium-high heat; grease with vegetable oil if necessary (or spray with cooking spray before heating).

2. In large bowl, stir all ingredients except blueberries and syrup until blended. Stir in blueberries.

3. For each pancake, pour batter by slightly less than 1/4 cupfuls onto hot griddle. Cook about 1 1/2 minutes or until puffed and dry around edges. Turn; cook other sides until golden brown. Serve with syrup.

1 PANCAKE: Calories 110 (Calories from Fat 50); Total Fat 6g (Saturated Fat 2.5g; Trans Fat 0g); Cholesterol 40mg; Sodium 250mg; Total Carbohydrate 12g (Dietary Fiber 0g; Sugars 3g); Protein 3g; % DAILY VALUE: Vitamin A 4%; Vitamin C 0%; Calcium 6%; Iron 4%; EXCHANGES: 1 Starch, 1 Fat; CARBOHYDRATE CHOICES: 1

holiday inspiration

Yum! Besides the maple syrup, offer blueberry pancake syrup, blueberry pie filling and whipped cream for topping.

BRUNCH POTATOES ALFREDO *with* ROASTED PEPPERS

prep 10 min   *total time* 55 min   *makes* 10 servings

7 cups frozen country-style shredded hash brown potatoes (from 30-oz bag), thawed
1 jar (7 oz) roasted red bell peppers, drained, chopped
4 medium green onions, sliced (1/4 cup)
1 container (10 oz) refrigerated Alfredo pasta sauce
1 1/2 cups shredded Swiss cheese (6 oz)
Additional sliced green onions and bell peppers, if desired

1. Heat oven to 350°F. Spray 11 × 7-inch or 12 × 8-inch glass baking dish with cooking spray.

2. Place potatoes, bell peppers and green onions in baking dish; mix lightly. Top with Alfredo sauce; sprinkle with cheese.

3. Bake uncovered 40 to 45 minutes or until golden brown. Sprinkle with additional green onions and bell peppers just before serving.

1 SERVING: Calories 290 (Calories from Fat 120); Total Fat 14g (Saturated Fat 8g; Trans Fat 0g); Cholesterol 45mg; Sodium 200mg; Total Carbohydrate 32g (Dietary Fiber 3g; Sugars 2g); Protein 10g; % DAILY VALUE: Vitamin A 25%; Vitamin C 30%; Calcium 25%; Iron 4%; EXCHANGES: 2 Starch, 1/2 High-Fat Meat, 2 Fat; CARBOHYDRATE CHOICES: 2

make-ahead magic

To make ahead, assemble all of the ingredients in the baking dish; cover and refrigerate up to 12 hours. You don't need to thaw the potatoes because they'll thaw while in the fridge.

holiday inspiration

To serve this right away, get a jump-start by quickly thawing the potatoes in the microwave. Simply microwave them in a microwavable bowl uncovered on High for 3 to 5 minutes, stirring once.

CHOCOLATE CHIP–BANANA PANCAKES

prep 15 min   *total time* 15 min   *makes* 12 pancakes

2 eggs
1 1/2 cups all-purpose flour
2 tablespoons sugar
2 teaspoons baking powder
1/2 teaspoon salt
1 1/4 cups milk
2 tablespoons butter or margarine, melted
1 teaspoon vanilla
1 large banana, peeled, chopped
1/2 cup miniature semisweet chocolate chips

1. Heat griddle to 375°F or heat skillet over medium-high heat; grease with vegetable oil if necessary (or spray with cooking spray before heating).

2. In large bowl, beat eggs with wire whisk until lightly beaten. Beat in remaining ingredients except banana and chocolate chips just until smooth. Stir in banana and chocolate chips.

3. For each pancake, pour batter by slightly less than 1/4 cupfuls onto hot griddle. Cook about 1 1/2 minutes or until puffed and dry around edges. Turn; cook other sides until golden brown.

1 PANCAKE: Calories 160 (Calories from Fat 50); Total Fat 6g (Saturated Fat 3g; Trans Fat 0g); Cholesterol 40mg; Sodium 220mg; Total Carbohydrate 23g (Dietary Fiber 1g; Sugars 9g); Protein 4g; **% DAILY VALUE:** Vitamin A 4%; Vitamin C 0%; Calcium 8%; Iron 6%; **EXCHANGES:** 1 Starch, 1/2 Other Carbohydrate, 1 Fat; **CARBOHYDRATE CHOICES:** 1 1/2

holiday inspiration

Dress up these delicious pancakes with fresh currants or sliced fresh strawberries and a dollop of whipped cream. Don't forget those chocolate lovers—put a bowl of extra chips on the table for happy sprinkling.

CHRISTMAS BREAKFAST CREPES

prep 45 min *total time* 45 min *makes* 6 servings

Strawberry Topping

3 cups sliced strawberries (about 1 1/2 pints)

1/2 cup sugar

Crepes

1 1/2 cups all-purpose flour

1 tablespoon sugar

1/2 teaspoon baking powder

1/2 teaspoon salt

2 cups milk

2 tablespoons butter or margarine, melted

1 teaspoon finely shredded lime peel

2 tablespoons lime juice

2 eggs

Lime Cream Filling

2/3 cup whipping (heavy) cream

1 package (8 oz) cream cheese, softened

1/2 cup sugar

1 tablespoon finely shredded lime peel

1. In large bowl, toss strawberries and 1/2 cup sugar. Let stand at room temperature at least 20 minutes.

2. Meanwhile, in medium bowl, mix flour, 1 tablespoon sugar, the baking powder and salt. Stir in milk, butter, 1 teaspoon lime peel, the lime juice and eggs. Beat with egg beater until smooth.

3. Lightly grease 6- to 8-inch skillet with butter. Heat over medium heat until bubbly. Pour batter by slightly less than 1/4 cupfuls into skillet. Immediately rotate skillet until thin layer of batter covers bottom. Cook until light golden brown. Run wide spatula around edge to loosen; turn and cook other side until light brown. Repeat with remaining batter, greasing skillet as needed. Stack crepes, placing waxed paper between each; cool.

4. In chilled small bowl, beat whipping cream with electric mixer on high speed until stiff; set aside. In medium bowl, beat cream cheese on high speed until fluffy; stir in 1/2 cup sugar and 1 tablespoon lime peel. Gently stir in whipped cream. Spoon about 2 tablespoons of the filling down center of each crepe; fold sides over filling. To serve, place 2 crepes on each of 6 plates. Spoon strawberries over crepes.

1 **SERVING:** Calories 600 (Calories from Fat 260); Total Fat 29g (Saturated Fat 17g; Trans Fat 1g); Cholesterol 160mg; Sodium 440mg; Total Carbohydrate 72g (Dietary Fiber 3g; Sugars 46g); Protein 12g; % **DAILY VALUE:** Vitamin A 25%; Vitamin C 40%; Calcium 20%; Iron 15%; **EXCHANGES:** 2 Starch, 1 Fruit, 1 1/2 Other Carbohydrate, 1 High-Fat Meat, 4 Fat; **CARBOHYDRATE CHOICES:** 5

make-ahead magic

To make ahead, unfilled crepes can be tightly covered with foil and refrigerated up to 48 hours before serving.

holiday inspiration

We eat with our eyes first and just a little bit of garnish makes these crepes so special. Try arranging thin strips of lime peel and a dollop of whipped cream on top of each serving—Christmas green that packs a punch!

MORNING GLORY OVEN FRENCH TOAST

prep 25 min   *total time* 40 min   *makes* 6 servings

Cranberry-Raspberry Topping

1 box (10 oz) frozen raspberries, thawed

1 cup granulated sugar

1 cup fresh or frozen cranberries

French Toast

3 eggs

3/4 cup milk

1 tablespoon granulated sugar

1/4 teaspoon salt

1/4 teaspoon ground cinnamon

18 slices French bread, 1/2 inch thick

Powdered sugar, if desired

1. Drain raspberries, reserving 1/2 cup juice. In 2-quart saucepan, mix juice and 1 cup sugar. Heat to boiling; boil 5 minutes. Stir in raspberries and cranberries; reduce heat. Simmer about 3 minutes, stirring occasionally, until cranberries are tender but do not burst. Serve warm or cool.

2. Heat oven to 500°F. In small bowl, beat eggs, milk, 1 tablespoon granulated sugar, the salt and cinnamon with fork.

3. Dip bread into egg mixture; place on plate. Lightly grease cookie sheet with shortening or cooking spray. Heat cookie sheet in oven 1 minute; remove from oven. Place dipped bread on hot cookie sheet.

4. Bake 5 to 8 minutes or until bottoms are golden brown. Turn bread; bake 2 to 4 minutes longer or until golden brown. Sprinkle with powdered sugar. Serve with topping.

1 SERVING: Calories 490 (Calories from Fat 60); Total Fat 7g (Saturated Fat 2g; Trans Fat 0.5g); Cholesterol 110mg; Sodium 700mg; Total Carbohydrate 93g (Dietary Fiber 7g; Sugars 43g); Protein 13g; % DAILY VALUE: Vitamin A 4%; Vitamin C 10%; Calcium 15%; Iron 20%; EXCHANGES: 2 Starch, 1 Fruit, 3 Other Carbohydrate, 1 Lean Meat, 1 Fat; CARBOHYDRATE CHOICES: 6

holiday inspiration

Add a little panache to your table!

- Cover the table or countertop with holiday gift wrap or cut holiday shapes from gift wrap (using cookie cutters as patterns) to scatter on a tablecloth. Add candles for a festive setting.

- Top it off with an easy centerpiece made by filling a basket or copper bowl with small evergreen branches, pinecones, whole oranges and grapefruit, unshelled nuts and cinnamon sticks.

ROASTED BEEF TENDERLOIN

prep 15 min *total time* 1 hr 15 min *makes* 6 servings

2 1/2-lb beef tenderloin
1 tablespoon olive or vegetable oil
1/2 teaspoon coarsely ground pepper
1/2 teaspoon dried marjoram leaves
1/4 teaspoon coarse kosher salt, coarse sea salt or
   regular salt

1. Heat oven to 425°F. Turn small end of beef under about 6 inches. Tie turned-under portion of beef with string at about 1 1/2-inch intervals. Place in shallow roasting pan. Brush with oil. Sprinkle with pepper, marjoram and salt. Insert ovenproof meat thermometer so tip is in thickest part of beef.

2. For medium-rare, roast 35 to 40 minutes or until thermometer reads 135°F. Cover loosely with foil and let stand 15 to 20 minutes until thermometer reads 145°F. (Temperature will continue to rise about 10°F, and beef will be easier to carve.) For medium, roast uncovered 45 to 50 minutes or until thermometer reads 150°F. Cover beef loosely with foil and let stand 15 to 20 minutes until thermometer reads 160°F. Remove string from beef before carving. Serve with pan drippings, if desired.

1 SERVING: Calories 230 (Calories from Fat 110); Total Fat 12g (Saturated Fat 4g; Trans Fat 0g); Cholesterol 80mg; Sodium 170mg; Total Carbohydrate 0g (Dietary Fiber 0g; Sugars 0g); Protein 30g; % DAILY VALUE: Vitamin A 0%; Vitamin C 0%; Calcium 0%; Iron 15%; EXCHANGES: 4 Lean Meat; CARBOHYDRATE CHOICES: 0

HERB-BUTTER TENDERLOIN Mix softened butter with a mixture of chopped fresh herbs like basil, oregano and chives. Top servings of hot steak with a dollop of softened herb butter. Sprinkle with additional chopped fresh herbs or whole herb leaves if desired.

HORSERADISH-SAUCED TENDERLOIN Top servings of hot steak with a spoonful of Horseradish Sauce (page 69), and sprinkle with a mixture of coarsely ground fresh peppercorns and chopped fresh parsley.

PESTO TENDERLOIN Top servings of hot steak with purchased pesto, chopped seeded plum (Roma) tomatoes and shavings of Parmesan or Asiago cheese.

holiday inspiration

For your wine-loving guests, here is a novel multi-purpose party favor. Write your menu on each bottle of wine with a china or dry-erase marker. Set a bottle at each place setting. Not only will your guests be tempted by the menu, they'll also get to take the wine home.

CROWN ROAST *of* PORK *with* STUFFING

prep 30 min   *total time* 4 hrs 10 min   *makes* 16 servings

8- to 10-lb pork crown roast (about 16 to 18 ribs)
2 teaspoons salt
1 teaspoon pepper
Apple-Cranberry Stuffing or Bread Stuffing (page 73)

1. Heat oven to 325°F. Sprinkle pork with salt and pepper. Place pork, with bone ends up, on rack in shallow roasting pan. Wrap bone ends in foil to prevent excessive browning. Insert ovenproof meat thermometer so tip is in thickest part of pork and does not touch bone or rest in fat. Place small heatproof bowl or crumpled foil in crown to hold shape of roast evenly.

2. Roast uncovered 2 hours 40 minutes to 3 hours 20 minutes. Meanwhile, make Apple-Cranberry Stuffing. About 1 hour before pork is done, remove bowl or foil and fill center of crown with stuffing. Cover stuffing with foil for first 30 minutes of roasting.

3. Remove pork from oven when thermometer reads 150°F, cover with tent of foil and let stand 15 to 20 minutes or until thermometer reads 160°F. (Temperature will continue to rise about 10°F, and pork will be easier to carve.) Remove foil from bone ends; place paper frills on bone ends. To carve, cut roast between ribs.

1 SERVING: Calories 410 (Calories from Fat 200); Total Fat 22g (Saturated Fat 9g; Trans Fat 0.5g); Cholesterol 125mg; Sodium 690mg; Total Carbohydrate 17g (Dietary Fiber 1g; Sugars 4g); Protein 37g; % DAILY VALUE: Vitamin A 8%; Vitamin C 2%; Calcium 4%; Iron 10%; EXCHANGES: 1 Starch, 5 Lean Meat, 1 Fat; CARBOHYDRATE CHOICES: 1

holiday inspiration

This spectacular special roast is usually available during the holidays, so call the meat department ahead of time to make sure or to order one. And don't worry, those fancy paper frills come with the roast.

RIB ROAST *with* HERB RUB

prep 20 min *total time* 2 hrs 55 min *makes* 8 servings

Herb Rub

3/4 cup chopped fresh parsley

1 1/2 tablespoons chopped fresh or 1 1/2 teaspoons
  dried thyme leaves

1 1/2 tablespoons chopped fresh or 1 1/2 teaspoons
  dried rosemary leaves

1 tablespoon olive or vegetable oil

2 cloves garlic, finely chopped

Roast

4- to 6-lb beef rib roast (small end)

1 clove garlic, cut in half

1/4 cup Dijon mustard

Horseradish Sauce

1 cup sour cream

1 tablespoon plus 1 teaspoon horseradish sauce

1 tablespoon plus 1 teaspoon Dijon mustard

1/4 teaspoon coarsely ground pepper

1. Heat oven to 325°F. In small bowl, mix all herb rub ingredients. Line shallow roasting pan with foil. Place beef, fat side up, on rack in roasting pan. Rub garlic halves over beef. Spread 1/4 cup mustard over top and sides of beef. Spread herb rub over top and sides of beef. Insert ovenproof meat thermometer so tip is in center of thickest part of beef and does not touch bone.

2. For medium-rare, roast 1 hour 45 minutes to 2 hours 15 minutes or until thermometer reads 135°F. Remove beef from pan onto carving board. Cover beef loosely with foil and let stand 15 to 20 minutes until thermometer reads 145°F. (Temperature will continue to rise about 10°F, and beef will be easier to carve.) For medium, roast uncovered 2 hours 15 minutes to 2 hours 45 minutes or until thermometer reads 150°F. Cover beef loosely with foil and let stand 15 to 20 minutes or until thermometer reads 160°F.

3. Meanwhile, in small bowl, mix all sauce ingredients. Cover; refrigerate at least 1 hour to blend flavors. Serve beef with sauce.

1 SERVING: Calories 340 (Calories from Fat 210); Total Fat 23g (Saturated Fat 10g; Trans Fat 1g); Cholesterol 100mg; Sodium 340mg; Total Carbohydrate 3g (Dietary Fiber 0g; Sugars 1g); Protein 29g; % DAILY VALUE: Vitamin A 15%; Vitamin C 8%; Calcium 6%; Iron 20%; EXCHANGES: 4 Medium-Fat Meat, 1 Fat; CARBOHYDRATE CHOICES: 0

new twist

Instead of the horseradish sauce, your family may like gravy better. In 2-quart saucepan, mix 2 tablespoons beef drippings and 2 tablespoons all-purpose flour until smooth; gradually stir in 1 cup beef broth or water. Heat to boiling, stirring constantly; boil and stir 1 minute.

holiday inspiration

Find yourself always hoping someone else will carve the meat? Here are some tips that will make you a confident carver, not to mention the star of the show!

- The 15-minute stand time lets the juices set up, making carving much easier.

- Don't cover the roast too tightly during standing because the steam will soften the surface of the beef and you won't get those crisp, caramelized sections people like to fight over!

- Always use a sharp knife and cut beef across the grain at a slanted angle into slices.

BURGUNDY BEEF STEW

prep 15 min *total time* 2 hrs 5 min *makes* 8 servings

6 slices bacon, cut into 1-inch pieces

2-lb beef boneless chuck eye, rolled rump or bottom round roast, cut into 1-inch pieces

1/2 cup all-purpose flour

1 1/2 cups dry red wine or beef broth

1 1/2 teaspoons chopped fresh or 1/2 teaspoon dried thyme leaves

1 1/4 teaspoons salt

1 teaspoon beef bouillon granules

1/4 teaspoon pepper

1 clove garlic, chopped

1 dried bay leaf

2 tablespoons butter or margarine

1 package (8 oz) sliced mushrooms

4 medium onions, sliced (2 cups)

Chopped fresh parsley, if desired

1. In 4-quart Dutch oven, cook bacon over medium heat, stirring occasionally, until crisp. Remove bacon with slotted spoon, reserving drippings in Dutch oven. Drain bacon on paper towels; crumble bacon.

2. Coat beef with flour. Cook beef in bacon drippings over medium heat, stirring occasionally, until brown. Drain excess fat from Dutch oven. Add wine and just enough water to cover beef. Stir in thyme, salt, bouillon granules, pepper, garlic and bay leaf. Heat to boiling; reduce heat. Cover; simmer about 1 hour 30 minutes or until beef is tender.

3. In 12-inch skillet, melt butter over medium heat. Cook mushrooms and onions in butter, stirring occasionally, until onions are tender. Stir mushroom mixture and bacon into beef mixture. Cover; simmer 10 minutes. Remove bay leaf. Garnish stew with parsley.

1 SERVING: Calories 250 (Calories from Fat 130); Total Fat 14g (Saturated Fat 5g; Trans Fat 0.5g); Cholesterol 55mg; Sodium 630mg; Total Carbohydrate 13g (Dietary Fiber 2g; Sugars 3g); Protein 18g; % DAILY VALUE: Vitamin A 4%; Vitamin C 4%; Calcium 2%; Iron 15%; EXCHANGES: 1 Starch, 2 Medium-Fat Meat, 1/2 Fat; CARBOHYDRATE CHOICES: 1

SWEET *and* SPICY RUBBED HAM

prep 10 min *total time* 1 hr 55 min *makes* 20 servings

6- to 8-lb fully cooked smoked bone-in ham

1/2 cup packed brown sugar

1/3 cup maple-flavored syrup

1/2 teaspoon ground mustard

1/8 teaspoon ground cinnamon

1/8 teaspoon ground ginger

1/8 teaspoon ground cloves

Dash ground nutmeg

1. Heat oven to 325°F. Line shallow roasting pan with foil. Place ham, cut side down, on rack in pan. Insert ovenproof meat thermometer in thickest part of ham.

2. Bake uncovered about 1 hour 30 minutes or until thermometer reads 140°F. Meanwhile, in small bowl, mix remaining ingredients. Brush over ham during last 30 minutes of baking.

3. Cover ham loosely with foil and let stand 10 to 15 minutes for easier carving.

1 SERVING: Calories 140 (Calories from Fat 35); Total Fat 4g (Saturated Fat 1.5g; Trans Fat 0g); Cholesterol 40mg; Sodium 890mg; Total Carbohydrate 10g (Dietary Fiber 0g; Sugars 8g); Protein 15g; % DAILY VALUE: Vitamin A 0%; Vitamin C 0%; Calcium 0%; Iron 6%; EXCHANGES: 1/2 Other Carbohydrate, 2 Lean Meat; CARBOHYDRATE CHOICES: 1/2

holiday inspiration

Wine and food experts agree, if you wouldn't drink the wine, don't use it in your recipe! And good wines don't have to be pricey. Use your favorite dry red in the Burgundy Beef Stew, whether it's Cabernet, Zinfandel, Pinot Noir or Merlot.

holiday inspiration

- Although this ham is delicious on its own, you may want to offer some type of condiment or sauce for all those "dipping and dunking" friends. Honey mustard, Dijon mustard, chutney and fruit are all good bets.

- Give garnish a go! A simple garnish of red grapes, watercress and cinnamon sticks is so easy and impressive.

Become a meat thermometer pro! Some meat thermometers are too top-heavy to stand up by themselves in the pork tenderloins. If the thermometer will not stand vertically, try inserting it almost horizontally, or sideways, into the pork. Using an instant-read thermometer is another option; check for doneness at the minimum time given. Instant-read thermometers are not ovenproof and can't be left in the pork.

HERB-CRUSTED PORK TENDERLOIN

prep 15 min *total time* 1 hr 5 min *makes* 6 servings

2 pork tenderloins (about 3/4 lb each)

1 cup soft bread crumbs (about 1 1/2 slices bread)

1/4 cup chopped fresh parsley

2 tablespoons chopped fresh or 1/2 teaspoon dried thyme leaves

1 tablespoon olive or vegetable oil

1/2 teaspoon salt

1/2 teaspoon fennel seed

1/4 teaspoon coarsely ground pepper

2 cloves garlic, finely chopped

1. Heat oven to 450°F. Spray shallow roasting pan and rack with cooking spray. Place pork tenderloins on rack in pan.

2. In small bowl, mix remaining ingredients. Spoon crumb mixture evenly over pork. Insert ovenproof meat thermometer so tip is in the thickest part of pork. Cover pork loosely with foil.

3. Bake 20 minutes; remove foil. Bake uncovered 10 to 15 minutes longer or until thermometer reads 155°F. Cover pork loosely with foil and let stand 10 to 15 minutes or until thermometer reads 160°F. (Temperature will continue to rise about 5°F, and pork will be easier to carve.)

1 SERVING: Calories 170 (Calories from Fat 60); Total Fat 7g (Saturated Fat 2g; Trans Fat 0g); Cholesterol 65mg; Sodium 280mg; Total Carbohydrate 4g (Dietary Fiber 0g; Sugars 0g); Protein 25g; % DAILY VALUE: Vitamin A 6%; Vitamin C 4%; Calcium 2%; Iron 10%; EXCHANGES: 3 1/2 Very Lean Meat, 1 Fat; CARBOHYDRATE CHOICES: 0

BREAD STUFFING

prep 20 min *total time* 20 min
makes 10 servings (1/2 cup each)

3/4 cup butter or margarine
2 large stalks celery (with leaves), chopped
    (1 1/2 cups)
1 large onion, chopped (1 cup)
10 cups soft bread cubes (about 15 slices bread)
1 1/2 teaspoons chopped fresh or 1/2 teaspoon dried
    thyme leaves
1 teaspoon salt
1/2 teaspoon ground sage
1/4 teaspoon pepper

1. In 4-quart Dutch oven, melt butter over medium-high heat. Cook celery and onion in butter, stirring occasionally, until tender; remove from heat.

2. In large bowl, toss celery mixture and remaining ingredients. Use to stuff one 12- to 15-pound turkey. After stuffing turkey, place any remaining stuffing in a 1- or 2-quart casserole that has been greased with shortening or cooking spray; cover and refrigerate. Bake stuffing in casserole with turkey for the last 35 to 40 minutes of baking or until heated through.

1 SERVING: Calories 230 (Calories from Fat 140); Total Fat 15g (Saturated Fat 7g; Trans Fat 1g); Cholesterol 35mg; Sodium 530mg; Total Carbohydrate 19g (Dietary Fiber 1g; Sugars 2g); Protein 3g; % DAILY VALUE: Vitamin A 10%; Vitamin C 2%; Calcium 6%; Iron 6%; EXCHANGES: 1 Starch, 3 Fat; CARBOHYDRATE CHOICES: 1

LIGHTER BREAD STUFFING For 6 grams of fat and 135 calories per serving, decrease butter to 1/4 cup. In 4-quart Dutch oven, heat butter and 1/2 cup chicken broth to boiling over medium-high heat. Cook celery and onion in broth mixture.

APPLE-CRANBERRY STUFFING Add 3 cups finely chopped apples and 1 cup fresh or frozen cranberries with the bread cubes. 12 servings (1/2 cup each).

CORNBREAD STUFFING Substitute cornbread cubes for the soft bread cubes. 10 servings (1/2 cup each).

GIBLET STUFFING Place giblets (except liver*) and neck from turkey or chicken in 2-quart saucepan. Add enough water to cover; season with salt and pepper. Simmer over low heat 1 to 2 hours or until tender. Drain giblets. Remove meat from neck and finely chop with giblets; add with the remaining stuffing ingredients. 12 servings (1/2 cup each).

*The liver is very strongly flavored and should not be used to make the stuffing. Discard it, or reserve for another use.

MUSHROOM STUFFING Cook 2 cups sliced mushrooms (about 5 oz) with the celery and onion. 11 servings (1/2 cup each).

ORANGE-APPLE STUFFING Add 1 cup diced orange sections or mandarin orange segments and 1 cup finely chopped apples with the bread cubes. 12 servings (1/2 cup each).

OYSTER STUFFING Add 2 cans (8 oz each) oysters, drained and chopped, or 2 cups shucked oysters, drained and chopped, with the remaining stuffing ingredients. 12 servings (1/2 cup each).

SAUSAGE STUFFING Omit salt. In 10-inch skillet, cook 1 lb bulk pork sausage over medium heat, stirring occasionally, until no longer pink; drain, reserving drippings. Substitute drippings for part of the butter. Add cooked sausage with the remaining stuffing ingredients. 12 servings (1/2 cup each).

HERB and GARLIC ROAST LEG of LAMB

prep 15 min *total time* 2 hrs 50 min
makes 10 to 12 servings

1/4 cup finely chopped fresh parsley

1 tablespoon chopped fresh or 1 teaspoon dried rosemary leaves, crushed

1 tablespoon chopped fresh or 1 teaspoon dried thyme leaves, crushed

3 tablespoons olive or vegetable oil

2 teaspoons kosher salt

1/2 teaspoon pepper

2 cloves garlic, finely chopped

5- to 6-lb boneless leg of lamb

1. Heat oven to 325°F. In small bowl, stir all ingredients except lamb until well mixed.

2. Place lamb in shallow roasting pan (keep netting or string on lamb). Spread herb mixture over entire surface of lamb. Insert ovenproof meat thermometer so tip is in thickest part of lamb and does not rest in fat.

3. Bake uncovered 2 hours 5 minutes to 2 hours 15 minutes for medium-rare or until thermometer reads 140°F. (For medium doneness, bake until thermometer reads 155°F.)

4. Remove from oven; cover loosely with foil. Let stand 15 to 20 minutes or until thermometer reads 145°F (or 160°F for medium doneness). Remove netting or string before serving. Serve with pan drippings if desired.

1 SERVING: Calories 260 (Calories from Fat 130); Total Fat 14g (Saturated Fat 4g; Trans Fat 1g); Cholesterol 100mg; Sodium 430mg; Total Carbohydrate 0g (Dietary Fiber 0g; Sugars 0g); Protein 31g; % DAILY VALUE: Vitamin A 4%; Vitamin C 2%; Calcium 0%; Iron 15%; EXCHANGES: 4 1/2 Lean Meat; CARBOHYDRATE CHOICES: 0

holiday inspiration

Salt is salt, right? Not quite. There are many different types of salt besides regular table salt and they've become very trendy and some are expensive. Kosher salt is coarser grained than regular table salt. Look for it next to regular table salt, which, by the way, can be used instead of the kosher salt.

turkey primer

The holidays are a wonderful occasion to gather family and friends around the table for a celebration feast. Whether you're making a turkey dinner as a first-timer or as a more experienced cook, this primer provides the basic essentials to assure success. Above all, remember the joy of the season and enjoy!

buying the bird

Here is the easy-to-remember rule: Buy 1 pound uncooked whole turkey per person (includes yummy leftovers, too). The amount of sliced cooked turkey is about 50 percent of the weight of the whole bird. Choosing a fresh versus frozen bird is a matter of personal preference, but if time is too short to thaw a frozen bird, then fresh is the perfect solution.

storing the bird

Fresh whole turkeys can be refrigerated up to 2 days. Fresh or purchased frozen turkeys can be frozen up to 1 year.

thawing the bird

Thaw turkeys slowly in the refrigerator or in cold water. Don't thaw on the counter or in the sink because bacteria thrive at room temperature. Place the turkey in a dish, baking pan with sides or plastic bag to catch any drips during thawing, and thaw for the times listed in the chart below.

REFRIGERATOR AND COLD-WATER THAWING METHODS

Whole Turkey Weight	Thawing Time in Refrigerator	Thawing Time in Cold Water*
8 to 12 pounds	1 to 2 days	4 to 6 hours
12 to 16 pounds	2 to 3 days	6 to 8 hours
16 to 20 pounds	3 to 4 days	8 to 10 hours
20 to 24 pounds	4 to 5 days	10 to 12 hours

*Change water as needed to keep water cold.

stuffing the bird

- Just about any kind of bread makes great stuffing, but top choices include white bread and cornbread. If you're short on time, use purchased stuffing cubes or mix.

- Don't stuff the turkey ahead of time; do it just before roasting (this prevents any bacteria in the raw poultry from contaminating the stuffing).

- Use about 3/4 cup stuffing per pound. Don't pack it in the cavity because it expands during roasting.

- Put stuffing (either the whole recipe or what's left after stuffing the bird) in a casserole; cover and bake it during the last 30 to 45 minutes of turkey roasting or until hot in the center. For a crisper, browned top, uncover the stuffing during the last 15 to 20 minutes.

- Always remove stuffing from the bird before carving it or it won't cool quickly enough, letting bacteria grow more easily.

- Stuffing doesn't have to be made with bread. Try adding a couple of quartered onions and a clove or two of garlic to the cavity, or use wedges of fresh lemon and orange and fresh herbs.

how to get a turkey ready for roasting

1. Turn turkey breast-side down for easier filling of neck cavity. Fill neck cavity lightly with stuffing.

2. Fasten neck skin to back of turkey with skewer.

3. Turn turkey breast-side up. Fold wings across back of turkey so tips are touching.

4. Fill body cavity lightly with stuffing.

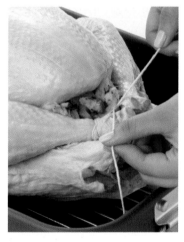

5. Tuck legs under band of skin at tail (if present), or tie together with heavy string, then tie to tail if desired.

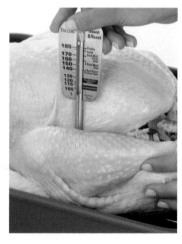

6. Insert ovenproof thermometer so tip is in thickest part of inside thigh and does not touch bone.

TIMETABLE FOR ROASTING TURKEY

Weight of Turkey	Oven Temperature	Roasting Time*
Whole Turkey (not stuffed)		Roast until thermometer reads 180°F and a leg moves easily when lifted or twisted. Thermometer placed in the center of stuffing will read 165°F when done. Remove from the oven; cover with foil to keep warm. Let stand about 15 minutes for easiest carving.
8 to 12 pounds	325°F	2 3/4 to 3 hours
12 to 14 pounds	325°F	3 to 3 3/4 hours
14 to 18 pounds	325°F	3 3/4 to 4 1/4 hours
18 to 20 pounds	325°F	4 1/4 to 4 1/2 hours
20 to 24 pounds	325°F	4 1/2 to 5 hours
Whole Turkey (stuffed)		
8 to 12 pounds	325°F	3 to 3 1/2 hours
12 to 14 pounds	325°F	3 1/2 to 4 hours
14 to 18 pounds	325°F	4 to 4 1/4 hours
18 to 20 pounds	325°F	4 1/4 to 4 3/4 hours
20 to 24 pounds	325°F	4 3/4 to 5 1/4 hours
Whole Turkey Breast (bone-in)		Roast until thermometer reads 170°F and juice of turkey is no longer pink when cut into the center. Remove from the oven; cover with foil to keep warm. Let stand about 15 minutes for easiest carving.
2 to 4 pounds	325°F	1 1/2 to 2 hours
3 to 5 pounds	325°F	1 1/2 to 2 1/2 hours
5 to 7 pounds	325°F	2 to 2 1/2 hours

*Times given are for unstuffed birds unless noted. Stuffed birds other than turkey require 15 to 30 minutes longer. Begin checking turkey doneness about 1 hour before end of recommended roasting time. For purchased prestuffed turkeys, follow package directions instead of this timetable.

turkey deep-frying dos and don'ts

Deep-frying is the trendy way to cook turkey in record time! This method makes for a super-moist, juicy bird with crispy skin. For a safe and successful experience, read through these important guidelines. Learn more about deep-frying turkey at the National Turkey Federation Web site: www.turkeyfed.org.

dos:

- Use only peanut, canola and safflower oils because they can withstand high temperatures.

- Follow the use-and-care directions for your fryer; review all safety tips.

- Place the fryer on a level dirt or grassy area away from the house or garage. Never fry a turkey indoors, including in a garage or any structure attached to a building. If only concrete is available, place a large sheet of cardboard over area to prevent oil stains.

- Before frying, determine the amount of oil needed by placing the turkey in the basket and place in the pot. Add water until it reaches 1 to 2 inches above the turkey. Remove the turkey; record the water level, using a ruler to measure the distance from the top of the pot to the surface of the water. Pour out the water and dry the pot thoroughly.

- Wear long sleeves and pants and oven mitts to protect from steam and oil spattering.

- Immediately wash hands, utensils, equipment and surfaces that have come in contact with the raw turkey.

- Have a working fire extinguisher nearby for added safety.

- Serve the turkey right after cooking; refrigerate leftovers within 2 hours of cooking.

- Cool oil completely before disposing of or storing.

don'ts:

- Never fry on wooden decks or other structures that could catch fire.

- Never leave the hot oil unattended, and do not allow children or pets near the cooking area.

- Do not fry a stuffed turkey.

carving the bird

Place turkey, breast up, on a cutting board. Remove ties or skewers. Let the bird stand for 15 to 20 minutes before cutting; this resting period allows the meat to become more firm, so carving smooth, even slices is easier. Use a sharp carving knife and meat fork for best results.

 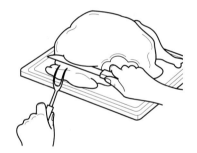 

1. While gently pulling leg away from body, cut through joint between thigh and body. Separate drumstick and thigh by cutting through connecting joint.*

2. Make a deep horizontal cut into breast just above wing.

3. Insert fork in top of breast and, starting halfway up breast, carve thin slices down to the horizontal cut, working from outer edge of bird to the center. Remove wings by cutting through joint between wing and body.

* Serve drumsticks and thighs whole or carve them. To carve, remove meat from drumstick by slicing at an angle, and slice thigh by cutting even slices parallel to the bone.

ROAST TURKEY

prep 30 min *total time* 4 hrs 30 min
makes 12 to 15 servings

12- to 15-lb turkey, thawed if frozen
Bread Stuffing (page 73)
3 tablespoons butter or margarine, melted

1. Heat oven to 325°F. From turkey, remove bag of giblets and neck if present. Rinse cavity; pat dry with paper towels.

2. Make Bread Stuffing. Stuff turkey just before roasting, not ahead of time. Turn turkey breast side down for easier filling of neck cavity. Fill neck cavity lightly with stuffing; fasten neck skin to back of turkey with skewer. Turn turkey breast side up. Fold wings across back of turkey so tips are touching. Fill body cavity lightly with stuffing. (Do not pack stuffing because it will expand during roasting.) Place any remaining stuffing in a 1- or 2-quart casserole that has been greased with shortening or cooking spray; cover and refrigerate. Bake stuffing in casserole with turkey for the last 35 to 40 minutes of roasting or until heated through.

3. Tuck legs under band of skin at tail (if present), or tie together with heavy string, then tie to tail if desired. On rack in shallow roasting pan, place turkey, breast side up. Brush butter over turkey. Insert ovenproof meat thermometer so tip is in thickest part of inside thigh and does not touch bone. (Do not add water or cover turkey.)

4. Roast uncovered 3 hours to 3 hours 45 minutes. After roasting about 2 hours, place a tent of foil loosely over turkey when it begins to turn golden, and cut band of skin or remove tie holding legs to allow inside of thighs to cook through.

5. Turkey is done when thermometer reads 180°F and legs move easily when lifted or twisted. Thermometer placed in center of stuffing will read 165°F when done. If a meat thermometer is not used, begin testing for doneness after about 2 hours 30 minutes. When turkey is done, place on warm platter and cover with foil to keep warm. Let stand about 15 minutes for easiest carving. Cover and refrigerate any remaining turkey and stuffing separately.

1 **SERVING:** Calories 590 (Calories from Fat 340); Total Fat 38g (Saturated Fat 14g; Trans Fat 2g); Cholesterol 180mg; Sodium 600mg; Total Carbohydrate 16g (Dietary Fiber 1g; Sugars 1g); Protein 47g; % **DAILY VALUE:** Vitamin A 15%; Vitamin C 0%; Calcium 8%; Iron 15%; **EXCHANGES:** 1 Starch, 6 1/2 Lean Meat, 3 1/2 Fat; **CARBOHYDRATE CHOICES:** 1

BEST BRINED TURKEY BREAST

prep 10 min *total time* 14 hrs 40 min
makes 8 servings

9 cups hot water
3/4 cup salt
1/2 cup sugar
4- to 6-lb bone-in whole turkey breast, thawed if frozen
1 onion, cut into eighths
2 fresh rosemary sprigs
4 fresh thyme sprigs
3 dried bay leaves
6 tablespoons butter or margarine, melted
1/4 cup dry white wine or chicken broth

1. In 6-quart container or stockpot, mix water, salt and sugar; stir until sugar and salt are dissolved. Add turkey. Cover; refrigerate at least 12 hours but no longer than 24 hours.

2. Heat oven to 325°F. Remove turkey from brine; rinse thoroughly under cool running water and pat dry.

3. Place onion on center of rack in large shallow roasting pan, top with rosemary, thyme and bay leaves. Place turkey, skin side up, over onion and herbs.

4. In small bowl, mix butter and wine. Soak 16-inch square of cheesecloth in butter mixture until completely saturated; cover turkey completely with cheesecloth. Roast 1 hour 30 minutes.

5. Remove cheesecloth. Insert ovenproof meat thermometer so tip is in thickest part of turkey and does not touch bone. Roast 30 to 60 minutes longer or until thermometer reads 170°F and juice of turkey is clear when center is cut. Using the pan drippings to make gravy isn't recommended because the gravy will be too salty.

1 SERVING: Calories 310 (Calories from Fat 140); Total Fat 15g (Saturated Fat 5g; Trans Fat 0g); Cholesterol 125mg; Sodium 640mg; Total Carbohydrate 0g (Dietary Fiber 0g; Sugars 0g); Protein 43g; % DAILY VALUE: Vitamin A 6%; Vitamin C 0%; Calcium 2%; Iron 8%; EXCHANGES: 6 Very Lean Meat, 2 1/2 Fat; CARBOHYDRATE CHOICES: 0

holiday inspiration

- You've tried roasting, deep-frying and grilling the bird, now give brining a try! Brining is becoming a popular way of making the holiday bird. It's the process of soaking a turkey in a saltwater bath overnight, which draws water into the cells of the turkey so it stays juicy when cooked.

- Cheesecloth can be found in the cooking accessories section of supermarkets or gourmet cooking stores. If you can't find it, just baste the turkey with the butter and wine mixture after an hour of roasting and every 30 minutes after that until the turkey is done. Take the bird out of the oven and close the oven door when basting so the oven heat doesn't escape.

CHEESY CHICKEN TORTELLINI

prep 30 min *total time* 30 min *makes* 5 servings

1 package (7 oz) dried cheese-filled tortellini
1 tablespoon vegetable oil
1 lb boneless skinless chicken breasts, cut into thin slices
1/4 cup butter or margarine
1 small green bell pepper, chopped (1/2 cup)
2 shallots, finely chopped
1 clove garlic, finely chopped
1/4 cup all-purpose flour
1/4 teaspoon pepper
1 3/4 cups milk
1/2 cup shredded mozzarella cheese (2 oz)
1/2 cup shredded Swiss cheese (2 oz)
1/4 cup grated Parmesan or Romano cheese (1 oz)

1. Cook and drain tortellini as directed on package.

2. Meanwhile, in 3-quart saucepan, heat oil over medium-high heat. Cook chicken in oil, stirring frequently, until no longer pink in center. Remove chicken from saucepan; keep warm.

3. In same saucepan, melt butter over medium-high heat. Cook bell pepper, shallots and garlic in butter, stirring frequently, until bell pepper is crisp-tender. Stir in flour and pepper. Cook over medium heat, stirring constantly, until mixture is bubbly; remove from heat. Stir in milk. Heat to boiling, stirring constantly. Boil and stir 1 minute; remove from heat.

4. Stir in mozzarella and Swiss cheeses until melted. Stir in tortellini and chicken until coated. Sprinkle with Parmesan cheese.

1 SERVING: Calories 540 (Calories from Fat 240); Total Fat 27g (Saturated Fat 13g; Trans Fat 1g); Cholesterol 135mg; Sodium 700mg; Total Carbohydrate 35g (Dietary Fiber 1g; Sugars 6g); Protein 39g; **% DAILY VALUE:** Vitamin A 15%; Vitamin C 10%; Calcium 45%; Iron 10%; **EXCHANGES:** 2 1/2 Starch, 4 1/2 Lean Meat, 2 1/2 Fat; **CARBOHYDRATE CHOICES:** 2

new twist

Morph this into a meatless meal! Skip the chicken and add 1 chopped medium red bell pepper with the shallots. Then, stir in 1 can (14 ounces) quartered artichoke hearts, drained well, with the cheeses.

holiday inspiration

Serve this dish with warm crusty bread to dip into the cheesy sauce and, for dessert, small scoops of sorbet in chocolate cups bought at the store.

CHICKEN BREASTS *with* WILD RICE ALFREDO

prep 25 min *total time* 2 hrs 5 min *makes* 6 servings

1 1/2 cups uncooked wild rice, rinsed and drained
1 can (14 oz) roasted garlic-seasoned chicken broth
1 cup water
1 teaspoon dried thyme leaves
2 tablespoons butter or margarine
6 boneless skinless chicken breasts (about 2 lb)
1 package (8 oz) sliced fresh mushrooms (3 cups)
1 jar (7 oz) roasted red bell peppers, drained, chopped
1 jar (1 lb) Alfredo pasta sauce (2 cups)

1. In 2-quart saucepan, heat wild rice, broth and water to boiling over high heat. Reduce heat to low. Cover; simmer 45 to 60 minutes or until rice kernels are open and almost tender; drain if necessary. Stir in thyme. Spread rice in ungreased 13 × 9–inch (3-quart) glass baking dish.

2. Heat oven to 350°F. Meanwhile, in 12-inch skillet, heat butter over medium-high heat. Cook chicken in butter 8 to 10 minutes, turning once, until brown. Place on cooked rice. Add mushrooms to skillet. Cook 3 to 5 minutes, stirring occasionally, until lightly browned. Stir in bell peppers and Alfredo sauce; pour over chicken.

3. Bake uncovered 45 to 55 minutes or until mixture is bubbly and juice of chicken is clear when center of thickest part is cut (170°F).

1 **SERVING:** Calories 670 (Calories from Fat 300); Total Fat 34g (Saturated Fat 17g; Trans Fat 1.5g); Cholesterol 175mg; Sodium 740mg; Total Carbohydrate 42g (Dietary Fiber 4g; Sugars 4g); Protein 48g; % **DAILY VALUE:** Vitamin A 50%; Vitamin C 35%; Calcium 25%; Iron 15%; EXCHANGES: 3 Starch, 5 1/2 Lean Meat, 3 Fat; **CARBOHYDRATE CHOICES:** 3

new twist

Go with green! Offer haricots verts (often labeled as petite or thin) or regular green beans on the side. Drizzle the beans with extra-virgin olive oil and sprinkle with toasted slivered almonds.

holiday inspiration

Not every grocery store carries everything you may need for a recipe so sometimes innovation is in order. If you can't find chicken broth with garlic, make your own. Just finely chop 2 cloves of garlic and stir into regular chicken broth.

holiday inspiration

- Yes, comfort food can be made when you're short on time. Buy uncooked chicken breast strips for stir-fry; it's already cut up.

- For casual get-togethers, dish up portions into oversized coffee mugs or shallow soup bowls. Use a bagged complete salad kit to make an easy side.

CREAMY CHICKEN and DUMPLINGS

prep 20 min *total time* 40 min *makes* 4 servings

1 tablespoon vegetable oil

1 lb boneless skinless chicken breasts, cut into 1-inch pieces

1 3/4 cups water

1 cup milk

1 package (about 1.2 oz) chicken gravy mix

3/4 teaspoon dried marjoram leaves

1/2 teaspoon salt

1 bag (1 lb) frozen broccoli, carrots and cauliflower

1 2/3 cups Original Bisquick mix

1/2 cup milk

Chopped fresh parsley, if desired

1. In 4-quart Dutch oven, heat oil over medium heat. Cook chicken in oil, stirring frequently, until golden brown. Stir in water, 1 cup milk, the gravy mix, marjoram, salt and frozen vegetables. Heat to boiling; reduce heat.

2. In medium bowl, stir Bisquick mix and 1/2 cup milk until soft dough forms. Drop dough by 12 spoonfuls onto chicken mixture (do not drop directly into liquid).

3. Cook uncovered over low heat 10 minutes. Cover; cook 10 minutes longer. Sprinkle with parsley.

1 SERVING: Calories 470 (Calories from Fat 150); Total Fat 17g (Saturated Fat 4.5g; Trans Fat 1.5g); Cholesterol 75mg; Sodium 1560mg; Total Carbohydrate 46g (Dietary Fiber 4g; Sugars 10g); Protein 35g; % DAILY VALUE: Vitamin A 70%; Vitamin C 30%; Calcium 25%; Iron 20%; EXCHANGES: 2 Starch, 1/2 Other Carbohydrate, 1 Vegetable, 4 Very Lean Meat, 2 1/2 Fat; CARBOHYDRATE CHOICES: 3

CREAMY CRAB *au* GRATIN

prep 15 min *total time* 30 min *makes* 4 servings

1 1/2 cups sliced fresh mushrooms (4 oz)

2 medium stalks celery, sliced (1 cup)

1 can (14 oz) chicken broth

3/4 cup half-and-half

3 tablespoons all-purpose flour

1/2 teaspoon red pepper sauce

2 cups chopped cooked crabmeat or 2 packages (8 oz each) refrigerated imitation crabmeat chunks

1 cup soft bread crumbs (about 1 1/2 slices bread)

1. Heat oven to 400°F. Lightly spray 11 × 7-inch (2-quart) glass baking dish with cooking spray.

2. Spray 3-quart saucepan with cooking spray; heat over medium heat. Cook mushrooms and celery in saucepan about 4 minutes, stirring constantly, until celery is tender. Stir in broth. Heat to boiling; reduce heat.

3. In small bowl, beat half-and-half, flour and pepper sauce with wire whisk until smooth; stir into vegetable mixture. Heat to boiling, stirring constantly. Boil and stir 1 minute. Stir in crabmeat.

4. Spoon crabmeat mixture into baking dish. Top with bread crumbs. Bake uncovered about 15 minutes or until thoroughly heated.

1 SERVING: Calories 200 (Calories from Fat 70); Total Fat 8g (Saturated Fat 3.5g; Trans Fat 0g); Cholesterol 85mg; Sodium 740mg; Total Carbohydrate 13g (Dietary Fiber 1g; Sugars 3g); Protein 19g; % DAILY VALUE: Vitamin A 6%; Vitamin C 4%; Calcium 15%; Iron 10%; EXCHANGES: 1 Starch, 2 1/2 Very Lean Meat, 1 Fat; CARBOHYDRATE CHOICES: 1

holiday inspiration

Your health-conscious friends and family will love this great-tasting gratin. Dress it up a little by placing each serving in individual gratin dishes or ceramic ramekins. Fresh sugar snap peas or pea pods would go along nicely.

LEMON- and PARMESAN-CRUSTED SALMON

prep 10 min *total time* 35 min *makes* 4 servings
see photo on page 52, top

1 salmon fillet (1 1/4 lb)

2 tablespoons butter or margarine, melted

1/4 teaspoon salt

3/4 cup fresh white medium- to firm-textured bread crumbs (1 slice)*

1/4 cup grated Parmesan cheese

2 tablespoons thinly sliced green onions

2 teaspoons grated lemon peel

1/4 teaspoon dried thyme leaves

1. Heat oven to 375°F. Spray shallow baking pan with cooking spray. Pat salmon dry with paper towel. Place salmon, skin side down, in pan. Brush with 1 tablespoon of the butter. Sprinkle with salt.

2. In small bowl, mix bread crumbs, cheese, onions, lemon peel and thyme. Stir in remaining 1 tablespoon butter. Press bread crumb mixture evenly on salmon.

3. Bake uncovered 15 to 25 minutes or until salmon flakes easily with fork. Serve immediately.

*Soft-textured bread is not recommended because it's too moist and won't create a crisp crumb topping.

1 SERVING: Calories 290 (Calories from Fat 140); Total Fat 16g (Saturated Fat 6g; Trans Fat 0g); Cholesterol 115mg; Sodium 420mg; Total Carbohydrate 4g (Dietary Fiber 0g; Sugars 0g); Protein 33g; **% DAILY VALUE:** Vitamin A 8%; Vitamin C 4%; Calcium 10%; Iron 8%; **EXCHANGES:** 5 Lean Meat, 1/2 Fat; **CARBOHYDRATE CHOICES:** 0

holiday inspiration

This excellent salmon is easy, elegant and impressive! Serve with steamed or grilled asparagus spears and buttered small red potatoes.

CHAMPAGNE SHRIMP RISOTTO

prep 10 min *total time* 25 min *makes* 6 servings

1 lb uncooked medium shrimp in shells, thawed if frozen

2 tablespoons butter or margarine

1 medium onion, thinly sliced

1/2 cup brut champagne, dry white wine or chicken broth

1 1/2 cups uncooked Arborio or medium-grain white rice

2 cups chicken broth

1 cup clam juice or water

2 cups chopped arugula, watercress or spinach

1/3 cup grated Parmesan cheese

1/2 teaspoon ground pepper

Chopped fresh parsley, if desired

1. Peel shrimp. Make a shallow cut lengthwise down back of each shrimp; wash out vein.

2. In 12-inch skillet or 4-quart Dutch oven, melt butter over medium-high heat. Cook onion in butter, stirring frequently, until tender. Reduce heat to medium. Add shrimp. Cook uncovered about 8 minutes, turning once, until shrimp are pink. Remove shrimp from skillet; keep warm.

3. Add champagne to onion in skillet; cook until liquid has evaporated. Stir in rice. Cook uncovered over medium heat about 5 minutes, stirring frequently, until edges of rice kernels are translucent. Meanwhile, in 2-quart saucepan, heat broth and clam juice over medium heat. Pour 1/2 cup broth mixture over rice. Cook uncovered, stirring occasionally, until liquid is absorbed. Repeat with remaining broth mixture, 1/2 cup at a time, until rice is tender and creamy.

4. About 5 minutes before risotto is done, stir in shrimp, arugula, cheese and pepper. Sprinkle with parsley before serving.

1 SERVING: Calories 300 (Calories from Fat 60); Total Fat 7g (Saturated Fat 3.5g; Trans Fat 0g); Cholesterol 85mg; Sodium 640mg; Total Carbohydrate 43g (Dietary Fiber 0g; Sugars 1g); Protein 16g; **% DAILY VALUE:** Vitamin A 15%; Vitamin C 2%; Calcium 15%; Iron 20%; **EXCHANGES:** 3 Starch, 1 Very Lean Meat, 1 Fat; **CARBOHYDRATE CHOICES:** 3

new twist

Leave out the shrimp and serve this as a lovely main course for your vegetarian friends.

holiday inspiration

Even though you may be tempted, don't rush the process! When making risotto, adding the broth a little at a time ensures that the dish will be creamy while allowing the grains to remain separate. It's worth the wait.

ALMOND-CRUSTED SHRIMP

prep 20 min *total time* 55 min *makes* 4 servings

1/4 cup all-purpose flour

1/2 teaspoon salt

1 egg

2 tablespoons water

3/4 cup panko or plain dry bread crumbs

1/3 cup sliced almonds

16 uncooked peeled deveined extra-large shrimp
(about 1 lb), thawed if frozen and peel left on tails

1/4 cup butter or margarine, melted

1. Heat oven to 375°F. Generously spray 15 × 10 × 1-inch pan with cooking spray.

2. Pat shrimp dry with paper towel. In shallow dish, mix flour and salt. In another shallow dish, beat egg and water with fork or wire whisk until well mixed. In third shallow dish, mix bread crumbs and almonds.

3. Dip each shrimp into flour, turning to coat. Then dip into egg, coating well. Finally, cover with bread crumb mixture, spooning mixture over shrimp and pressing to coat. Place coated shrimp in pan. Drizzle with butter.

4. Bake uncovered 30 to 35 minutes or until shrimp are pink.

1 SERVING: Calories 440 (Calories from Fat 200); Total Fat 22g (Saturated Fat 7g; Trans Fat 0.5g); Cholesterol 245mg; Sodium 1250mg; Total Carbohydrate 34g (Dietary Fiber 3g; Sugars 3g); Protein 27g; % DAILY VALUE: Vitamin A 15%; Vitamin C 0%; Calcium 15%; Iron 30%; EXCHANGES: 2 Starch, 3 Very Lean Meat, 4 Fat; CARBOHYDRATE CHOICES: 2

holiday inspiration

• Just a little change from the ordinary can make a big difference. Bravo to panko bread crumbs! Also known as Japanese bread crumbs, panko crumbs are coarser than the regular, more granular-looking crumbs, resulting in lighter, crunchier coatings or toppings and a more textured, striking appearance.

• Angel hair pasta tossed with extra-virgin olive oil, grated Parmesan cheese and chopped fresh parsley or basil makes an excellent match with the crunchy shrimp.

ROASTED-VEGETABLE LASAGNA

prep 50 min *total time* 1 hr 25 min *makes* 10 servings

Roasted Vegetables

Olive oil cooking spray

1 medium onion, cut into 8 wedges, separated into pieces

2 medium bell peppers, cut into 1-inch pieces

2 medium zucchini, sliced (3 cups)

8 oz mushrooms, sliced (3 cups)

1/2 teaspoon salt

1/4 teaspoon pepper

Tomato Sauce

1 large onion, chopped (1 cup)

2 tablespoons finely chopped garlic

1 can (28 oz) crushed tomatoes, undrained

3 tablespoons chopped fresh or 1 tablespoon dried basil leaves

3 tablespoons chopped fresh or 1 tablespoon dried oregano leaves

1 teaspoon sugar

1/2 teaspoon salt

1/2 teaspoon crushed red pepper flakes

Noodles and Cheese

12 uncooked lasagna noodles

4 cups shredded mozzarella cheese (1 lb)

1 cup shredded Parmesan cheese (4 oz)

1. Heat oven to 450°F. Spray 15 × 10 × 1-inch pan with cooking spray. Place onion pieces in pan in single layer; spray onion with cooking spray. Roast uncovered 10 minutes. Add bell peppers, zucchini and mushrooms to pan, arranging in single layer. Spray vegetables with cooking spray; sprinkle with 1/2 teaspoon salt and the pepper. Roast uncovered 20 to 25 minutes, turning vegetables once, until tender.

2. Meanwhile, spray 2-quart saucepan with cooking spray. Cook chopped onion and garlic in saucepan over medium heat 2 minutes, stirring occasionally. Stir in remaining sauce ingredients. Heat to boiling; reduce heat. Simmer uncovered 15 to 20 minutes or until slightly thickened.

3. Cook and drain noodles as directed on package. Rinse noodles with cold water; drain. In medium bowl, mix cheeses.

4. Reduce oven temperature to 400°F. Spray 13 × 9–inch (3-quart) glass baking dish with cooking spray. Spread 1/4 cup of the sauce in dish; top with 3 noodles. Layer with 3/4 cup sauce, 1 1/4 cups vegetables and 1 cup cheese mixture. Repeat layers 3 more times with remaining noodles, sauce, vegetables and cheese mixture.

5. Bake uncovered 20 to 25 minutes or until hot. Let stand 10 minutes before cutting.

1 SERVING: Calories 330 (Calories from Fat 120); Total Fat 13g (Saturated Fat 8g; Trans Fat 0g); Cholesterol 30mg; Sodium 870mg; Total Carbohydrate 31g (Dietary Fiber 4g; Sugars 6g); Protein 21g; **% DAILY VALUE:** Vitamin A 20%; Vitamin C 30%; Calcium 50%; Iron 15%; EXCHANGES: 1 1/2 Starch, 2 Vegetable, 2 Medium-Fat Meat, 1/2 Fat; CARBOHYDRATE CHOICES: 2

new twist

- Don't make the sauce from scratch—no one will ever know that you used 1 jar (1 pound 10 ounces) tomato pasta sauce instead of the scratch tomato sauce.

- Mix up the mushrooms! Try a combination of shiitake, oyster and chanterelle mushrooms instead of just plain white button mushrooms.

- Serve this lasagna as a vegetarian entrée, or add grilled Italian sausages on the side.

make-ahead magic

To make ahead, cover unbaked lasagna tightly with foil and refrigerate up to 24 hours or freeze up to 2 months. If refrigerated, bake 25 to 35 minutes or until hot. If frozen, thaw in refrigerator overnight; bake 25 to 35 minutes or until hot.

holiday inspiration

This yummy lasagna is weeknight heaven! If you can only find sausage with casings, no problem—take the casings off and toss them out, then just crumble the sausage into the skillet. Even though the directions say to refrigerate it up to 24 hours, you can bake it right after you assemble it, too.

DO-AHEAD RAVIOLI-SAUSAGE LASAGNA

prep 20 min   *total time* 9 hrs 30 min   *makes* 8 servings

1 1/4 lb bulk Italian pork sausage
1 jar (26 to 28 oz) tomato pasta sauce (any variety)
1 bag (25 to 27.5 oz) frozen cheese-filled ravioli
2 1/2 cups shredded mozzarella cheese (10 oz)
2 tablespoons grated Parmesan cheese

1. In 10-inch skillet, cook sausage over medium-high heat 5 to 7 minutes, stirring occasionally, until no longer pink; drain.

2. In ungreased 13 × 9–inch pan, spread 1/2 cup of the pasta sauce. Arrange single layer of frozen ravioli over sauce; evenly pour 1 cup of the pasta sauce over ravioli. Sprinkle evenly with 1 1/2 cups sausage and 1 cup of the mozzarella cheese. Repeat layers with remaining ravioli, pasta sauce and sausage.

3. Cover tightly with foil and refrigerate at least 8 hours but no longer than 24 hours.

4. Heat oven to 350°F. Bake covered 45 minutes. Remove foil; sprinkle with remaining 1 1/2 cups mozzarella cheese and the Parmesan cheese. Bake uncovered about 15 minutes longer or until cheese is melted and lasagna is hot in center. Let stand 10 minutes before serving.

1 SERVING: Calories 540 (Calories from Fat 280); Total Fat 31g (Saturated Fat 13g; Trans Fat 0g); Cholesterol 150mg; Sodium 1870mg; Total Carbohydrate 34g (Dietary Fiber 2g; Sugars 8g); Protein 31g; % DAILY VALUE: Vitamin A 20%; Vitamin C 10%; Calcium 50%; Iron 15%; EXCHANGES: 2 Starch, 3 1/2 High-Fat Meat, 1/2 Fat; CARBOHYDRATE CHOICES: 2

SLOW COOKER BUTTERNUT SQUASH SOUP

prep 15 min   *total time* 6 hrs 45 min   *makes* 6 servings

2 tablespoons butter or margarine
1 medium onion, chopped (1/2 cup)
1 butternut squash (2 lb), peeled, cubed
2 cups water
1/2 teaspoon dried marjoram leaves
1/4 teaspoon ground black pepper
1/8 teaspoon ground red pepper (cayenne)
2 extra-large vegetarian vegetable bouillon cubes
1 package (8 oz) cream cheese, cubed

1. In 10-inch skillet, melt butter over medium heat. Cook onion in butter, stirring occasionally, until crisp-tender.

2. In 3 1/2- to 4-quart slow cooker, mix onion and remaining ingredients except cream cheese.

3. Cover; cook on Low heat setting 6 to 8 hours.

4. In blender or food processor, place one-third to one-half of the soup mixture at a time. Cover; blend on high speed until smooth. Return mixture to slow cooker. Using wire whisk, stir in cream cheese. Cover; cook on Low heat setting about 30 minutes, stirring occasionally with wire whisk, until cheese is melted and soup is smooth.

1 SERVING: Calories 230 (Calories from Fat 160); Total Fat 17g (Saturated Fat 10g; Trans Fat 0.5g); Cholesterol 50mg; Sodium 930mg; Total Carbohydrate 15g (Dietary Fiber 2g; Sugars 6g); Protein 5g; % DAILY VALUE: Vitamin A 210%; Vitamin C 15%; Calcium 8%; Iron 8%; EXCHANGES: 1 Starch, 3 1/2 Fat; CARBOHYDRATE CHOICES: 1

holiday inspiration

- This wonderfully rich and flavorful soup became a staff favorite while being tested in our kitchens. Sprinkle with chopped toasted walnuts, pecans or pumpkin seeds, and pair with an artisanal bread and a salad of mixed baby greens.

- For easier peeling, place whole squash in microwave oven. Microwave on High 2 to 4 minutes or until tip of knife can pierce skin easily. Cool slightly before peeling.

THREE-BEAN CHRISTMAS CHILI

prep 20 min *total time* 35 min *makes* 6 servings

1 can (28 oz) whole tomatoes, undrained

1 can (15 to 16 oz) garbanzo beans, drained

1 can (15 to 16 oz) kidney beans, drained

1 can (15 to 16 oz) butter beans, drained

1 can (15 oz) tomato sauce

3 small red, orange or yellow bell peppers, cut into 1-inch pieces

1 Anaheim or jalapeño chile, seeded, chopped

1 to 2 tablespoons chili powder

2 teaspoons ground cumin

1/4 teaspoon pepper

1/2 cup sour cream

3 tablespoons salsa

Chopped fresh cilantro, if desired

1. In 4-quart Dutch oven, mix all ingredients except sour cream, salsa and cilantro. Heat to boiling, breaking up tomatoes; reduce heat. Cover; simmer 15 to 20 minutes or until bell peppers are tender.

2. Meanwhile, in small bowl, mix sour cream and salsa. Serve chili with sour cream mixture. Sprinkle with cilantro.

1 SERVING: Calories 370 (Calories from Fat 60); Total Fat 7g (Saturated Fat 2.5g; Trans Fat 0g); Cholesterol 15mg; Sodium 1050mg; Total Carbohydrate 59g (Dietary Fiber 16g; Sugars 10g); Protein 19g; % DAILY VALUE: Vitamin A 70%; Vitamin C 90%; Calcium 15%; Iron 40%; EXCHANGES: 2 1/2 Starch, 1/2 Other Carbohydrate, 2 Vegetable, 1 Very Lean Meat, 1 Fat; CARBOHYDRATE CHOICES: 4

SEAFOOD BISQUE

prep 10 min *total time* 25 min *makes* 8 servings

1/3 cup butter or margarine

1/3 cup all-purpose flour

2 cans (14 oz each) chicken broth

4 cups (1 qt) half-and-half

1/2 cup dry white wine or water

1/2 cup chopped drained roasted red bell peppers (from 7-oz jar)

12 oz cod fillet, cut into 1-inch pieces

12 oz uncooked peeled deveined medium shrimp, thawed if frozen and tail shells removed

1/2 cup basil pesto

1/4 teaspoon salt

1/8 teaspoon freshly ground pepper

1. In 4-quart Dutch oven, melt butter over medium-high heat. Stir in flour. Gradually stir in broth, half-and-half and wine. Stir in bell peppers and cod. Heat to boiling, stirring occasionally.

2. Stir in shrimp. Simmer uncovered 2 to 3 minutes or until shrimp are pink. Stir in pesto, salt and pepper.

1 SERVING: Calories 420 (Calories from Fat 280); Total Fat 31g (Saturated Fat 15g; Trans Fat 1g); Cholesterol 150mg; Sodium 860mg; Total Carbohydrate 11g (Dietary Fiber 0g; Sugars 6g); Protein 22g; % DAILY VALUE: Vitamin A 35%; Vitamin C 20%; Calcium 20%; Iron 10%; EXCHANGES: 1/2 Starch, 3 Very Lean Meat, 6 Fat; CARBOHYDRATE CHOICES: 1

holiday inspiration

Why not invite the gang over for a tree-trimming party? Double the chili recipe, making it in a 6-quart Dutch oven, and serve a "make it your way" chili bar. Put out sour cream, salsa, shredded cheeses, chopped red onion, chopped ripe olives, chopped avocado and, for the bold, hot sauce. Have baskets filled with croutons, tortilla chips, muffins and breadsticks for chili dipping. For an extra treat, buy bread bowls or tortilla bowls (available at your supermarket) to serve the chili in.

BettyCrocker.com

new twist

As you dish up the soup, sprinkle chopped fresh
basil leaves and a little freshly shredded Parmesan
cheese on each serving. Or for a simple yet
"showy" garnish for each serving, tie a chive
around an additional cooked shrimp. Cooked
shrimp works great in this recipe, too. Just add it
to the bisque and simmer until heated through.

fruits of the season
cranberries and pomegranates

cranberries

Cranberries, with their crimson color and mouth-puckering tartness, are ever-present during the holiday season. This perennial vine, along with Concord grapes and blueberries, is purely native to North America. Native Americans used cranberries along with game and other ingredients to make pemmican, a highly nutritious jerky-like food that traveled well. They also concocted poultices and used the juice and skins to dye beautiful rugs and blankets. The first recipes using cranberries date back to the eighteenth century—and new recipes are continually being created. Cranberries are grown in Wisconsin, Massachusetts, New Jersey, Oregon and Washington. It's not widely known, but cranberry production is very environmentally friendly. Growing marshes (or bogs) and the surrounding area preserve wetlands and provide excellent habitat for myriad plant and animal life.

In cranberry lore, they were thought to have special powers to calm nerves. Cranberries are good source of antioxidants and vitamin C, and a glass of juice per day may help promote urinary tract health. This wonderful little fruit is used in sauces, beverages, desserts and stuffing and in the dried form as a snack and recipe ingredient. You'll also find it gracing a Christmas tree as garland or plunged into a vase for added beauty in a cut flower arrangement! For fun, how about this bit of trivia: firm cranberries bounce and go their merry way along the production line, but the soft unusable ones just go "thud"! Try Classic Cranberry Mold with your turkey dinner and, for snacking, Cranberry-Orange Chex® Mix.

user guide

- Fresh cranberries are available September through December.

- Look for bright red fruit without blemishes; throw out any bruised berries.

- Refrigerate fresh berries up to 1 month, or freeze whole berries up to 1 year. Do not thaw before using; follow the recipe using frozen berries.

- Twelve ounces of cranberries equals 3 cups.

CRANBERRY-ORANGE CHEX MIX

prep 10 min *total time* 40 min *makes* 10 cups snack

3 cups Corn Chex® cereal
3 cups Rice Chex® cereal
3 cups Wheat Chex® Cereal
1 cup sliced almonds
1/4 cup butter or margarine
1/4 cup packed brown sugar
1/4 cup frozen (thawed) orange juice concentrate
1/2 cup dried cranberries

1. Heat oven to 300°F. In large bowl, mix cereals and almonds; set aside.

2. In 1-cup microwavable measuring cup, place butter; cover with microwavable paper towel. Microwave on High 30 to 50 seconds or until melted. Stir in brown sugar and orange juice concentrate. Microwave uncovered on High 30 seconds; stir. Pour over cereal mixture, stirring until evenly coated. Spread in large ungreased roasting pan.

3. Bake uncovered 30 minutes, stirring after 15 minutes. Stir in dried cranberries. Spread on waxed paper or foil to cool. Store in airtight container.

CLASSIC CRANBERRY MOLD

prep 20 min *total time* 6 hrs 50 min *makes* 8 servings

2 cups water
3/4 cup sugar
3 cups fresh or frozen cranberries
1 box (6-serving size) raspberry-flavored gelatin
1 can (8 oz) crushed pineapple in syrup, undrained
1 medium stalk celery, chopped (1/2 cup), if desired
1/2 cup chopped walnuts or pistachio nuts, if desired
Salad greens, if desired

1. In 2-quart saucepan, heat water and sugar to boiling, stirring occasionally; boil 1 minute. Stir in cranberries. Heat to boiling; boil 5 minutes, stirring occasionally. Stir in gelatin until dissolved. Stir in pineapple, celery and walnuts. Cool at room temperature about 30 minutes.

2. Pour into ungreased 6-cup mold, 8 individual molds or stemmed goblets. Cover; refrigerate at least 6 hours until firm. Unmold onto salad greens. Garnish with celery leaves and additional cranberries if desired.

pomegranates

Pomegranates, with their interior compartments filled with ruby red, sweet-tart sacs that shine like jewels, are an architectural wonder. Larger than apples, pomegranates have a leathery, deep red to purplish red rind. Steadily gaining in popularity, this unique fruit dates back thousands of years to the B.C.E. era and is thought to have originated in Persia. Legend indicates pomegranates represented health, fertility and rebirth and that they had mystical healing powers. In addition to being a food source, they were used as art in decoration and the juice was used as a dye. Pomegranates are now grown in California, Asia and the Mediterranean and have been discovered to be a good source of antioxidants, potassium and vitamin C.

Bright red pomegranate seeds are excellent snacks and add a festive finishing touch to salads, sauces, desserts, vegetables and even chichi cocktails! Look for pomegranate juice in the refrigerated section of your supermarket and pomegranate-spiked beverages in the beverage section. Left whole, they add an exotic, yet rustic touch to centerpieces and gift baskets. If you've never eaten pomegranate seeds, give them a whirl with Glorious Pomegranate-Orange Sauce or Pomegranate and Citrus Broccoli Salad.

user guide

- Fresh pomegranates are available September through January.

- Look for deep red fruit that are firm and heavy for their size; avoid those with blemishes, cracks and soft spots.

- Refrigerate whole fruit in a plastic bag for up to 2 months. Seeds can be refrigerated in resealable food-storage plastic bags up to 2 weeks or frozen up to 6 months.

- To remove the seeds, cut the crown end off the pomegranate, and then make 4 to 6 lengthwise cuts, 1/4 inch deep, in the rind. Put the pomegranate in a bowl and cover with cool water; let stand 5 minutes. Holding the pomegranate under the water, break it apart into sections, separating the seeds from the pithy white membrane. The edible sacs will sink to the bottom of the bowl, and the bitter, inedible membrane will float to the top. Throw out the membrane and the rind. Drain the seeds in a colander; gently pat dry with paper towels. Be careful during this process because the juice can stain permanently.

- A medium pomegranate should give you about 1 cup seeds.

GLORIOUS POMEGRANATE-ORANGE SAUCE

prep 10 min *total time* 10 min *makes* 1 cup sauce

1/2 cup butter or margarine
1/3 cup sugar
1/3 cup frozen (thawed) orange juice concentrate
1/4 cup pomegranate seeds

1. In 1-quart saucepan, melt butter over medium heat. Add sugar and orange juice concentrate, stirring until sugar is dissolved. Remove from heat; cool slightly.

2. Beat sauce with wire whisk until thick and shiny. Stir in pomegranate seeds.

POMEGRANATE *and* CITRUS BROCCOLI SALAD

prep 20 min *total time* 20 min
makes 9 servings (1/2 cup each)

1/2 cup mayonnaise or salad dressing
1/4 cup orange juice
1 teaspoon sugar
1/2 teaspoon salt
Dash pepper
3 cups coarsely chopped broccoli florets (about 8 oz)
1 medium orange, peeled, cut into bite-size chunks (about 1 cup)
3/4 cup pomegranate seeds (from 1 pomegranate)
1/3 cup roasted salted sunflower nuts
2 tablespoons chopped red onion

1. In large serving bowl, mix mayonnaise, orange juice, sugar, salt and pepper.

2. Add remaining ingredients; toss until well coated. Store covered in refrigerator.

ROASTED VEGETABLE MEDLEY

prep 25 min   *total time* 1 hr 20 min
makes 10 servings (1/2 cup each)

2 tablespoons olive or vegetable oil

1 tablespoon chopped fresh or 1 teaspoon dried
   sage leaves

1 clove garlic, finely chopped

1/2 lb Brussels sprouts, cut in half

1/2 lb parsnips, peeled, cut into 1 1/2-inch pieces

1/4 lb ready-to-eat baby-cut carrots

1 small butternut squash (2 lb), peeled, seeded
   and cut into 1-inch pieces

1/2 teaspoon salt

1. Heat oven to 425°F. In small bowl, mix oil, sage and garlic.

2. In ungreased 15 × 10 × 1-inch pan, place remaining ingredients except salt. Pour oil mixture over vegetables. Sprinkle with salt; stir to coat.

3. Cover with foil. Roast 20 minutes; remove foil. Roast uncovered 30 to 35 minutes longer, stirring occasionally, until vegetables are crisp-tender.

1 SERVING: Calories 90 (Calories from Fat 25); Total Fat 3g (Saturated Fat 0g; Trans Fat 0g); Cholesterol 0mg; Sodium 130mg; Total Carbohydrate 14g (Dietary Fiber 3g; Sugars 5g); Protein 2g; % DAILY VALUE: Vitamin A 160%; Vitamin C 20%; Calcium 4%; Iron 4%; EXCHANGES: 1 Starch, 1/2 Fat; CARBOHYDRATE CHOICES: 1

new twist

Parsnips are one of the underdogs of the vegetable world. This under-appreciated root vegetable looks like a white carrot with creamy-yellow to white flesh. When cooked it is sweeter than a carrot. If you must, however, carrots can be substituted!

CHEESY BACON BRUSSELS SPROUTS

prep 25 min *total time* 1 hr
makes 10 servings (1/2 cup each)

1 1/4 lb Brussels sprouts (1 to 1 1/2 inch), cut in half (5 cups)*
6 slices bacon, cut into 1-inch pieces
1 tablespoon butter or margarine
1 large onion, finely chopped (1 cup)
1 tablespoon all-purpose flour
1/4 teaspoon dried thyme leaves
1/4 teaspoon pepper
3/4 cup half-and-half
2 teaspoons chicken bouillon granules
1/3 cup shredded Parmesan cheese
1/2 cup shredded Cheddar cheese

1. Heat oven to 350°F. In 3-quart saucepan, place Brussels sprouts; add enough water just to cover. Heat to boiling; boil 6 to 8 minutes or until crisp-tender. Drain and return to saucepan; set aside.

2. Meanwhile, in 10-inch skillet, cook bacon over medium heat, stirring occasionally, until crisp. Remove bacon with slotted spoon; drain on paper towels and set aside. Drain all but 1 tablespoon bacon fat from skillet.

3. Add butter to bacon fat in skillet. Heat over medium-high heat until butter is melted. Add onion; cook 2 to 3 minutes, stirring frequently, until crisp-tender. Add flour, thyme and pepper; cook and stir until well blended. Gradually stir in half-and-half and bouillon granules. Heat to boiling, stirring constantly; boil and stir 1 minute. Remove from heat; stir in Parmesan cheese.

4. Pour sauce over Brussels sprouts in saucepan; mix gently. Spoon into 2-quart casserole. Bake uncovered 25 to 30 minutes, sprinkling with crumbled bacon and Cheddar cheese for last 10 minutes of baking, until hot and bubbly.

*Remove any discolored outer leaves and trim discolored portion of stem ends of Brussels sprouts.

1 SERVING: Calories 130 (Calories from Fat 70); Total Fat 8g (Saturated Fat 4g; Trans Fat 0g); Cholesterol 20mg; Sodium 330mg; Total Carbohydrate 8g (Dietary Fiber 3g; Sugars 3g); Protein 6g; % DAILY VALUE: Vitamin A 10%; Vitamin C 20%; Calcium 8%; Iron 2%; EXCHANGES: 1 Vegetable, 1/2 High-Fat Meat, 1 Fat; CARBOHYDRATE CHOICES: 1/2

CHEESY BACON GREEN BEANS Omit Brussels sprouts. In Step 1, place 1 bag (1 lb) frozen cut green beans and 2 tablespoons water in 2-quart microwavable casserole. Cover and microwave on High 5 minutes; drain and set aside. Continue as directed.

holiday inspiration

Don't let anyone give you any attitude—this vegetable with the funny little name delivers big on flavor! Brussels sprouts look and taste like miniature green cabbage and they're cute and fun to boot.

APPLESAUCE–SWEET POTATO BAKE

prep 10 min   *total time* 1 hr 15 min   *makes* 6 servings

1 lb dark-orange sweet potatoes (about 3 medium)
1 cup applesauce
1/3 cup packed brown sugar
1/4 cup chopped nuts
1/2 teaspoon ground cinnamon
2 tablespoons butter or margarine

1. In 3-quart saucepan, place sweet potatoes; add enough water (salted if desired) to cover. Heat to boiling; reduce heat. Cover; simmer 30 to 35 minutes or until tender; drain. Remove skins; cut each sweet potato lengthwise in half.

2. Heat oven to 375°F. In ungreased 2-quart casserole or 8-inch square baking dish, place sweet potatoes, cut sides up. Spread applesauce over sweet potatoes.

3. In small bowl, mix brown sugar, nuts and cinnamon; sprinkle over applesauce. Dot with butter. Cover; bake about 30 minutes or until hot.

1 SERVING: Calories 210 (Calories from Fat 60); Total Fat 7g (Saturated Fat 2.5g; Trans Fat 0g); Cholesterol 10mg; Sodium 125mg; Total Carbohydrate 35g (Dietary Fiber 3g; Sugars 28g); Protein 2g; % DAILY VALUE: Vitamin A 180%; Vitamin C 15%; Calcium 4%; Iron 4%; EXCHANGES: 1/2 Starch, 2 Other Carbohydrate, 1 Fat; CARBOHYDRATE CHOICES: 2

new twist

- Substitute 1 can (17 oz) vacuum-packed sweet potatoes, cut lengthwise in half, for the fresh sweet potatoes and skip Step 1.

- For a festive topping, why not try sprinkling the sweet potatoes with one of these tasty morsels?
    Dried cranberries
    Miniature marshmallows
    Toasted coconut
    Toasted pecans or almonds
    French-fried onion rings or crushed croutons

DO-AHEAD GARLIC MASHED POTATOES

prep 15 min   *total time* 1 hr 15 min   *makes* 8 servings

3 lb round red or white potatoes (about 9 medium), peeled, cut into pieces
6 cloves garlic, peeled
3/4 cup milk
1/2 cup whipping (heavy) cream
1/2 cup butter or margarine
1 teaspoon salt
Dash pepper

1. In 3-quart saucepan, place potatoes and garlic; add enough water to cover. Heat to boiling; reduce heat. Cover; cook 20 to 25 minutes or potatoes are until tender. (Cooking time will vary depending on size of potato pieces and type of potato used.) Drain and return to saucepan.

2. Heat potatoes over low heat about 1 minute, shaking pan often to keep potatoes from sticking and burning, to dry potatoes (this will help make mashed potatoes fluffier). Mash potatoes and garlic in pan with potato masher or electric mixer on low speed 1 to 2 minutes or until no lumps remain.

3. In 1-quart saucepan, heat milk, whipping cream, butter, salt and pepper over medium-low heat, stirring occasionally, until butter is melted; reserve and refrigerate 1/4 cup mixture. Add remaining milk mixture in small amounts to potatoes, mashing after each addition, until potatoes are light and fluffy.

4. Spray 2-quart casserole with cooking spray. Spoon potatoes into casserole; cover and refrigerate up to 24 hours. Potatoes can be baked immediately following directions in Step 5.

5. Heat oven to 350°F. Pour reserved milk mixture over potatoes. Bake uncovered 40 to 45 minutes or until hot. Stir potatoes before serving.

1 SERVING: Calories 300 (Calories from Fat 150); Total Fat 17g (Saturated Fat 9g; Trans Fat 1g); Cholesterol 50mg; Sodium 400mg; Total Carbohydrate 33g (Dietary Fiber 3g; Sugars 2g); Protein 4g; % DAILY VALUE: Vitamin A 15%; Vitamin C 10%; Calcium 6%; Iron 4%; EXCHANGES: 2 Starch, 3 Fat; CARBOHYDRATE CHOICES: 2

holiday inspiration

Potato lovers know there is absolutely no bad
way to make a spud! This supreme potato dish
will bring rave reviews. Save a bit of time by
using jarred garlic—just check the label for the
correct amount to use.

Explore the options for making this beautiful and sophisticated side dish:

- Two cans (15 ounces each) canned pear halves can be substituted for the fresh pears. Drain liquid from pears and drain pears, flat sides down, on paper towels. Follow directions in Step 1—except fill hollow with cheese now. Roast 15 minutes or until pears and cheese are hot; sprinkle pears with nuts.

- Blue cheese, garlic-and-herb spreadable cheese or chives-and-onion cream cheese can be substituted for the Gorgonzola cheese.

holiday inspiration

The ripe firm pears should not be hard, but should also not be as soft and ambrosial as a pear would be for eating out of hand. If your pears are too hard, let them ripen a day or two longer. These delicious pears would also make an elegant first course or can be placed on salad greens for a unique salad.

ROASTED ROSEMARY-GORGONZOLA PEARS

prep 20 min *total time* 50 min *makes* 8 servings

4 unpeeled ripe firm pears, cut in half lengthwise, cored*

1 tablespoon olive or vegetable oil

1/2 teaspoon kosher (coarse) salt

1/4 teaspoon coarse ground pepper

1 teaspoon chopped fresh or 1/2 teaspoon dried rosemary leaves, crushed

1/3 cup finely crumbled Gorgonzola cheese

1/4 cup chopped walnuts, toasted (page 110)

1. Heat oven to 375°F. Cut thin slice from rounded side of pear halves, if necessary, so they'll rest level in pan. In 13 × 9–inch pan, arrange pear halves, cut sides up. Brush tops of pears with oil; sprinkle with salt, pepper and rosemary.

2. Roast uncovered 15 minutes. Fill cored hollow of each pear half with 2 teaspoons cheese. Roast uncovered 10 to 15 minutes longer or until pears are tender and cheese is soft. Sprinkle with walnuts. Drizzle with additional olive oil if desired.

*A melon baller or the tip of a teaspoon works well to core the pears. Be sure to make a hollow big enough to hold 2 teaspoons of the cheese.

1 SERVING: Calories 120 (Calories from Fat 50); Total Fat 6g (Saturated Fat 1.5g; Trans Fat 0g); Cholesterol 0mg; Sodium 230mg; Total Carbohydrate 13g (Dietary Fiber 3g; Sugars 9g); Protein 2g; % DAILY VALUE: Vitamin A 0%; Vitamin C 2%; Calcium 4%; Iron 2%; EXCHANGES: 1 Fruit, 1 Fat; CARBOHYDRATE CHOICES: 1

ROMA TOMATOES *with* ASPARAGUS *and* HOLLANDAISE

prep 25 min   *total time* 30 min   *makes* 12 servings

6 medium plum (Roma) tomatoes (2 1/2 to
   3 inches long)

36 thin asparagus spears (1/4 inch diameter)

1 cup milk

1 package (0.9 oz) hollandaise sauce mix

1/4 cup butter or margarine

1/2 cup shredded Parmesan cheese (2 oz)

1. Cut tomatoes in half lengthwise. Seed tomatoes, using teaspoon; remove flesh, leaving 1/4-inch-thick shell. Cut thin slice from rounded side of tomato halves, if necessary, so they'll rest level in pan. Drain tomatoes, hollow sides down, on paper towels.

2. Break off tough ends of asparagus. From tip end, cut off top 3 inches of each spear (reserve remaining portions of spear for another use). In 1-quart saucepan, heat 1 inch water to boiling. Add asparagus pieces. Heat to boiling and boil 2 minutes; drain and set aside.

3. In same 1-quart saucepan, beat milk and sauce mix with wire whisk until smooth. Add butter. Heat to boiling over medium heat, stirring constantly. Reduce heat to low. Cook 1 minute, stirring constantly, until thickened and smooth.

4. Set oven control to broil. In 13 × 9–inch pan, place tomato halves. In each tomato half, arrange 3 asparagus pieces lengthwise with tips extended over stem end of tomato. Spoon 1 tablespoon sauce over asparagus-filled tomato halves, allowing some sauce to fill tomato hollow. Sprinkle with cheese.

5. Broil with tops 4 to 6 inches from heat 2 to 4 minutes or until tomatoes are hot and cheese just begins to brown. If desired, heat remaining sauce until hot; serve with tomatoes.

1 SERVING: Calories 90 (Calories from Fat 50); Total Fat 6g (Saturated Fat 3g; Trans Fat 0g); Cholesterol 15mg; Sodium 170mg; Total Carbohydrate 5g (Dietary Fiber 0g; Sugars 3g); Protein 4g; % DAILY VALUE: Vitamin A 15%; Vitamin C 10%; Calcium 10%; Iron 2%; EXCHANGES: 1/2 Vegetable, 1/2 Medium-Fat Meat, 1 Fat; CARBOHYDRATE CHOICES: 1/2

holiday inspiration

Isn't it great to find recipes like this? They look fabulous, like you've spent the whole day making them, but they're super easy to make! Serve with Roasted Beef Tenderloin (page 66) or grilled steak or chicken.

ITALIAN CHRISTMAS VEGGIES

prep 20 min   *total time* 20 min   *makes* 6 servings

1/3 cup fat-free Italian dressing

2 medium zucchini, cut into 1/4-inch slices

1 medium red bell pepper, cut into 1/2-inch slices

1 cup sliced fresh mushrooms

1 cup sliced onion

2 tablespoons dry white wine or chicken broth

3 tablespoons shredded Parmesan cheese

1. In 10-inch skillet, cook dressing, zucchini, bell pepper, mushrooms and onion over medium-high heat about 5 minutes, stirring frequently, until dressing has almost evaporated.

2. Stir in wine. Cover; cook about 2 minutes or until vegetables are crisp-tender. Sprinkle with cheese.

1 SERVING: Calories 50 (Calories from Fat 10); Total Fat 1g (Saturated Fat 0.5g; Trans Fat 0g); Cholesterol 0mg; Sodium 210mg; Total Carbohydrate 7g (Dietary Fiber 2g; Sugars 4g); Protein 3g; % DAILY VALUE: Vitamin A 35%; Vitamin C 40%; Calcium 6%; Iron 4%; EXCHANGES: 1 Vegetable; CARBOHYDRATE CHOICES: 1/2

new twist

Vibrant colors and lots of flavor make this recipe an entertaining shoo-in:

- For a little variety, use a yellow summer squash in place of one of the zucchini.

- Create a meatless meal by spooning the vegetables over polenta slices, cheese-filled ravioli or spaghetti.

CARIBBEAN CRUNCH SQUASH

prep 15 min *total time* 1 hr 15 min *makes* 4 servings

1 buttercup squash (2 to 2 1/2 lb)
2 tablespoons butter or margarine, melted
2 tablespoons peach or apricot preserves
2 tablespoons graham cracker crumbs
2 tablespoons shredded coconut
1/4 teaspoon ground ginger
1/8 teaspoon ground allspice
1/8 teaspoon pepper

1. Heat oven to 350°F. Cut squash into quarters; remove seeds and fibers. In ungreased 13 × 9-inch pan, place squash, cut sides up.

2. In small bowl, mix butter and preserves. Brush about half of preserves mixture over cut sides of squash pieces. In another small bowl, mix remaining ingredients; sprinkle over squash. Drizzle with remaining preserves mixture.

3. Bake uncovered 45 to 60 minutes or until tender.

1 SERVING: Calories 180 (Calories from Fat 70); Total Fat 8g (Saturated Fat 4g; Trans Fat 0g); Cholesterol 15mg; Sodium 65mg; Total Carbohydrate 24g (Dietary Fiber 5g; Sugars 13g); Protein 2g; % DAILY VALUE: Vitamin A 100%; Vitamin C 15%; Calcium 2%; Iron 4%; EXCHANGES: 1/2 Starch, 1 Other Carbohydrate, 1 1/2 Fat; CARBOHYDRATE CHOICES: 1 1/2

new twist

- Depending on where you live, varieties of squash can vary. Two acorn squash (1 to 1 1/2 pounds each) can be substituted for the buttercup squash.

- Certain flavors are destined for one another, and so it is with grilled pork chops, a pork roast or a pork tenderloin—any one of them would be perfect to go along with this sweetly spiced squash.

TORTELLINI-BROCCOLI SALAD

prep 20 min *total time* 1 hr 20 min *makes* 4 servings

1 package (7 oz) dried cheese-filled tortellini
1/4 cup balsamic or cider vinegar
1 tablespoon chopped fresh or 1 teaspoon dried basil leaves
2 tablespoons olive or vegetable oil
1/4 teaspoon paprika
1/8 teaspoon salt
1 clove garlic, finely chopped
1 medium carrot, sliced (1/2 cup)
2 cups broccoli florets
2 medium green onions, sliced (2 tablespoons)

1. Cook and drain tortellini as directed on package. Rinse with cold water; drain.

2. In tightly covered container, shake remaining ingredients except carrot, broccoli and onions to make vinaigrette.

3. In large glass or plastic bowl, mix carrot, broccoli, onions and vinaigrette. Add tortellini; toss until evenly coated. Cover; refrigerate at least 1 hour to blend flavors.

1 SERVING: Calories 280 (Calories from Fat 100); Total Fat 11g (Saturated Fat 3.5g; Trans Fat 0g); Cholesterol 35mg; Sodium 540mg; Total Carbohydrate 34g (Dietary Fiber 3g; Sugars 2g); Protein 10g; % DAILY VALUE: Vitamin A 70%; Vitamin C 60%; Calcium 10%; Iron 8%; EXCHANGES: 2 Starch, 1 Vegetable, 1/2 High-Fat Meat, 1 Fat; CARBOHYDRATE CHOICES: 2

holiday inspiration

- Rather than chopping the vegetables, why not buy presliced carrots, broccoli and onions from the salad bar or look for precut veggies in the produce department?

- To save more time, use 1/3 cup purchased balsamic vinaigrette dressing or another vinaigrette dressing you really like.

- If you have leftover holiday ham, turkey or beef, chop it and add it to make a main-meal salad!

HEAVENLY FRUIT SALAD

prep 20 min   *total time* 20 min   *makes* 6 servings
see photo on page 52, bottom

1/4 cup orange juice

1/4 cup honey

1/2 teaspoon ground cinnamon

1 medium jicama, peeled, cut into 1/4-inch slices

3 oranges, peeled, sliced

3 kiwifruit, peeled, sliced

1/4 cup pomegranate seeds or dried cranberries

1. In tightly covered container, shake orange juice, honey and cinnamon.

2. Cut jicama slices with star-shaped cookie cutter.

3. In serving bowl, mix jicama, oranges and kiwifruit. Toss with orange-honey dressing. Sprinkle with pomegranate seeds.

1 SERVING: Calories 160 (Calories from Fat 0); Total Fat 0g (Saturated Fat 0g; Trans Fat 0g); Cholesterol 0mg; Sodium 5mg; Total Carbohydrate 37g (Dietary Fiber 8g; Sugars 23g); Protein 2g; % DAILY VALUE: Vitamin A 4%; Vitamin C 160%; Calcium 6%; Iron 6%; EXCHANGES: 1 Starch, 1 Fruit, 1/2 Other Carbohydrate; CARBOHYDRATE CHOICES: 2 1/2

holiday inspiration

Bright red pomegranate seeds add a sparkling touch to any salad. Pomegranates are larger than apples and have a leathery, deep red to purplish red rind. Though not beautiful on the outside, but they have a spectacular interior packed full of sparkling, juicy, ruby-colored seeds that are slightly sweet and refreshingly tart. See page 96 to learn how to cut open and remove seeds.

GREEN BEANS *with* SHIITAKE MUSHROOMS

prep 35 min   *total time* 35 min   *makes* 6 servings

1 1/2 lb fresh green beans

1/4 cup slivered almonds

6 oz fresh shiitake mushrooms

1 tablespoon olive or vegetable oil

1 tablespoon sesame oil

3 cloves garlic, finely chopped

2 tablespoons soy sauce

1. Remove ends of beans. Leave beans whole, or cut into 1-inch pieces. Place steamer basket in 1/2 inch water in saucepan or skillet (water should not touch bottom of basket). Place green beans in steamer basket. Cover tightly and heat to boiling; reduce heat. Steam 10 minutes.

2. In ungreased heavy skillet, cook almonds over medium-low heat 5 to 7 minutes, stirring frequently until browning begins, then stirring constantly until golden brown and fragrant.

3. Remove tough stems of mushrooms; cut mushrooms into 1/4-inch slices. In 12-inch skillet, heat olive and sesame oils over medium heat. Cook mushrooms and garlic in oils 3 minutes, stirring occasionally. Stir in soy sauce and green beans. Cook 2 to 3 minutes or until green beans are crisp-tender. Sprinkle with almonds.

1 SERVING: Calories 120 (Calories from Fat 70); Total Fat 7g (Saturated Fat 1g; Trans Fat 0g); Cholesterol 0mg; Sodium 310mg; Total Carbohydrate 9g (Dietary Fiber 4g; Sugars 3g); Protein 4g; % DAILY VALUE: Vitamin A 10%; Vitamin C 4%; Calcium 6%; Iron 8%; EXCHANGES: 2 Vegetable, 1 1/2 Fat; CARBOHYDRATE CHOICES: 1/2

holiday inspiration

Know your mushrooms! Once cultivated only in
Japan and Korea, shiitake mushrooms are now
cultivated in the United States. The meaty flesh
has a full-bodied, some say even steaklike, flavor.
The stems are tough but add a wonderful flavor to
stocks and sauces (throw out stems after they've
been used for flavoring). Your favorite kind of
mushrooms can be substituted for the shiitake.

make-ahead magic

The Parmesan Fans can be made up to 2 days
ahead of time and stored in a tightly covered
container at room temperature.

HOLIDAY SALAD *with* PARMESAN FANS

prep 20 min *total time* 30 min *makes* 6 servings

Parmesan Fans

6 wonton wrappers (3 1/2-inch square)

1 tablespoon Italian dressing

2 teaspoons grated Parmesan cheese

Salad

1 bag (5 oz) spring mix salad greens or 6 cups assorted greens

1/4 cup Italian dressing

1/3 cup red or green pistachio nuts, coarsely chopped

1. Heat oven to 350°F. Place wonton wrappers on cutting board. In each wrapper, cut 3/8- to 1/2-inch strips to within 1/2 inch of bottom (see illustration **a** at right). Make 2 or 3 pleats in the same direction on bottom edge of each wrapper to form fan base (see illustration **b** at right); spread strips gently to form fan shape. Carefully transfer fans to cookie sheet. Brush with 1 tablespoon dressing; sprinkle with cheese.

2. Bake 4 to 6 minutes or until light brown. Cool completely.

3. In medium bowl, toss salad greens and 1/4 cup dressing. Arrange greens on 6 salad plates; sprinkle with nuts. Place fans upright in salad.

1 SERVING: Calories 120 (Calories from Fat 80); Total Fat 9g (Saturated Fat 1g; Trans Fat 0g); Cholesterol 0mg; Sodium 200mg; Total Carbohydrate 8g (Dietary Fiber 1g; Sugars 2g); Protein 3g; **% DAILY VALUE:** Vitamin A 15%; Vitamin C 8%; Calcium 4%; Iron 4%; **EXCHANGES:** 1/2 Starch, 1 Vegetable, 1 1/2 Fat; **CARBOHYDRATE CHOICES:** 1/2

a. For each wrapper, cut 3/8- to 1/2-inch strips to within 1/2 inch of bottom.

b. Make 2 or 3 pleats in the same direction on bottom edge of wrapper.

CHRISTMAS SALAD *with* BALSAMIC VINAIGRETTE

prep 20 min *total time* 20 min *makes* 6 servings

Vinaigrette

1/3 cup olive or vegetable oil

1/4 cup balsamic or red wine vinegar

2 tablespoons sugar

1 teaspoon Dijon mustard

1 clove garlic, finely chopped

Salad

1 bag (10 oz) mixed baby greens or Italian-blend salad greens

1 avocado, pitted, peeled and sliced

1/3 cup pistachio nuts

1/4 cup dried cranberries

1. In small bowl, beat all vinaigrette ingredients with wire whisk until smooth.

2. In large bowl, toss all salad ingredients with vinaigrette just before serving.

1 SERVING: Calories 250 (Calories from Fat 180); Total Fat 20g (Saturated Fat 2.5g; Trans Fat 0g); Cholesterol 0mg; Sodium 65mg; Total Carbohydrate 14g (Dietary Fiber 4g; Sugars 9g); Protein 3g; % DAILY VALUE: Vitamin A 30%; Vitamin C 20%; Calcium 4%; Iron 8%; EXCHANGES: 1/2 Other Carbohydrate, 1 Vegetable, 4 Fat; CARBOHYDRATE CHOICES: 1

APPLE-GORGONZOLA SALAD Omit avocado, pistachio nuts and cranberries and instead, toss the greens and dressing with 1 medium green apple, chopped (1 cup), 1/2 cup crumbled Gorgonzola or blue cheese (2 oz) and 1/3 cup walnuts, toasted.*

MUSHROOM-TOMATO SALAD Omit avocado, pistachio nuts and cranberries and instead, toss the greens and dressing with 2 cups fresh mushrooms, sliced, 1 1/2 cups grape tomatoes, cut in half and 1/3 cup finely sliced purple onion.

STRAWBERRY-ALMOND SALAD Omit avocado, pistachio nuts and cranberries and instead, toss the greens and dressing with 2 cups quartered strawberries, 1 package (4 oz) goat cheese crumbles and 1/3 cup slivered almonds, toasted.*

*To toast nuts, heat oven to 350°F. Spread nuts in ungreased shallow pan. Bake 6 to 10 minutes, stirring occasionally, until light brown. Watch carefully because nuts brown quickly. Or cook nuts in ungreased heavy skillet over medium heat 5 to 7 minutes, stirring frequently until nuts begin to brown, then stirring constantly until light brown.

make-ahead magic

The vinaigrette can be made up to 2 days ahead of time. Cover tightly and refrigerate until serving time.

BettyCrocker.com

Top to bottom: Christmas Salad with
Balsamic Vinaigrette, Apple-Gorgonzola Salad
and Strawberry-Almond Salad

134

146

CANDY CANE LANE

MELT-IN-YOUR-MOUTH SUGAR COOKIES

prep 4 hrs 25 min *total time* 4 hrs 25 min
makes about 5 dozen cookies

1 1/2 cups powdered sugar
1 cup butter or margarine, softened
1 teaspoon vanilla
1/2 teaspoon almond extract
1 egg
2 1/2 cups all-purpose flour
1 teaspoon baking soda
1 teaspoon cream of tartar
Creamy Vanilla Glaze (at right)
or
Royal Icing (at right)
or
Shiny Decorator's Glaze (at right)

1. In large bowl, beat powdered sugar, butter, vanilla, almond extract and egg with electric mixer on medium speed, or mix with spoon. Stir in flour, baking soda and cream of tartar. Cover; refrigerate at least 2 hours.

2. Heat oven to 375°F. Lightly grease cookie sheet with shortening or cooking spray. Divide dough in half. Roll each half 1/4 inch thick on lightly floured surface. Cut into desired shapes with 2 1/2-inch cookie cutters. Place about 2 inches apart on cookie sheet.

3. Bake 7 to 8 minutes or until edges are light brown. Remove from cookie sheet to wire rack. Cool completely, about 30 minutes. Frost with Creamy Vanilla Glaze; decorate as desired (see new twist, opposite).

1 COOKIE: Calories 70 (Calories from Fat 30); Total Fat 3g (Saturated Fat 1.5g; Trans Fat 0g); Cholesterol 10mg; Sodium 45mg; Total Carbohydrate 9g (Dietary Fiber 0g; Sugars 5g); Protein 0g; % DAILY VALUE: Vitamin A 2%; Vitamin C 0%; Calcium 0%; Iron 0%; EXCHANGES: 1/2 Other Carbohydrate, 1/2 Fat; CARBOHYDRATE CHOICES: 1/2

CREAMY VANILLA GLAZE

1 cup powdered sugar
1/2 teaspoon vanilla
1 tablespoon water or 1 to 2 tablespoons milk

In small bowl, mix all ingredients with spoon until smooth and spreadable.

ROYAL ICING

1 package (16 oz) powdered sugar (4 1/2 cups)
1/3 cup warm water (105°F to 115°F)
3 tablespoons meringue powder
1 teaspoon vanilla or almond extract
1/2 teaspoon cream of tartar
Food colors, if desired

In large bowl, beat all ingredients except food colors with electric mixer on low speed until mixed. Beat on high speed 7 to 10 minutes or until very stiff. Divide and tint with food colors.

SHINY DECORATOR'S GLAZE

2 cups powdered sugar
2 tablespoons water
2 tablespoons light corn syrup
1/2 teaspoon almond extract

In small bowl, beat all ingredients with electric mixer on low speed until smooth.

new twist

Express your artistic abilities by painting, marbling or flocking cookies. Paint cookies with Egg Yolk Paint (below) before baking, or with Food Color Paint or Milk Paint (below) before or after baking, using fine-tip paintbrushes.

- EGG YOLK PAINT: Stir together 1 egg yolk and 1/4 teaspoon water. Divide mixture among several small custard cups. Tint with food color to get the color you want (Egg Yolk Paint creates opaque, bright colors). Paint on cookie dough before baking. If paint thickens while standing, add a few drops of water. For food-safety reasons, use Egg Yolk Paint only on cookie dough that will be baked; don't paint on baked cookies.

- FOOD COLOR PAINT: Stir together small amounts of water and food color. Paint on cookie dough before baking, or use to paint designs on frosted cookies that are set.

- MILK PAINT: Stir together small amounts of evaporated milk and food color. Paint on cookie dough before baking or on frosted cookies that are set.

- MARBLING: Using a fine-tip brush, paint a different color of Milk Paint or Food Color Paint on freshly iced, glazed or frosted cookies. Or drizzle or pipe on frosting, or squeeze on decorating gels sold in tubes at supermarkets. (Don't allow glaze, frosting or icing to dry or harden before marbling, or this technique won't work.) Use a brush or toothpick to swirl the colors or create marbleized patterns. Let paint or gel dry completely before storing cookies.

- FLOCKING: Using tinted Creamy Vanilla Glaze, Shiny Decorator's Glaze or Royal Icing, pipe or drizzle a design on completely dried and hardened glazed or frosted cookie. Sprinkle colored sugar over design while design is still fresh (don't allow design to dry or harden before flocking or this technique won't work). Shake off any excess sugar. Or instead of adding a design, you can flock the entire surface of a freshly glazed or frosted cookie.

holiday inspiration

Get savvy about glaze to make your own designer cookies!

- CREAMY VANILLA GLAZE (page 114) is an all-purpose, versatile, white-colored glaze (using 2% milk, whole milk or half-and-half will make it whiter than if skim milk is used). To make a thinner glaze, add more milk. For a colored glaze, stir in liquid food color, 1 drop at a time, until you get the color you want (too much liquid color will break down the frosting, causing it to separate and curdle). For intense, vivid color, use paste food color.

- ROYAL ICING (page 114) is a stiff decorator icing and makes very crisp lines. When decorating cookies, first pipe a thin border of Royal Icing around the outside edge and let dry. Then fill in the cookies with thinned Royal Icing or frosting, using a small metal spatula or medium-size paintbrush. The icing doesn't drip over the edges, so you'll have cookies that look professionally decorated.

- SHINY DECORATOR'S GLAZE (page 114) adds a smooth and glossy sheen to your holiday cookies. Thin the glaze with a little water and drizzle or pour over cookies for a fast and shiny finish. Vanilla can be used instead of the almond extract, but the glaze won't be as white. If you love the flavor of vanilla and do a lot of decorating, consider buying clear vanilla, which is available online or in cake decorating supply stores.

Top to bottom: Gingerbread Cookies and
Espresso Thumbprint Cookies (page 135)

GINGERBREAD COOKIES

prep 1 hr 5 min *total time* 3 hrs 35 min
makes about 2 1/2 dozen 2 1/2-inch cookies

Cookies

1 cup packed brown sugar

1/3 cup shortening

1 1/2 cups full-flavor molasses

2/3 cup cold water

7 cups all-purpose flour

2 teaspoons baking soda

2 teaspoons ground ginger

1 teaspoon ground allspice

1 teaspoon ground cinnamon

1 teaspoon ground cloves

1/2 teaspoon salt

Decorator's Frosting, if desired

2 cups powdered sugar

2 tablespoons milk or half-and-half

1/2 teaspoon vanilla

Food color, if desired

1. In large bowl, beat brown sugar, shortening, molasses and water with electric mixer on medium speed, or mix with spoon. Stir in remaining cookie ingredients. Cover; refrigerate at least 2 hours until firm.

2. Heat oven to 350°F. Lightly grease cookie sheet with shortening or cooking spray. Roll one-fourth of dough at a time 1/4 inch thick on floured surface. Cut into desired shapes. Place about 2 inches apart on cookie sheet.

3. Bake 10 to 12 minutes or until no indentation remains when touched. Immediately remove from cookie sheet to wire rack. Cool completely, about 30 minutes.

4. In small bowl, mix all frosting ingredients with spoon until smooth and spreadable. Decorate cookies with frosting and, if desired, colored sugars and candies.

1 COOKIE: Calories 200 (Calories from Fat 25); Total Fat 2.5g (Saturated Fat 0.5g; Trans Fat 0g); Cholesterol 0mg; Sodium 135mg; Total Carbohydrate 42g (Dietary Fiber 0g; Sugars 16g); Protein 3g; % DAILY VALUE: Vitamin A 0%; Vitamin C 0%; Calcium 4%; Iron 15%; EXCHANGES: 1 Starch, 1 1/2 Other Carbohydrate, 1/2 Fat; CARBOHYDRATE CHOICES: 3

holiday inspiration

When using cookie cutters that have one wide end and one narrow end, alternate the placement of it as you cut out the cookies. In other words, cut the first cookie with the wide end of the cutter toward you, then cut the next cookie with the narrow end toward you. This way, you can get more cookies out of one batch of dough.

SHORTBREAD

prep 45 min   *total time* 1 hr 15 min
makes about 2 dozen cookies

3/4 cup butter or margarine, softened
1/4 cup sugar
1 3/4 cups all-purpose flour
1/2 teaspoon almond extract, if desired

1. Heat oven to 350°F. In large bowl, beat butter and sugar with electric mixer on medium speed, or mix with spoon. Stir in flour and almond extract. (If dough is crumbly, mix in additional 1 to 2 tablespoons butter or margarine, softened.)

2. On lightly floured surface, roll dough into 9 × 6–inch rectangle, 1/2 inch thick. Cut into 1 1/2-inch squares with knife or cut with 1 1/2-inch cookie cutters. On ungreased cookie sheet, place squares or shapes about 1 inch apart.

3. Bake 12 to 14 minutes or until set. Remove from cookie sheet to wire rack. Cool completely, about 30 minutes.

1 COOKIE: Calories 90 (Calories from Fat 50); Total Fat 6g (Saturated Fat 3g; Trans Fat 0g); Cholesterol 15mg; Sodium 40mg; Total Carbohydrate 9g (Dietary Fiber 0g; Sugars 2g); Protein 1g; % DAILY VALUE: Vitamin A 4%; Vitamin C 0%; Calcium 0%; Iron 2%; EXCHANGES: 1/2 Starch, 1 Fat; CARBOHYDRATE CHOICES: 1/2

BROWN SUGAR SHORTBREAD Substitute packed brown sugar for the sugar and vanilla for the almond extract.

Top to bottom: Shortbread Ornaments, Shortbread Buttons and Shortbread Trees

holiday inspiration

If you like pastel colors for cookie dough, tint using liquid food colors. For brightly colored doughs, you'll get the best results with paste food colors. Paste food color is available in craft and specialty kitchen stores. To color the doughs for Shortbread Buttons, Shortbread Ornaments and Shortbread Trees, we used paste food colors, kneading the color into the dough in a 1-quart resealable bag. This is an activity kids love!

new twist

Create your own shortbread masterpieces! Try Shortbread Buttons, Ornaments or Trees, and your cookies will get oohs and aahs!

- SHORTBREAD BUTTONS: Tint cookie dough with food color. Roll dough 1/4 inch thick; cut with 1 1/2-inch round cookie cutter. Make button holes with toothpick or end of straw; bake as directed. About 3 dozen cookies.

- SHORTBREAD ORNAMENTS: Divide into 3 equal parts. Tint each part dough with food colors to make bright red, green and purple. Roll dough between sheets of waxed paper to 1/4-inch thickness; cut with 3-inch round biscuit cutter. Cut dough rounds with knife or pizza cutter to form 1/4-inch strips. Combine different colors of dough strips to form striped round ornaments. Pinch small pea-size amount of dough; place on ornament to form top. Punch hole near top with end of plastic straw to hang ornament; bake as directed. Decorate with decorating gels if desired. About 2 dozen cookies.

- SHORTBREAD TREES: Divide into 6 equal parts. Mix 2 parts dough, 2 tablespoons chopped pistachio nuts and enough green food color to tint dough a light green. Mix another 2 parts dough and enough green food color to tint dough a medium green. Mix remaining 2 parts dough and enough green food color to tint dough a deep green. Pat light green dough into 9 × 2–inch rectangle, 3/4 inch thick, on plastic wrap. Pat medium green dough into 9 × 1 3/4–inch rectangle, 1/2 inch thick; place on top of light green dough. Pat deep green dough into 9 × 3/4–inch roll, 1/2 inch thick; place on top of medium green dough. Shape dough into triangle so that it looks like a tree shape (don't worry if layers aren't perfect). Wrap dough in plastic wrap and refrigerate about 2 hours or until firm. Cut dough into 1/4-inch slices. Place about 1 inch apart on ungreased cookie sheet. Bake 10 to 12 minutes or until set. Cool on cookie sheet 1 minute before removing to wire rack. About 2 dozen cookies.

Shortbread is so simple and yet so scrumptious! With a little imagination, you can turn these melt-in-your-mouth cookies into decorated delights.

- Dip edges of shortbread cookies into melted chocolate and then into chopped pistachio nuts.

- Drizzle tops of shortbread cookies with melted semisweet chocolate chips or white vanilla baking chips.

- Roll or pat the dough into two 4-inch circles, 1/2 inch thick. Scallop the edges using your fingers or a small spoon. Decorate with whole nuts and melted white vanilla baking chips or sprinkle lightly with cocoa in desired design.

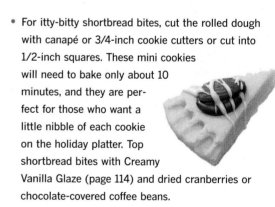

- For itty-bitty shortbread bites, cut the rolled dough with canapé or 3/4-inch cookie cutters or cut into 1/2-inch squares. These mini cookies will need to bake only about 10 minutes, and they are perfect for those who want a little nibble of each cookie on the holiday platter. Top shortbread bites with Creamy Vanilla Glaze (page 114) and dried cranberries or chocolate-covered coffee beans.

- For shortbread cookies with a textured top, use a meat mallet to lightly pound the rolled dough.

CHOCOLATE CRINKLES

prep 1 hr 35 min *total time* 5 hrs 5 min
makes about 6 dozen cookies

2 cups granulated sugar
1/2 cup vegetable oil
2 teaspoons vanilla
4 oz unsweetened baking chocolate, melted, cooled
4 eggs
2 cups all-purpose flour
2 teaspoons baking powder
1/2 teaspoon salt
1 cup powdered sugar

1. In large bowl, mix granulated sugar, oil, vanilla and chocolate. Stir in eggs, one at a time. Stir in flour, baking powder and salt. Cover; refrigerate at least 3 hours.

2. Heat oven to 350°F. Grease cookie sheet with shortening or cooking spray. Place powdered sugar in small bowl. Drop dough by teaspoonfuls into powdered sugar; roll in sugar to coat. Shape dough into balls. Place about 2 inches apart on cookie sheet.

3. Bake 10 to 12 minutes or until almost no indentation remains when touched. Remove from cookie sheet to wire rack. Cool completely, about 30 minutes.

1 COOKIE: Calories 70 (Calories from Fat 25); Total Fat 2.5g (Saturated Fat 1g; Trans Fat 0g); Cholesterol 10mg; Sodium 35mg; Total Carbohydrate 10g (Dietary Fiber 0g; Sugars 7g); Protein 0g; % DAILY VALUE: Vitamin A 0%; Vitamin C 0%; Calcium 0%; Iron 0%; EXCHANGES: 1/2 Other Carbohydrate, 1/2 Fat; CARBOHYDRATE CHOICES: 1/2

from the heart

GIVE A LITTLE DOUGH THIS HOLIDAY. Homemade cookie dough that's ready to bake makes an especially thoughtful gift for someone who appreciates homemade taste. Place the dough in a decorative tin that also can be used to store the cookies. Be sure to tuck in a little note of baking instructions.

Sending a homemade treat to out-of-town friends and family? Here are some tips for mailing your cookies:

• Wrap cookies in pairs, back to back, and place them flat or on end in a can, box or other sturdy container. Or place cookies in single layers with waxed paper in between.

• Fill each container about 3/4 full, then cushion the top with crushed waxed paper or foil to prevent shaking and breakage.

• Pack containers in a foil-lined corrugated or fiberboard packing box. Fill with crumpled newspapers, shredded paper or foam packing peanuts.

Top to bottom: Peppermint Swirls (page 140), Peanut Butter–Chocolate
Cookies (page 125), Chocolate Crinkles, Lemon Cookie Tarts (page 143),
Snickerdoodles (page 125) and Candy Cane Cookies (page 142)

Top to bottom: Thumbprint Cookies, Lemon-Almond
Thumbprint Cookies and Fudgy Peanut Cookies

THUMBPRINT COOKIES

prep 1 hr *total time* 1 hr *makes* about 3 dozen cookies

1/4 cup packed brown sugar
1/4 cup shortening
1/4 cup butter or margarine, softened
1/2 teaspoon vanilla
1 egg yolk
1 cup all-purpose flour
1/4 teaspoon salt
1 egg white
1 cup finely chopped nuts
About 6 tablespoons jelly or jam (any flavor)

1. Heat oven to 350°F. In medium bowl, beat brown sugar, shortening, butter, vanilla and egg yolk with electric mixer on medium speed, or mix with spoon. Stir in flour and salt.

2. Shape dough into 1-inch balls. In small bowl, beat egg white slightly with fork. Place nuts in another small bowl. Dip each ball into egg white, then roll in nuts. On ungreased cookie sheet, place balls about 1 inch apart. Press thumb or end of wooden spoon into center of each cookie to make indentation, but do not press all the way to the cookie sheet.

3. Bake about 10 minutes or until light brown. Quickly remake indentations with end of wooden spoon if necessary. Immediately remove from cookie sheet to wire rack. Fill each thumbprint with about 1/2 measuring teaspoon of the jelly.

1 COOKIE: Calories 80 (Calories from Fat 45); Total Fat 5g (Saturated Fat 1.5g; Trans Fat 0g); Cholesterol 10mg; Sodium 30mg; Total Carbohydrate 7g (Dietary Fiber 0g; Sugars 3g); Protein 1g; **% DAILY VALUE:** Vitamin A 0%; Vitamin C 0%; Calcium 0%; Iron 0%; **EXCHANGES:** 1/2 Other Carbohydrate, 1 Fat; **CARBOHYDRATE CHOICES:** 1/2

FUDGY PEANUT COOKIES Roll balls of dough in finely chopped salted dry-roasted peanuts. Cool cookies completely, fill indentations with purchased hot fudge topping or hazelnut spread with cocoa (from 13-oz jar) instead of the jelly.

LEMON-ALMOND THUMBPRINT COOKIES Roll balls of dough in finely chopped slivered almonds. Fill indentations with Lemon Curd (page 262) or purchased lemon curd instead of the jelly.

from the heart

WHAT TO DO when you want to bring cookies to a family with both adults and kids and they each like different things? Make the lemon-almond version for the big people and the gooey-filled fudgy peanut version for the kids.

RUSSIAN TEA CAKES

prep 1 hr 5 min *total time* 1 hr 35 min
makes about 4 dozen cookies

1 cup butter or margarine, softened
1/2 cup powdered sugar
1 teaspoon vanilla
2 1/4 cups all-purpose flour
1/4 teaspoon salt
3/4 cup finely chopped nuts
Additional powdered sugar

1. Heat oven to 400°F. In large bowl, beat butter, 1/2 cup powdered sugar and the vanilla with electric mixer on medium speed, or mix with spoon. Stir in flour and salt. Stir in nuts.

2. Shape dough into 1-inch balls. On ungreased cookie sheet, place balls about 2 inches apart.

3. Bake 8 to 9 minutes or until set but not brown. In small bowl, place additional powdered sugar. Immediately remove cookies from cookie sheet; roll in powdered sugar. Cool completely on wire rack, about 30 minutes. Roll in powdered sugar again.

1 COOKIE: Calories 80 (Calories from Fat 45); Total Fat 5g (Saturated Fat 2g; Trans Fat 0g); Cholesterol 10mg; Sodium 40mg; Total Carbohydrate 8g (Dietary Fiber 0g; Sugars 3g); Protein 0g; **% DAILY VALUE:** Vitamin A 2%; Vitamin C 0%; Calcium 0%; Iron 0%; **EXCHANGES:** 1/2 Other Carbohydrate, 1 Fat; **CARBOHYDRATE CHOICES:** 1/2

LEMON TEA CAKES Substitute lemon extract for the vanilla and add 1 teaspoon grated lemon peel with the flour. Crush 1/2 cup lemon drops in food processor or blender. Stir in 1/4 cup of the crushed lemon drops with the flour; reserve remaining candy. Bake as directed. Immediately roll baked cookies in powdered sugar; wait 10 minutes, then roll in reserved crushed lemon drops. Reroll, if desired.

PEPPERMINT TEA CAKES Crush 3/4 cup hard peppermint candies in food processor or blender. Stir in 1/4 cup of the crushed candies with the flour; reserve remaining candy. Bake as directed. Immediately roll baked cookies in powdered sugar; wait 10 minutes, then roll in reserved crushed candy. Reroll, if desired.

Top to bottom: Peppermint Tea Cakes, Russian Tea Cakes and Lemon Tea Cakes

holiday inspiration

This is the cookie of many names! Whether you call them Russian Tea Cakes, Swedish Tea Cakes, Snowballs, Mexican Wedding Cakes or Butterballs, these rich and buttery cookies have become a holiday favorite. Try one of the flavor options, too—they're scrumptious!

SNICKERDOODLES

prep 50 min *total time* 50 min

makes about 4 dozen cookies

see photo on page 121

1 1/2 cups sugar

1/2 cup butter or margarine, softened

1/2 cup shortening

2 eggs

2 3/4 cups all-purpose flour

2 teaspoons cream of tartar

1 teaspoon baking soda

1/4 teaspoon salt

1/4 cup sugar

1 tablespoon ground cinnamon

1. Heat oven to 400°F. In large bowl, beat 1 1/2 cups sugar, the butter, shortening and eggs with electric mixer on medium speed, or mix with spoon. Stir in flour, cream of tartar, baking soda and salt.

2. Shape dough into 1 1/4-inch balls. In small bowl, mix 1/4 cup sugar and the cinnamon. Roll balls in cinnamon-sugar mixture. On ungreased cookie sheet, place balls 2 inches apart.

3. Bake 8 to 10 minutes or until set. Immediately remove from cookie sheet to wire rack.

1 COOKIE: Calories 100 (Calories from Fat 40); Total Fat 4.5g (Saturated Fat 1.5g; Trans Fat 0g); Cholesterol 15mg; Sodium 55mg; Total Carbohydrate 13g (Dietary Fiber 0g; Sugars 7g); Protein 1g; **% DAILY VALUE:** Vitamin A 0%; Vitamin C 0%; Calcium 0%; Iron 2%; **EXCHANGES:** 1 Other Carbohydrate, 1 Fat; **CARBOHYDRATE CHOICES:** 1

holiday inspiration

Look in the spice section of your store for jars or plastic bottles of sugar-cinnamon mixture—it's ready to go!

PEANUT BUTTER-CHOCOLATE COOKIES

prep 50 min *total time* 50 min

makes about 3 dozen cookies

see photo on page 121

1/2 cup granulated sugar

1/2 cup packed brown sugar

1/2 cup creamy peanut butter

1/2 cup butter or margarine, softened

1 egg

1 1/2 cups all-purpose flour

3/4 teaspoon baking soda

1/2 teaspoon baking powder

Additional granulated sugar

About 3 dozen milk chocolate candy drops or pieces

1. Heat oven to 375°F. In large bowl, beat 1/2 cup granulated sugar, the brown sugar, peanut butter, butter and egg with electric mixer on medium speed, or mix with spoon. Stir in flour, baking soda and baking powder.

2. Shape dough into 1-inch balls. In small bowl, place additional granulated sugar. Roll balls in granulated sugar. Place about 2 inches apart on ungreased cookie sheet.

3. Bake 8 to 10 minutes or until edges are light brown. Immediately press 1 chocolate candy in center of each cookie. Remove from cookie sheet to wire rack.

1 COOKIE: Calories 120 (Calories from Fat 50); Total Fat 6g (Saturated Fat 2.5g; Trans Fat 0g); Cholesterol 15mg; Sodium 75mg; Total Carbohydrate 14g (Dietary Fiber 0g; Sugars 10g); Protein 2g; **% DAILY VALUE:** Vitamin A 2%; Vitamin C 0%; Calcium 0%; Iron 2%; **EXCHANGES:** 1 Other Carbohydrate, 1 Fat; **CARBOHYDRATE CHOICES:** 1

new twist

Add razzle-dazzle by rolling the balls of dough in colored sugar instead of regular granulated sugar.

GINGERSNAPS

prep 1 hr 15 min *total time* 2 hrs 45 min
makes about 4 dozen cookies

1 cup packed brown sugar
3/4 cup shortening
1/4 cup molasses
1 egg
2 1/4 cups all-purpose flour
2 teaspoons baking soda
1 teaspoon ground cinnamon
1 teaspoon ground ginger
1/2 teaspoon ground cloves
1/4 teaspoon salt
Granulated sugar

1. In large bowl, beat brown sugar, shortening, molasses and egg with electric mixer on medium speed, or mix with spoon. Stir in remaining ingredients except granulated sugar. Cover; refrigerate at least 1 hour.

2. Heat oven to 375°F. Lightly grease cookie sheet with shortening or cooking spray.

3. In small bowl, place granulated sugar. Shape dough by rounded teaspoonfuls into balls; dip tops into granulated sugar. Place balls, sugared sides up, about 3 inches apart on cookie sheet.

4. Bake 9 to 12 minutes or just until set. Remove from cookie sheet to wire rack. Cool completely, about 30 minutes.

1 COOKIE: Calories 80 (Calories from Fat 30); Total Fat 3.5g (Saturated Fat 1g; Trans Fat 0.5g); Cholesterol 0mg; Sodium 70mg; Total Carbohydrate 11g (Dietary Fiber 0g; Sugars 6g); Protein 0g; % DAILY VALUE: Vitamin A 0%; Vitamin C 0%; Calcium 0%; Iron 2%; EXCHANGES: 1 Other Carbohydrate, 1/2 Fat; CARBOHYDRATE CHOICES: 1

BLACK-AND-WHITE GINGERSNAPS Make Snowcapped Gingersnaps (at right) as directed—but don't sprinkle with crystallized ginger. After white coating is set, dip half of each cookie into melted chocolate-flavored candy coating (almond bark) so that chocolate covers half of white coating. Place on waxed paper; let stand until chocolate is set.

GINGER COOKIE CUTOUTS Roll the chilled dough for Gingersnaps, one-fourth at a time, on lightly floured cloth-covered surface. Cut into desired shapes with floured cookie cutters. Bake as directed. Frost and decorate cooled cookies if desired.

LACED GINGERSNAPS Cover cookie sheet with waxed paper. Heat 1/2 cup semisweet chocolate chips or white vanilla baking chips and 1 teaspoon shortening until melted. Drizzle over cookies.

SNOWCAPPED GINGERSNAPS Cover cookie sheet with waxed paper. Place 3 packages (6 oz each) white chocolate baking bars, broken up, and 1 tablespoon shortening in microwavable bowl. Microwave uncovered on Medium-High (70%) for 1 minute 30 seconds to 2 minutes, stirring every 15 seconds, until smooth. Dip half of each cooled cookie into melted mixture; sprinkle with chopped crystallized ginger if desired. Place on waxed paper; let stand until coating is firm.

TRIPLE-GINGER GINGERSNAPS Add 1/4 cup finely chopped crystallized ginger and 1 tablespoon grated gingerroot to the dough before shaping into balls.

new twist

If you don't have time to shape the dough into balls, divide dough into 4 equal parts. Shape each part into a roll, 1 inch in diameter and about 12 inches long. Place rolls on greased cookie sheet; flatten slightly to about 5/8-inch thickness. Sprinkle with sugar. Bake 10 to 12 minutes or just until set. While warm, slice diagonally into about 1-inch strips. Drizzle with melted white vanilla baking chips if desired.

SLICE-IT-EASY COOKIES

prep 1 hr 35 min *total time* 6 hrs 5 min
makes about 7 dozen cookies

1 cup butter or margarine, softened
1 cup sugar
1 1/2 teaspoons vanilla
2 eggs
3 cups all-purpose flour
1 teaspoon salt
1/2 teaspoon baking soda

1. In large bowl, beat butter, sugar, vanilla and eggs with electric mixer on medium speed, or mix with spoon. Stir in remaining ingredients. Divide into 3 equal parts. Shape each part into roll, about 1 1/2 inches in diameter. Wrap and refrigerate at least 4 hours.

2. Heat oven to 400°F. Cut rolls into 1/8-inch slices. On ungreased cookie sheet, place slices about 1 inch apart.

3. Bake 8 to 10 minutes or just until golden brown around edges. Immediately remove from cookie sheet to wire rack. Cool completely, about 30 minutes.

1 COOKIE: Calories 45 (Calories from Fat 20); Total Fat 2.5g (Saturated Fat 1g; Trans Fat 0g); Cholesterol 10mg; Sodium 50mg; Total Carbohydrate 6g (Dietary Fiber 0g; Sugars 2g); Protein 0g; % DAILY VALUE: Vitamin A 0%; Vitamin C 0%; Calcium 0%; Iron 0%; EXCHANGES: 1/2 Other Carbohydrate. 1/2 Fat; CARBOHYDRATE CHOICES: 1/2

CHRISTMAS TREES Shape each roll into a triangle; coat sides with green sugar. Refrigerate and cut into slices as directed. Cut tree trunks from several slices; attach trunks to unbaked trees on cookie sheet, overlapping slightly. Sprinkle with candy decorations. Bake as directed. About 6 dozen cookies.

HOLIDAY COOKIE TARTS Cut out centers of half of the unbaked cookie slices with 3/4-inch holiday cutters, or design your own patterns. Place slice with cutout on top of slice without cutout; press edges to seal. Spoon 1/2 teaspoon red jelly or jam into cutout. Bake as directed. Lightly sprinkle powdered sugar over cookies. About 3 1/2 dozen sandwich cookies.

PEPPERMINT PINWHEELS Using half of Slice-It-Easy Cookie dough, divide dough in half again. Into 1 half, stir 1/2 teaspoon peppermint extract and 1/4 teaspoon red or green food color. Cover both halves and refrigerate 1 hour. Roll plain dough into 9 × 8–inch rectangle on lightly floured surface. Repeat with colored dough; place on plain dough. Roll doughs together until about 1/4 inch thick. Roll up tightly, beginning at 9-inch side. Refrigerate at least 4 hours; cut into slices and bake as directed. About 3 dozen cookies.

RIBBON BAR COOKIES Decrease vanilla to 1 teaspoon; add 1 teaspoon peppermint extract. Divide dough in half. Stir 1/2 teaspoon red or green food color into 1 half. Cover both halves and refrigerate 1 hour. Shape each half into 2 strips, each about 9 × 2 1/2 inches, on very lightly floured surface. Layer strips, alternating colors; press together. Refrigerate, cut into slices and bake as directed. About 5 1/2 dozen cookies.

new twist

For a kaleidoscope of color, coat rolls with Rainbow Dust (page 292) or any type of colored sugar or multicolored shot. Refrigerate, cut into slices and bake as directed.

RUM-CASHEW BISCOTTI

prep 25 min *total time* 2 hrs
makes about 3 dozen biscotti

Biscotti

2/3 cup granulated sugar
1/2 cup vegetable oil
2 teaspoons rum extract
2 eggs
2 1/2 cups all-purpose flour
1 cup unsalted cashew pieces
1 teaspoon baking powder
1/4 teaspoon baking soda
1/4 teaspoon salt

Rum Glaze

1/2 cup powdered sugar
2 teaspoons eggnog or half-and-half
1 teaspoon rum or 1/2 teaspoon rum extract

1. Heat oven to 350°F. In large bowl, beat granulated sugar, oil, 2 teaspoons rum extract and the eggs with spoon. Stir in remaining biscotti ingredients.

2. Turn dough onto lightly floured surface. Knead until smooth. On ungreased cookie sheet, shape half of dough at a time into 10 × 3–inch rectangle.

3. Bake 25 to 30 minutes or until toothpick inserted in center comes out clean. Cool on cookie sheet 15 minutes. Cut crosswise into 1/2-inch slices. Place slices, cut sides down, on cookie sheet.

4. Bake about 15 minutes, turning once, until crisp and light brown. Immediately remove from cookie sheet to wire rack. Cool completely, about 45 minutes. In small bowl, mix all glaze ingredients with spoon until smooth and thin enough to drizzle. Drizzle glaze over biscotti.

1 BISCOTTI: Calories 110 (Calories from Fat 45); Total Fat 5g (Saturated Fat 1g; Trans Fat 0g); Cholesterol 10mg; Sodium 45mg; Total Carbohydrate 13g (Dietary Fiber 0g; Sugars 6g); Protein 2g; **% DAILY VALUE:** Vitamin A 0%; Vitamin C 0%; Calcium 0%; Iron 4%; **EXCHANGES:** 1 Other Carbohydrate, 1 Fat; **CARBOHYDRATE CHOICES:** 1

CHOCOLATE-DIPPED BISCOTTI Heat 3 oz semi-sweet baking chocolate or white chocolate baking bar and 1/2 teaspoon shortening until melted and smooth. Drizzle chocolate over biscotti, or dip half of each biscotti into melted chocolate. Immediately sprinkle with your choice of crushed hard peppermint candy, chopped pistachio or other nuts, decorator sugar crystals, chopped candied ginger or holiday candy decorations. Place on waxed paper until chocolate is set.

MERRY CHERRY BISCOTTI Substitute vanilla for the rum extract in dough and glaze. Omit cashews. Add 3/4 cup dried cherry-flavored dried cranberries or 3/4 cup chopped candied cherries and 1/2 cup chopped slivered almonds.

PISTACHIO BISCOTTI Substitute vanilla for the rum extract in dough and glaze. Omit cashews. Add 1/2 cup coarsely chopped pistachio nuts.

from the heart

BISCOTTI ARE THE TRENDY ITALIAN COOKIES that are baked twice—first as a loaf, then a second time sliced—until they are dry and crisp. Great served with tea or coffee, and just right for munching, they make great gifts wrapped in cellophane and tied with festive ribbon. Pretty glass containers are ideal for giving biscotti. Tie curly ribbons on the containers, and add a handmade gift tag. Or package biscotti in cellophane, and tuck in a glass coffee mug. Because this is a hardy cookie, it's also a great one for mailing.

SPRITZ

prep 1 hr 50 min *total time* 2 hrs 20 min
makes about 5 dozen cookies

1 cup butter or margarine, softened
1/2 cup sugar
1 egg
2 1/2 cups all-purpose flour
1/4 teaspoon salt
1/4 teaspoon almond extract or vanilla
Few drops of food color, if desired

1. Heat oven to 400°F. In large bowl, beat butter, sugar and egg with electric mixer on medium speed, or mix with spoon. Stir in remaining ingredients.

2. Place dough in cookie press. On ungreased cookie sheet, form desired shapes.

3. Bake 5 to 8 minutes or until set but not brown. Immediately remove from cookie sheet to wire rack. Cool completely, about 30 minutes.

1 COOKIE: Calories 50 (Calories from Fat 30); Total Fat 3g (Saturated Fat 1.5g; Trans Fat 0g); Cholesterol 10mg; Sodium 30mg; Total Carbohydrate 6g (Dietary Fiber 0g; Sugars 2g); Protein 0g; % DAILY VALUE: Vitamin A 2%; Vitamin C 0%; Calcium 0%; Iron 0%; EXCHANGES: 1/2 Other Carbohydrate, 1/2 Fat; CARBOHYDRATE CHOICES: 1/2

CHOCOLATE SPRITZ Stir 2 oz unsweetened baking chocolate, melted and cooled, into butter-sugar mixture. Omit food color.

RUM BUTTER SPRITZ Substitute rum extract for the almond extract. Tint dough with food colors. After baking, spread cooled cookies with Rum Butter Glaze: Melt 1/4 cup butter or margarine in 1-quart saucepan; remove from heat. Stir in 1 cup powdered sugar and 1 teaspoon rum extract. Stir in 1 to 2 tablespoons hot water until glaze is spreadable. Tint glaze with food color to match cookies.

SPICY SPRITZ Stir in 1 teaspoon ground cinnamon, 1/2 teaspoon ground nutmeg and 1/4 teaspoon ground allspice with the flour.

new twist

After baking, decorate cookies with edible glitter, colored sugar, nonpareils, red cinnamon candies or finely chopped nuts. A drop of corn syrup will hold the decorations in place nicely.

BettyCrocker.com

ALMOND BONBONS

prep 1 hr 5 min   *total time* 1 hr 35 min
makes about 3 dozen cookies

Cookies
1 1/2 cups all-purpose flour
1/2 cup butter or margarine, softened
1/3 cup powdered sugar
2 tablespoons milk
1/2 teaspoon vanilla
1/2 package (7- or 8-oz size) almond paste

Almond Glaze
1 cup powdered sugar
1/2 teaspoon almond extract
4 to 5 teaspoons milk
Decorator sugar crystals, if desired

1. Heat oven to 375°F. In large bowl, beat flour, butter, 1/3 cup powdered sugar, 2 tablespoons milk and the vanilla with electric mixer on medium speed, or mix with spoon. Cut almond paste into 1/2-inch slices; cut each slice into fourths.

2. Shape 1-inch ball of dough around each piece of almond paste. Gently roll to form ball. On ungreased cookie sheet, place balls about 1 inch apart.

3. Bake 10 to 12 minutes or until set and bottom is golden brown. Remove from cookie sheet to wire rack. Cool completely, about 30 minutes.

4. In small bowl, mix all glaze ingredients with spoon until smooth. Dip tops of cookies into glaze; sprinkle with sugar crystals.

1 COOKIE: Calories 70 (Calories from Fat 30); Total Fat 3.5g (Saturated Fat 1.5g; Trans Fat 0g); Cholesterol 5mg; Sodium 20mg; Total Carbohydrate 10g (Dietary Fiber 0g; Sugars 6g); Protein 0g; % DAILY VALUE: Vitamin A 0%; Vitamin C 0%; Calcium 0%; Iron 0%; EXCHANGES: 1/2 Other Carbohydrate, 1 Fat; CARBOHYDRATE CHOICES: 1/2

new twist

For a flavorful twist, instead of almond paste, wrap the dough around:

- Candied cherries for Cherry Bonbons.
- Dried apricots for Apricot Bonbons.
- Dates for Date Bonbons.
- Malted milk balls for Malted Bonbons.
- Hazelnuts or macadamia nuts for Hazelnut Bonbons.

holiday inspiration

Add a winter wonderland touch by tinting the glaze with a few drops of food colors in pastel shades. When set, drizzle with additional white glaze. For gifts, pack small cookies in mini paper baking cups or fluted bonbon cups.

MINTY MIDDLE TREASURES

prep 45 min   *total time* 1 hr 15 min
makes about 2 dozen cookies
see photo on page 112, top

Cookies

1/2 cup granulated sugar

1/4 cup packed brown sugar

1/4 cup shortening

1/4 cup butter or margarine, softened

1/2 teaspoon vanilla

1 egg

1 2/3 cups all-purpose flour

1/2 teaspoon baking soda

1/4 teaspoon salt

About 2 dozen foil-wrapped thin rectangular
   chocolate mints, unwrapped

Almond Frosting

1 cup powdered sugar

1 tablespoon plus 1 to 2 teaspoons milk

1/4 teaspoon almond extract or vanilla

Food color, if desired

Candy sprinkles

1. Heat oven to 400°F. In large bowl, beat granulated sugar, brown sugar, shortening, butter, vanilla and egg with electric mixer on medium speed, or mix with spoon. Stir in flour, baking soda, salt.

2. Shape about 1 tablespoon dough around each mint. On ungreased cookie sheet, place cookies about 2 inches apart.

3. Bake 9 to 10 minutes or until light brown. Remove from cookie sheet to wire rack. Cool completely, about 30 minutes.

4. In small bowl, mix 1 cup powdered sugar, the milk, almond extract and a few drops of food color with spoon until thick enough to coat. Dip tops of cookies into frosting; sprinkle with candy sprinkles.

1 COOKIE: Calories 140 (Calories from Fat 50); Total Fat 6g (Saturated Fat 2.5g; Trans Fat 0g); Cholesterol 15mg; Sodium 70mg; Total Carbohydrate 21g (Dietary Fiber 0g; Sugars 14g); Protein 2g; % DAILY VALUE: Vitamin A 0%; Vitamin C 0%; Calcium 0%; Iron 4%; EXCHANGES: 1 1/2 Other Carbohydrate, 1 Fat; CARBOHYDRATE CHOICES: 1 1/2

holiday inspiration

Call it a Sweets Swap or a Cookie Exchange; you'll get to go home with the same great results—and lighten your baking load, too. Why not start this tradition of sharing with your friends this year? Here's how:

- Send out invitations a month in advance. Think about limiting your group to fewer than twelve people to make managing the event easier. You may want to mail labels for the sweets along with the invitations.

- Ask guests to bring their sweets on paper or plastic plates or in nonreturnable containers and covered with clear plastic wrap so the goodies are easily seen. Each person needs to bring enough treats to share and sample.

- Everyone will want the recipes, so have guests bring a copy; e-mail the recipes or print them out.

- As host, you will need to provide the space for guests and their treats. Be sure you have lots of piping-hot coffee and tea to go with the cookie samples.

ESPRESSO THUMBPRINT COOKIES

prep 1 hr 30 min   *total time* 1 hr 45 min
makes about 3 1/2 dozen cookies
see photo on page 116

Cookies

3/4 cup sugar

3/4 cup butter or margarine, softened

1/2 teaspoon vanilla

1 egg

1 3/4 cups all-purpose flour

3 tablespoons unsweetened baking cocoa

1/4 teaspoon salt

Espresso Filling

1/4 cup whipping (heavy) cream

2 teaspoons instant espresso coffee (dry)

1 cup (half 11.5-oz bag) milk chocolate chips

1 tablespoon coffee-flavored liqueur, if desired

Candy sprinkles or crushed hard peppermint candies,
   if desired

1. Heat oven to 350°F. In large bowl, beat sugar, butter, vanilla and egg with electric mixer on medium speed, or mix with spoon. Stir in flour, cocoa and salt.

2. Shape dough by rounded teaspoonfuls into 1-inch balls. On ungreased cookie sheet, place balls about 2 inches apart. Press thumb or end of wooden spoon into center of each cookie to make indentation, but do not press all the way to the cookie sheet.

3. Bake 7 to 11 minutes or until edges are firm. Quickly remake indentations with end of wooden spoon if necessary. Immediately remove from cookie sheet to wire rack. Cool completely, about 30 minutes.

4. Meanwhile, in 1-quart saucepan, heat whipping cream and coffee (dry) over medium heat, stirring occasionally, until steaming and coffee is dissolved. Remove from heat; stir in chocolate chips until melted. Stir in liqueur. Cool about 10 minutes or until thickened. Spoon rounded 1/2 teaspoon filling into indentation in each cookie. Top with candy sprinkles.

1 COOKIE: Calories 90 (Calories from Fat 45); Total Fat 5g (Saturated Fat 2.5g; Trans Fat 0g); Cholesterol 15mg; Sodium 40mg; Total Carbohydrate 10g (Dietary Fiber 0g; Sugars 6g); Protein 1g; **% DAILY VALUE:** Vitamin A 4%; Vitamin C 0%; Calcium 0%; Iron 2%; **EXCHANGES:** 1/2 Other Carbohydrate, 1 Fat; **CARBOHYDRATE CHOICES:** 1/2

from the heart

CREATE A GREAT GIFT BASKET for your favorite coffee lover. Combine these cookies with a coffee mug, favorite fresh coffee beans or ground coffee and Chocolate Spoons (page 284).

HOLIDAY MELTING MOMENTS

prep 1 hr 15 min *total time* 2 hrs 45 min
makes about 3 1/2 dozen cookies

Cookies

1 cup butter, softened (do not use margarine)
1 egg yolk
1 cup plus 2 tablespoons all-purpose flour
1/2 cup cornstarch
1/2 cup powdered sugar
2 tablespoons unsweetened baking cocoa
1/8 teaspoon salt

Vanilla Frosting

1 cup powdered sugar
2 tablespoons butter or margarine, softened
1 teaspoon vanilla
2 to 3 teaspoons milk
2 candy canes, about 6 inches long, finely crushed

1. In large bowl, beat 1 cup butter and egg yolk with electric mixer on medium speed, or mix with spoon. Stir in flour, cornstarch, 1/2 cup powdered sugar, the cocoa and salt. Cover; refrigerate about 1 hour or until firm.

2. Heat oven to 375°F. Shape dough into 1-inch balls. On ungreased cookie sheet, place balls about 2 inches apart.

3. Bake 10 to 12 minutes or until set but not brown. Remove from cookie sheet to wire rack. Cool completely, about 30 minutes.

4. In small bowl, mix all frosting ingredients except candy canes with spoon until smooth and spreadable. Frost cookies; sprinkle with crushed candy canes.

1 COOKIE: Calories 80 (Calories from Fat 45); Total Fat 5g (Saturated Fat 2.5g; Trans Fat 0g); Cholesterol 20mg; Sodium 40mg; Total Carbohydrate 9g (Dietary Fiber 0g; Sugars 5g); Protein 0g; % DAILY VALUE: Vitamin A 4%; Vitamin C 0%; Calcium 0%; Iron 0%; EXCHANGES: 1/2 Other Carbohydrate, 1 Fat; CARBOHYDRATE CHOICES: 1/2

holiday inspiration

Pssst . . . looking for a few cookie baking secrets?

- Have at least three or four cookie sheets on hand, so as you bake one sheet you can get another one ready to go. Use cookie sheets that are at least 2 inches narrower and shorter than the inside dimensions of your oven, so heat circulates around them.

- We recommend baking only one cookie sheet at a time, using the middle oven rack. If you want to bake two sheets at the same time, put one on the oven rack in the upper third of the oven and one on the oven rack in the lower third. Remember to switch their positions halfway through baking time.

- Check cookies at the minimum bake time. Even 1 minute can make a difference with cookies, especially those high in sugar and fat. The longer cookies bake, the more brown, crisp or hard they become.

- Always put cookie dough on completely cooled cookie sheets. Cookies spread too much if put on a hot, or even a warm, cookie sheet. You can cool cookie sheets quickly by popping them in the refrigerator or freezer or by running cold water over them (dry completely and grease again if needed).

HOLIDAY STARS

prep 1 hr 15 min *total time* 2 hrs 45 min
makes about 4 dozen cookies

1 cup granulated sugar
1/2 cup butter or margarine, softened
1/4 cup shortening
1 teaspoon vanilla
2 eggs
2 1/2 cups all-purpose flour
1 teaspoon baking powder
1/4 teaspoon salt
3/4 cup colored sugar

1. In large bowl, beat granulated sugar, butter, shortening, vanilla and eggs with electric mixer on medium speed, or mix with spoon. Stir in flour, baking powder and salt. Cover; refrigerate at least 1 hour.

2. Heat oven to 400°F. Roll dough 1/8 inch thick on well-floured surface. Cut with 2 1/2-inch star-shaped cookie cutter. On each cookie, cut slit between 2 points to just past the center (see illustration **a** below); spread to make 1/4-inch opening. Place on ungreased cookie sheet. Sprinkle with colored sugar.

3. Bake 6 to 8 minutes or until very light brown. Cool 1 minute; remove from cookie sheet to wire rack. Cool completely, about 30 minutes. Fit cookies together in pairs (see illustration **b** below).

1 COOKIE: Calories 80 (Calories from Fat 30); Total Fat 3.5g (Saturated Fat 1.5g; Trans Fat 0g); Cholesterol 15mg; Sodium 40mg; Total Carbohydrate 12g (Dietary Fiber 0g; Sugars 7g); Protein 0g; % DAILY VALUE: Vitamin A 0%; Vitamin C 0%; Calcium 0%; Iron 0%; EXCHANGES: 1 Other Carbohydrate, 1/2 Fat; CARBOHYDRATE CHOICES: 1

Top to bottom: Magic Window Cookies (page 139) and Holiday Stars

holiday inspiration

These 3-D cookies will be the talk of the town and the "star" of your cookie tray! For a "starry night" look, sprinkle clear, white or silver-colored edible glitter or colored decorator sugar crystals on a flat midnight blue or black serving platter; arrange cookies on platter. Place lighted votives around the platter to add to the illusion of a night sky filled with bright stars.

a. Cut a slit to just past the center.

b. Fit baked cookies together in pairs.

MAGIC WINDOW COOKIES

prep 1 hr 55 min *total time* 3 hrs 25 min

makes about 6 dozen 3-inch cookies

with Holiday Stars opposite

1 cup sugar

3/4 cup butter or margarine, softened

1 teaspoon vanilla

2 eggs

2 1/2 cups all-purpose flour

1 teaspoon baking powder

1/4 teaspoon salt

4 rolls (about 1 oz each) ring-shaped hard candies or other fruit-flavored hard candies

1. In large bowl, beat sugar, butter, vanilla and eggs with electric mixer on medium speed, or mix with spoon. Stir in flour, baking powder and salt. Cover; refrigerate about 1 hour or until firm.

2. Heat oven to 375°F. Cover cookie sheet with cooking parchment paper or foil. Roll one-third of dough at a time 1/8 inch thick on lightly floured cloth-covered surface. Cut into desired shapes. Place on parchment paper. Cut out designs from cookies using smaller cutters or your own patterns. Place whole or partially crushed pieces of candy in cutouts, depending on size and shape of design, mixing colors as desired. Be sure that you use candy pieces that are the same size in the cutouts so it melts evenly. (To crush candy, place in heavy food-storage plastic bag and tap lightly with rolling pin. Because candy melts easily, leave pieces as large as possible.)

3. Bake 7 to 9 minutes or until cookies are very light brown and candy is melted. If candy has not completely spread within cutout design, immediately spread with toothpick or knife. Cool completely on foil, about 30 minutes. Remove cookies gently to wire rack.

1 COOKIE: Calories 50 (Calories from Fat 20); Total Fat 2g (Saturated Fat 1g; Trans Fat 0g); Cholesterol 10mg; Sodium 30mg; Total Carbohydrate 8g (Dietary Fiber 0g; Sugars 4g); Protein 0g; **% DAILY VALUE:** Vitamin A 0%; Vitamin C 0%; Calcium 0%; Iron 0%; **EXCHANGES:** 1/2 Other Carbohydrate, 1/2 Fat; **CARBOHYDRATE CHOICES:** 1/2

holiday inspiration

These cookies take a little time to make but are truly works of art! Candies that are clear or almost clear and not opaque will give you the finished look of stained glass windows.

PEPPERMINT SWIRLS

prep 1 hr 5 min *total time* 1 hr 5 min
makes about 4 dozen cookies
see photo on page 120

1 cup butter or margarine, softened
1/3 cup powdered sugar
1 teaspoon vanilla
2 cups all-purpose flour
1/4 teaspoon peppermint extract
1/4 teaspoon red food color
2 tablespoons granulated sugar

1. Heat oven to 350°F. In large bowl, beat butter, powdered sugar and vanilla with electric mixer on medium speed, or mix with spoon. Stir in flour. Divide dough in half. Stir peppermint extract and food color into 1 half. Divide each color of dough in half.

2. Shape each piece of dough on generously floured surface into rope, 12 inches long. Place 2 ropes, 1 red and 1 white, side by side. Twist ropes. Repeat with remaining 2 pieces of dough.

3. Cut twisted ropes into 1/2-inch pieces; shape each into ball. On ungreased cookie sheet, place balls about 1 inch apart. Flatten to about 1/4-inch thickness with greased bottom of glass dipped in granulated sugar.

4. Bake 7 to 9 minutes or until set. Remove from cookie sheet to wire rack.

1 COOKIE: Calories 60 (Calories from Fat 35); Total Fat 4g (Saturated Fat 2g; Trans Fat 0g); Cholesterol 10mg; Sodium 25mg; Total Carbohydrate 5g (Dietary Fiber 0g; Sugars 1g); Protein 0g; % DAILY VALUE: Vitamin A 2%; Vitamin C 0%; Calcium 0%; Iron 0%; EXCHANGES: 1/2 Other Carbohydrate, 1 Fat; CARBOHYDRATE CHOICES: 1/2

holiday inspiration

Color your Christmas goodies with the colors of the rainbow! Paste food colors give the brightest colors. As a general rule, you need to use only half the amount of paste food color as liquid food color. So for this recipe, you would use only 1/8 teaspoon paste food color. Remove paste color with a toothpick and scrape it onto the dough. You may need to knead the dough with your hands in order to blend the color evenly throughout.

MERRY CHERRY FUDGIES

prep 1 hr 20 min *total time* 2 hrs 20 min
makes 2 dozen cookies

Cookies
1/4 cup butter or margarine, softened
1 package (3 oz) cream cheese, softened
3/4 cup all-purpose flour
1/4 cup powdered sugar
2 tablespoons unsweeted baking cocoa
1/2 teaspoon vanilla

Cherry Fudge Filling
2/3 cup granulated sugar
1/3 cup unsweetened baking cocoa
1/4 cup finely chopped red or green maraschino cherries, well drained
2 tablespoons butter or margarine, softened
1 egg

Cherry Glaze
1/2 cup powdered sugar
1 to 2 teaspoons red or green maraschino cherry juice
Additional red or green maraschino cherries, well drained and finely chopped, if desired

1. Heat oven to 350°F. In large bowl, beat 1/4 cup butter and the cream cheese with electric mixer on medium speed, or mix with spoon. Stir in flour, 1/4 cup powdered sugar, 2 tablespoons cocoa and the vanilla.

2. Place mini foil or paper baking cup, if desired, in each of 24 mini muffin cups, 1 3/4 × 1 inch. Divide dough into 24 equal pieces. Press each piece in bottom and up side of muffin cup. In small bowl, mix all filling ingredients. Spoon about 2 teaspoons filling into each cup.

3. Bake 18 to 20 minutes or until almost no indentation remains when filling is touched lightly. Cool 1 hour; loosen from cups with tip of knife. Remove from pan to wire rack. In small bowl, mix 1/2 cup powdered sugar and the cherry juice until smooth and spreadable. Drizzle glaze over cookies; sprinkle with additional chopped cherries.

1 COOKIE: Calories 100 (Calories from Fat 40); Total Fat 4.5g (Saturated Fat 2.5g; Trans Fat 0g); Cholesterol 20mg; Sodium 35mg; Total Carbohydrate 14g (Dietary Fiber 0g; Sugars 10g); Protein 1g; % DAILY VALUE: Vitamin A 4%; Vitamin C 0%; Calcium 0%; Iron 2%; EXCHANGES: 1 Other Carbohydrate, 1 Fat; CARBOHYDRATE CHOICES: 1

holiday inspiration

Instant flavor, instant color! Maraschino cherries are soaked in a sugar syrup and dyed red or green. Red cherries are flavored with almond; green cherries are flavored with mint.

Merry Cherry Fudgies

CANDY CANE COOKIES

prep 1 hr 30 min *total time* 6 hrs
makes about 4 1/2 dozen cookies
see photo on page 121

1 cup sugar
1 cup butter or margarine, softened
1/2 cup milk
1 teaspoon vanilla
1 teaspoon peppermint extract
1 egg
3 1/2 cups all-purpose flour
1 teaspoon baking powder
1/4 teaspoon salt
1/2 teaspoon red food color
2 tablespoons finely crushed hard peppermint candies
2 tablespoons sugar

1. In large bowl, beat 1 cup sugar, the butter, milk, vanilla, peppermint extract and egg with electric mixer on medium speed, or stir with spoon. Stir in flour, baking powder and salt. Divide dough in half. Stir food color into 1 half. Cover; refrigerate at least 4 hours.

2. Heat oven to 375°F. For each candy cane, shape 1 rounded teaspoon dough from each half into 4-inch rope by rolling back and forth on floured surface. Place 1 red and 1 white rope side by side; press together lightly and twist. Place on ungreased cookie sheet; curve top of cookie down to form handle of cane.

3. Bake 9 to 12 minutes or until set and very light brown. In small bowl, mix crushed candies and 2 tablespoons sugar; immediately sprinkle over baked cookies. Immediately remove from cookie sheet to wire rack. Cool completely, about 30 minutes.

1 COOKIE: Calories 80 (Calories from Fat 35); Total Fat 3.5g (Saturated Fat 2g; Trans Fat 0g); Cholesterol 15mg; Sodium 45mg; Total Carbohydrate 11g (Dietary Fiber 0g; Sugars 5g); Protein 1g; **% DAILY VALUE:** Vitamin A 2%; Vitamin C 0%; Calcium 0%; Iron 2%; **EXCHANGES:** 1 Other Carbohydrate, 1/2 Fat; **CARBOHYDRATE CHOICES:** 1

holiday inspiration

Easily chop hard candies by putting them into a resealable food-storage plastic bag and whack them with a meat mallet or rolling pin.

IRISH CREAM BARS

prep 20 min *total time* 2 hrs 50 min *makes* 24 bars
see photo on page 145

3/4 cup all-purpose flour
1/2 cup butter or margarine, softened
1/4 cup powdered sugar
2 tablespoons unsweetened baking cocoa
3/4 cup sour cream
1/2 cup granulated sugar
1/3 cup Irish cream liqueur
1 tablespoon all-purpose flour
1 teaspoon vanilla
1 egg
1/2 cup whipping (heavy) cream
Chocolate sprinkles, if desired

1. Heat oven to 350°F. In small bowl, mix 3/4 cup flour, the butter, powdered sugar and cocoa with spoon until soft dough forms. Press in bottom of ungreased 8- or 9-inch square pan. Bake 10 minutes.

2. In medium bowl, beat remaining ingredients except whipping cream and chocolate sprinkles with wire whisk until blended. Pour over baked layer. Bake 15 to 20 minutes or until filling is set. Cool slightly; refrigerate at least 2 hours before cutting.

3. For bars, cut into 6 rows by 4 rows. In chilled small bowl, beat whipping cream with electric mixer on high speed until stiff peaks form. Spoon whipped cream into decorating bag fitted with medium writing or star tip. Pipe dollop of cream onto each bar. Top with chocolate sprinkles. Store covered in refrigerator up to 48 hours.

1 BAR: Calories 110 (Calories from Fat 70); Total Fat 7g (Saturated Fat 4g; Trans Fat 0g); Cholesterol 35mg; Sodium 35mg; Total Carbohydrate 10g (Dietary Fiber 0g; Sugars 7g); Protein 1g; **% DAILY VALUE:** Vitamin A 6%; Vitamin C 0%; Calcium 0%; Iron 0%; **EXCHANGES:** 1/2 Other Carbohydrate, 1 1/2 Fat; **CARBOHYDRATE CHOICES:** 1/2

new twist

Instead of the Irish cream liqueur, substitute 1/3 cup Irish cream nondairy creamer (or 1/4 cup half-and-half plus 2 tablespoons cold coffee and 1 teaspoon almond extract).

LEMON COOKIE TARTS

prep 4 hrs 50 min *total time* 4 hrs 50 min
makes 4 dozen cookies
see photo on page 121

Cookies

1 cup butter or margarine, softened
1/2 cup granulated sugar
1/2 teaspoon vanilla
1 egg
2 cups all-purpose flour
1/4 teaspoon salt

Lemon Filling

3 eggs
1 1/2 cups granulated sugar
3 tablespoons all-purpose flour
1/2 teaspoon baking powder
2 teaspoons grated lemon peel
2 tablespoons lemon juice
1 tablespoon powdered sugar, if desired

1. In large bowl, beat butter, 1/2 cup granulated sugar, the vanilla and 1 egg with electric mixer on medium speed, or mix with spoon. Stir in 2 cups flour and the salt. Cover; refrigerate about 1 hour or until firm.

2. Meanwhile, in small bowl, beat all filling ingredients except powdered sugar with electric mixer on medium speed, or mix with wire whisk. Cover; refrigerate.

3. Heat oven to 350°F. Spray 48 mini muffin cups, 1 3/4 × 1 inch, with cooking spray. Shape dough into 48 one-inch balls. Place 1 ball in each muffin cup. Press dough into bottom and up side of cups. Spoon slightly less than 1 tablespoon filling into each cup.

4. Bake 18 to 20 minutes or until centers are puffed and edges are light brown. Cool in pan 30 minutes. With tip of knife, lift tarts from muffin cups to wire rack; cool completely. Just before serving, sprinkle tarts with powdered sugar.

1 COOKIE: Calories 90 (Calories from Fat 40); Total Fat 4.5g (Saturated Fat 2g; Trans Fat 0g); Cholesterol 30mg; Sodium 50mg; Total Carbohydrate 13g (Dietary Fiber 0g; Sugars 8g); Protein 1g; % DAILY VALUE: Vitamin A 4%; Vitamin C 0%; Calcium 0%; Iron 0%; EXCHANGES: 1 Other Carbohydrate, 1 Fat; CARBOHYDRATE CHOICES: 1

holiday inspiration

No guesswork here—one medium fresh lemon will give you about 2 to 3 tablespoons of juice and 2 to 3 teaspoons grated lemon peel. To get the most juice out of a lemon or lime, it should be at room temperature, or microwave it on High for about 20 seconds or so to warm it. Rolling a whole lemon back and forth on the counter while pressing gently also will give you more juice.

CONFETTI CARAMEL BARS

prep 15 min *total time* 3 hrs 5 min *makes* 32 bars

1 cup packed brown sugar

1 cup butter or margarine, softened

1 1/2 teaspoons vanilla

1 egg

2 cups all-purpose flour

1/2 cup light corn syrup

2 tablespoons butter or margarine

1 cup butterscotch-flavored chips

1 1/2 to 2 cups assorted candies and nuts (such as candy corn, candy-coated chocolate candies and salted peanuts)

1. Heat oven to 350°F. In large bowl, beat brown sugar, 1 cup butter, the vanilla and egg with electric mixer on medium speed, or mix with spoon. Stir in flour. Press evenly in bottom of ungreased 13 × 9–inch pan. Bake 20 to 22 minutes or until light brown. Cool 20 minutes.

2. In 1-quart saucepan, heat corn syrup, 2 tablespoons butter and the butterscotch chips over medium heat, stirring occasionally, until chips are melted; remove from heat. Cool 10 minutes.

3. Spread butterscotch mixture over crust. Sprinkle with candies and nuts; gently press into butterscotch mixture. Cover; refrigerate at least 2 hours until butterscotch mixture is firm. For bars, cut into 8 rows by 4 rows.

1 BAR: Calories 200 (Calories from Fat 90); Total Fat 10g (Saturated Fat 5g; Trans Fat 0g); Cholesterol 25mg; Sodium 70mg; Total Carbohydrate 26g (Dietary Fiber 0g; Sugars 17g); Protein 2g; **% DAILY VALUE:** Vitamin A 6%; Vitamin C 0%; Calcium 0%; Iron 4%; **EXCHANGES:** 2 Other Carbohydrate, 2 Fat; **CARBOHYDRATE CHOICES:** 2

holiday inspiration

A simple pan of bars can look extraordinary if you cut them into triangles or diamonds, and place the serving plate on confetti.

CHERRY-ALMOND TRIANGLES

prep 25 min *total time* 1 hr 40 min *makes* 24 triangles

Bars

1 jar (10 oz) maraschino cherries

1 cup all-purpose flour

1/2 cup butter or margarine, softened

1/4 cup powdered sugar

2 eggs

1 cup sliced almonds

1/2 cup granulated sugar

1/4 cup all-purpose flour

1/2 teaspoon baking powder

Cherry-Almond Glaze

1/2 cup powdered sugar

1/4 teaspoon almond extract

2 to 3 teaspoons maraschino cherry juice

1. Heat oven to 350°F. Drain cherries, reserving juice for cherry-almond glaze. Chop cherries; set aside.

2. In small bowl, mix 1 cup flour, the butter and 1/4 cup powdered sugar with spoon. Press in bottom of ungreased 9-inch square pan. Bake about 10 minutes or until set.

3. In medium bowl, beat eggs with fork. Stir in cherries and remaining bar ingredients. Spread over baked layer. Bake 20 to 25 minutes or until golden brown. Cool completely, about 45 minutes.

4. In small bowl, mix all glaze ingredients with spoon until smooth and thin enough to drizzle. Drizzle over bars. For bars, cut into 6 rows by 2 rows; cut each bar diagonally in half to form triangles.

1 TRIANGLE: Calories 140 (Calories from Fat 60); Total Fat 7g (Saturated Fat 2.5g; Trans Fat 0g); Cholesterol 30mg; Sodium 40mg; Total Carbohydrate 17g (Dietary Fiber 0g; Sugars 11g); Protein 2g; **% DAILY VALUE:** Vitamin A 4%; Vitamin C 0%; Calcium 2%; Iron 4%; **EXCHANGES:** 1 Other Carbohydrate, 1 1/2 Fat; **CARBOHYDRATE CHOICES:** 1

new twist

Here's another great secret from Betty! To make cutting bars easier, line the baking pan with foil. Turn the pan upside down and cut the foil 4 inches longer than the pan. Form foil over the pan bottom. Turn the pan right side up and position shaped foil inside the pan. When the bars have cooled, lift them from the pan, remove the foil and cut into bars.

Left to right, top to bottom: Cherry-Almond Triangles, Confetti Caramel Bars, Brandy Creme Brûlée Bars (page 147) and Irish Cream Bars (page 142)

PEPPERMINT BONBON BROWNIES

prep 35 min *total time* 3 hrs 25 min *makes* 48 brownies
see photo on page 112, bottom

Brownies

4 oz unsweetened baking chocolate

1 cup butter or margarine

2 cups granulated sugar

2 teaspoons vanilla

4 eggs

1 1/2 cups all-purpose flour

1/2 teaspoon salt

Peppermint Cream Cheese Filling

2 packages (8 oz each) cream cheese, softened

1/2 cup granulated sugar

2 teaspoons peppermint extract

1 egg

8 drops green food color

1/2 cup miniature semisweet chocolate chips

Chocolate Frosting

2 tablespoons butter or margarine

2 tablespoons corn syrup

2 tablespoons water

2 oz unsweetened baking chocolate

3/4 to 1 cup powdered sugar

1. Heat oven to 350°F. Grease bottom only of 13 × 9–inch pan with shortening or cooking spray. In 1-quart saucepan, melt 4 ounces chocolate and 1 cup butter over low heat, stirring frequently, until smooth; remove from heat. Cool 5 minutes.

2. Meanwhile, beat all Peppermint Cream Cheese Filling ingredients except chocolate chips with spoon until smooth. Stir in chocolate chips; set aside.

3. In large bowl, beat chocolate mixture, 2 cups sugar, the vanilla and 4 eggs with electric mixer on medium speed 1 minute, scraping bowl occasionally. Beat in flour and salt on low speed 30 seconds, scraping bowl occasionally. Beat on medium speed 1 minute.

4. Spread half of batter (about 2 1/2 cups) in pan. Spread filling over batter. Carefully spread remaining batter over filling. Gently swirl through batters with knife for marbled design.

5. Bake 45 to 50 minutes or until toothpick inserted in center comes out almost clean. Cool completely, about 2 hours.

6. In 1-quart saucepan, heat 2 tablespoons butter, the corn syrup and water to boiling; remove from heat. Add 2 ounces chocolate, stirring until melted. Stir in enough powdered sugar until spreadable. Spread over brownies. For brownies, cut into 8 rows by 6 rows. Store covered in refrigerator.

1 BROWNIE: Calories 180 (Calories from Fat 100); Total Fat 11g (Saturated Fat 6g; Trans Fat 0g); Cholesterol 45mg; Sodium 90mg; Total Carbohydrate 18g (Dietary Fiber 0g; Sugars 14g); Protein 2g; **% DAILY VALUE:** Vitamin A 6%; Vitamin C 0%; Calcium 0%; Iron 4%; **EXCHANGES:** 1 Other Carbohydrate, 2 1/2 Fat; **CARBOHYDRATE CHOICES:** 1

DOUBLE-PEPPERMINT BONBON BROWNIES Omit green food color and miniature chocolate chips from filling. After frosting brownies, sprinkle with a mixture of crushed red and green hard peppermint candies.

PEPPERMINT–WHITE CHOCOLATE BONBON BROWNIES Substitute 18 drops (about 1/2 teaspoon) red food color for the green food color in the filling. Omit miniature chocolate chips. Sprinkle filling layer with 1 cup white vanilla baking chips. Continue as directed.

BRANDY CREME BRÛLÉE BARS

prep 25 min *total time* 1 hr 45 min *makes* 36 bars
see photo on page 145

1 cup all-purpose flour

1/2 cup sugar

1/2 cup butter or margarine, softened

5 egg yolks

1/4 cup sugar

1 1/4 cups whipping (heavy) cream

1 tablespoon plus 1 teaspoon brandy or 1 1/2
    teaspoons brandy extract

1/3 cup sugar

1. Heat oven to 350°F. In small bowl, mix flour, 1/2 cup sugar and the butter with spoon. Press on bottom and 1/2 inch up sides of ungreased 9-inch square pan. Bake 20 minutes.

2. Reduce oven temperature to 300°F. In small bowl, beat egg yolks and 1/4 cup sugar with spoon until thick. Gradually stir in whipping cream and brandy. Pour over baked layer.

3. Bake 40 to 50 minutes or until custard is set and knife inserted in center comes out clean. Cool completely, about 30 minutes. For bars, cut into 6 rows by 6 rows. Place bars on cookie sheet lined with waxed paper.

4. In heavy 1-quart saucepan, heat 1/3 cup sugar over medium heat until sugar begins to melt. Stir until sugar is completely dissolved and caramel colored. Cool slightly until caramel has thickened slightly. Drizzle hot caramel over bars. (If caramel begins to harden, return to medium heat and stir until thin enough to drizzle.) After caramel on bars has hardened, cover and refrigerate bars up to 48 hours.

1 BAR: Calories 90 (Calories from Fat 50); Total Fat 6g (Saturated Fat 3g; Trans Fat 0g); Cholesterol 45mg; Sodium 20mg; Total Carbohydrate 9g (Dietary Fiber 0g; Sugars 6g); Protein 0g; **% DAILY VALUE:** Vitamin A 4%; Vitamin C 0%; Calcium 0%; Iron 0%; **EXCHANGES:** 1/2 Other Carbohydrate, 1 Fat; **CARBOHYDRATE CHOICES:** 1/2

holiday inspiration

These dazzling bars taste just like the popular restaurant dessert. When making them, use heavy whipping cream for the creamiest filling—it sets up beautifully and stays that way. Not all whipping cream has the word "heavy" on its label. Heavy whipping cream has a milk-fat content between 36 percent and 40 percent, compared to about 30 percent for light whipping cream.

from the heart

PLEASING ANYONE WHO ADORES CHOCOLATE is as easy as packing a dozen of these rich, dense, fudgy Peppermint Bonbon Brownies in a fun container and making the delivery. On second thought, maybe they'd like the whole pan!

171

179

HOLIDAY BREADS

CHAI-SPICED BREAD

prep 15 min   *total time* 3 hrs 55 min
makes 1 loaf (16 slices)

Bread
3/4 cup granulated sugar
1/2 cup butter or margarine, softened
2 eggs
1/2 cup prepared tea or water
1/3 cup milk
2 teaspoons vanilla
2 cups all-purpose flour
2 teaspoons baking powder
3/4 teaspoon ground cardamom
1/2 teaspoon salt
1/4 teaspoon ground cinnamon
1/8 teaspoon ground cloves

Glaze
1 cup powdered sugar
1/4 teaspoon vanilla
3 to 5 teaspoons milk
Additional ground cinnamon

1. Heat oven to 350°F. Grease bottom only of 8 × 4– or 9 × 5–inch loaf pan with shortening or cooking spray.

2. In large bowl, beat granulated sugar and butter with electric mixer on medium speed until fluffy. Beat in eggs, tea, 1/3 cup milk and 2 teaspoons vanilla on low speed until ingredients are well combined (will appear curdled). Stir in remaining bread ingredients just until moistened. Spread in pan.

3. Bake 50 to 60 minutes or until toothpick inserted in center comes out clean (do not underbake). Cool 10 minutes in pan on wire rack. Loosen sides of loaf from pan; remove from pan to wire rack. Cool 30 minutes.

4. In small bowl, stir powdered sugar, 1/4 teaspoon vanilla and 3 teaspoons of the milk, adding more milk by teaspoonfuls, until spreadable. Spread glaze over bread. Sprinkle with additional cinnamon. Cool completely, about 2 hours, before slicing. Wrap tightly and store at room temperature up to 4 days, or refrigerate up to 10 days.

1 SLICE: Calories 190 (Calories from Fat 60); Total Fat 7g (Saturated Fat 3g; Trans Fat 0g); Cholesterol 40mg; Sodium 180mg; Total Carbohydrate 30g (Dietary Fiber 0g; Sugars 17g); Protein 3g; **% DAILY VALUE:** Vitamin A 6%; Vitamin C 0%; Calcium 4%; Iron 6%; **EXCHANGES:** 1 Starch, 1 Other Carbohydrate, 1 Fat; **CARBOHYDRATE CHOICES:** 2

from the heart

CHAI IS THE HINDI WORD for tea made with milk and spices such as cardamom, cinnamon, cloves, ginger, nutmeg and pepper. For gift giving, pair a loaf of this bread with Chai Mix (page 268) and a couple of mugs, and package the items in a pretty brass container or basket.

PUMPKIN BREAD

prep 15 min *total time* 3 hrs 25 min
makes 2 loaves (24 slices each)

1 can (15 oz) pumpkin (not pumpkin pie mix)
1 2/3 cups sugar
2/3 cup vegetable oil
2 teaspoons vanilla
4 eggs
3 cups all-purpose or whole wheat flour
2 teaspoons baking soda
1 teaspoon salt
1 teaspoon ground cinnamon
1/2 teaspoon ground cloves
1/2 teaspoon baking powder
1/2 cup coarsely chopped nuts
1/2 cup raisins, if desired

1. Move oven rack to low position so that tops of pans will be in center of oven. Heat oven to 350°F. Grease bottoms only of two 8 × 4–inch loaf pans or one 9 × 5–inch loaf pan with shortening or cooking spray.

2. In large bowl, stir pumpkin, sugar, oil, vanilla and eggs until well mixed. Stir in remaining ingredients except nuts and raisins. Stir in nuts and raisins. Divide batter evenly between 8-inch pans or pour into 9-inch pan.

3. Bake 8-inch loaves 50 to 60 minutes, 9-inch loaf 1 hour 10 minutes to 1 hour 20 minutes, or until toothpick inserted in center comes out clean. Cool 10 minutes in pans on wire rack.

4. Loosen sides of loaves from pans; remove from pans to wire rack. Cool completely, about 2 hours, before slicing. Wrap tightly and store at room temperature up to 4 days, or refrigerate up to 10 days.

1 SLICE: Calories 100 (Calories from Fat 40); Total Fat 4.5g (Saturated Fat 0.5g; Trans Fat 0g); Cholesterol 20mg; Sodium 115mg; Total Carbohydrate 14g (Dietary Fiber 0g; Sugars 7g); Protein 2g; **% DAILY VALUE:** Vitamin A 30%; Vitamin C 0%; Calcium 0%; Iron 4%; **EXCHANGES:** 1 Other Carbohydrate, 1 Fat; **CARBOHYDRATE CHOICES:** 1

CRANBERRY BREAD Omit pumpkin, cinnamon, cloves and raisins. Stir in 1/2 cup milk and 2 teaspoons grated orange peel with the oil. Stir 3 cups fresh or frozen (thawed and drained) cranberries into batter. Bake 1 hour to 1 hour 10 minutes.

ZUCCHINI BREAD Substitute 3 cups shredded unpeeled zucchini (2 to 3 medium) for the pumpkin.

new twist

Mini loaves are great for gift giving! Batters can be baked in miniature loaf pans, muffin pans or small cake molds in special shapes. To determine how much batter a pan will hold, fill it to the top with water, then pour the water into a measuring cup. Check the chart to see how much batter you should use for the size pan you have. Let the baked breads cool for a few minutes, then loosen the edges with a table knife or metal spatula and carefully remove from the pans. Cool completely on a wire rack.

MINI NUT BREAD LOAVES BAKING GUIDE

Approximate Pan Size	Amount of Batter	Approximate Bake Time at 350°F
1/3 cup	1/4 cup	15 to 20 minutes
1/2 cup	1/3 cup	15 to 20 minutes
2/3 to 3/4 cup	1/2 cup	25 to 35 minutes
1 cup	3/4 cup	35 to 40 minutes

Top to bottom: Zucchini Bread, Pumpkin Bread and Cranberry Bread

CHOCOLATE-PISTACHIO BREAD

prep 15 min *total time* 4 hrs 25 min
makes 1 loaf (24 slices)

2/3 cup granulated sugar
1/2 cup butter or margarine, melted
1 cup milk
2 eggs
1 1/2 cups all-purpose flour
1 cup chopped pistachio nuts
1/2 cup semisweet chocolate chips
1/3 cup unsweetened baking cocoa
1 1/2 teaspoons baking powder
1/4 teaspoon salt
Decorator sugar crystals, if desired

1. Heat oven to 350°F. Generously grease bottom of 9 × 5–inch glass or shiny metal loaf pan with shortening; do not use dark-colored bakeware or bread will burn around edges. In large bowl, mix granulated sugar, butter, milk and egg until well blended. Stir in remaining ingredients except sugar crystals. Pour into pan. Sprinkle with sugar crystals.

2. Bake 60 to 70 minutes or until toothpick inserted in center comes out clean. Cool 10 minutes in pan on wire rack.

3. Loosen sides of loaf from pan; remove from pan to wire rack. Cool completely, about 3 hours, before slicing.

1 SLICE: Calories 150 (Calories from Fat 70); Total Fat 8g (Saturated Fat 3g; Trans Fat 0g); Cholesterol 20mg; Sodium 120mg; Total Carbohydrate 16g (Dietary Fiber 1g; Sugars 8g); Protein 3g; % DAILY VALUE: Vitamin A 4%; Vitamin C 0%; Calcium 4%; Iron 6%; EXCHANGES: 1/2 Starch, 1/2 Other Carbohydrate, 1 1/2 Fat; CARBOHYDRATE CHOICES: 1

DOUBLE CHOCOLATE–WALNUT BREAD Substitute chocolate milk for regular milk and walnuts for the pistachio nuts.

make-ahead magic

To make ahead, bake and cool the loaf, wrap tightly and refrigerate up to 10 days or freeze up to 3 months.

BANANA BREAD

prep 15 min   *total time* 3 hrs 25 min
makes 2 loaves (24 slices each)

1 1/4 cups sugar

1/2 cup butter or margarine, softened

2 eggs

1 1/2 cups mashed very ripe bananas (3 medium)

1/2 cup buttermilk

1 teaspoon vanilla

2 1/2 cups all-purpose flour

1 teaspoon baking soda

1 teaspoon salt

1 cup chopped nuts, if desired

1. Move oven rack to low position so that tops of pans will be in center of oven. Heat oven to 350°F. Grease bottoms only of two 8 × 4–inch loaf pans or one 9 × 5–inch loaf pan with shortening or cooking spray.

2. In large bowl, stir sugar and butter until well mixed. Stir in eggs until well mixed. Stir in bananas, buttermilk and vanilla; beat with spoon until smooth. Stir in flour, baking soda and salt just until moistened. Stir in nuts. Divide batter evenly between 8-inch pans or pour into 9-inch pan.

3. Bake 8-inch loaves about 1 hour, 9-inch loaf about 1 hour 15 minutes, or until toothpick inserted in center comes out clean. Cool 10 minutes in pans on wire rack.

4. Loosen sides of loaves from pans; remove from pans to wire rack. Cool completely, about 2 hours, before slicing. Wrap tightly and store at room temperature up to 4 days, or refrigerate up to 10 days.

1 SLICE: Calories 70 (Calories from Fat 20); Total Fat 2.5g (Saturated Fat 1g; Trans Fat 0g); Cholesterol 15mg; Sodium 95mg; Total Carbohydrate 12g (Dietary Fiber 0g; Sugars 6g); Protein 1g; % DAILY VALUE: Vitamin A 0%; Vitamin C 0%; Calcium 0%; Iron 0%; EXCHANGES: 1 Other Carbohydrate, 1/2 Fat; CARBOHYDRATE CHOICES: 1

BLUEBERRY-BANANA BREAD Omit nuts. Stir 1 cup fresh or frozen blueberries into batter.

new twist

For a quick and refreshingly different breakfast, top slices of banana bread with your favorite fruit-flavored yogurt, sliced fresh bananas and some chopped nuts.

To bake mini loaves, see the chart on page 152.

UPSIDE-DOWN TURTLE MUFFINS

prep 25 min   *total time* 50 min
makes 12 muffins

1/2 cup semisweet chocolate chips
3 tablespoons butter or margarine
1/3 cup buttermilk
1/3 cup packed brown sugar
1 teaspoon vanilla
1 egg
1 cup all-purpose flour
1 teaspoon baking soda
1/2 teaspoon salt
1/4 cup chopped pecans
24 milk chocolate-covered caramels
    (from 5.3-oz bag), unwrapped
36 small pecan halves

1. Heat oven to 400°F. Spray bottoms, sides and tops of 12 regular-size muffin cups with cooking spray.

2. In 1 1/2-quart heavy saucepan, melt chocolate chips and butter over low heat, stirring frequently; cool slightly. Stir in buttermilk, brown sugar, vanilla and egg.

3. In large bowl, mix flour, baking soda, salt and chopped pecans. Stir in chocolate mixture just until combined. Divide batter evenly among muffin cups. Push 1 caramel into center of batter in each muffin cup.

4. Bake 14 to 16 minutes or until toothpick inserted 1/2 inch from edge of muffin comes out clean. Cool 1 minute. Turn muffin pan upside down onto cookie sheet to remove muffins. Immediately place another caramel on bottom of each muffin. Leaving muffins upside down on cookie sheet, return to oven about 1 minute or until caramel is soft enough to add pecan halves.

5. Place 3 pecan halves on caramel on each muffin. Cool until caramel is slightly firm before serving, about 10 minutes. Serve warm if desired.

1 MUFFIN: Calories 240 (Calories from Fat 120); Total Fat 13g (Saturated Fat 5g; Trans Fat 0g); Cholesterol 25mg; Sodium 260mg; Total Carbohydrate 28g (Dietary Fiber 1g; Sugars 18g); Protein 3g; % DAILY VALUE: Vitamin A 2%; Vitamin C 0%; Calcium 4%; Iron 6%; EXCHANGES: 1 Starch, 1 Other Carbohydrate, 2 1/2 Fat; CARBOHYDRATE CHOICES: 2

new twist

Serve these warm ooey-gooey muffins with a scoop of dulce de leche or vanilla ice cream and a drizzle of Decadent Fudge Sauce (page 258) or Divine Caramel Sauce (page 261).

GINGERBREAD MUFFINS

prep 15 min   *total time* 35 min   *makes* 12 muffins

1/4 cup packed brown sugar

1/2 cup molasses

1/3 cup milk

1/3 cup vegetable oil

1 egg

2 cups all-purpose flour

1 teaspoon baking powder

1 teaspoon ground ginger

1/2 teaspoon salt

1/2 teaspoon baking soda

1/2 teaspoon ground cinnamon

1/4 teaspoon ground allspice

1. Heat oven to 400°F. Grease bottoms only of 12 regular size muffin cups with shortening, or place paper baking cup in each muffin cup.

2. In large bowl, beat brown sugar, molasses, milk, oil and egg with spoon. Stir in remaining ingredients just until flour is moistened. Divide batter evenly among muffin cups.

3. Bake 18 to 20 minutes or until toothpick inserted in center comes out clean. Immediately remove from pan to wire rack. Serve warm if desired.

1 MUFFIN: Calories 200 (Calories from Fat 60); Total Fat 7g (Saturated Fat 1g; Trans Fat 0g); Cholesterol 20mg; Sodium 210mg; Total Carbohydrate 32g (Dietary Fiber 0g; Sugars 13g); Protein 3g; % DAILY VALUE: Vitamin A 0%; Vitamin C 0%; Calcium 6%; Iron 10%; EXCHANGES: 1 Starch, 1 Other Carbohydrate, 1 Fat; CARBOHYDRATE CHOICES: 2

holiday inspiration

For a festive holiday finish:

- Dip muffin tops into melted butter and then into a mixture of ground cinnamon and sugar.

- Drizzle tops with melted white vanilla baking chips.

- Slice muffins in half, and fill with vanilla pudding or ice cream. Top with caramel or lemon sauce, and sprinkle with ground cinnamon or nutmeg.

CHERRY-STREUSEL MUFFINS

prep 20 min   *total time* 45 min   *makes* 12 muffins

Almond Streusel Topping

3 tablespoons packed brown sugar

3 tablespoons all-purpose flour

2 tablespoons finely chopped sliced almonds

1/4 teaspoon ground cinnamon

2 tablespoons firm butter or margarine

Muffins

1 jar (10 oz) maraschino cherries, drained, 1/4 cup juice reserved

1 1/3 cups all-purpose flour

2/3 cup granulated sugar

1 1/2 teaspoons baking powder

1/2 teaspoon salt

1/3 cup vegetable oil

1 teaspoon almond extract

1/2 teaspoon vanilla

2 eggs

3 tablespoons sliced almonds

1. Heat oven to 400°F. Place paper baking cup in each of 12 regular-size muffin cups.

2. In medium bowl, mix all topping ingredients except butter. Cut in butter, using pastry blender (or pulling 2 table knives through ingredients in opposite directions), until crumbly. Set aside.

3. Chop cherries; set aside. In large bowl, mix 1 1/3 cups flour, the granulated sugar, baking powder and salt. In small bowl, beat oil, reserved 1/4 cup cherry juice, almond extract, vanilla and eggs with fork until blended. Stir cherry juice mixture into flour mixture just until flour is moistened. Fold in cherries and almonds. Divide batter evenly among muffin cups. Sprinkle each with about 1 tablespoon topping.

4. Bake 19 to 23 minutes or until toothpick inserted in center comes out clean. Immediately remove from pan to wire rack. Serve warm if desired.

1 MUFFIN: Calories 250 (Calories from Fat 100); Total Fat 11g (Saturated Fat 2.5g; Trans Fat 0g); Cholesterol 40mg; Sodium 180mg; Total Carbohydrate 34g (Dietary Fiber 1g; Sugars 21g); Protein 3g; % DAILY VALUE: Vitamin A 2%; Vitamin C 0%; Calcium 6%; Iron 6%; EXCHANGES: 1 Starch, 1 1/2 Other Carbohydrate, 2 Fat; CARBOHYDRATE CHOICES: 2

holiday inspiration

Little frills here and there can add oomph! Look
for paper baking cups in festive colors, holiday
prints and metallic foils at your supermarket, party
store or paper warehouse.

SCONES

prep 15 min *total time* 35 min *makes* 8 scones

1 3/4 cups all-purpose flour

3 tablespoons sugar

2 1/2 teaspoons baking powder

1/2 teaspoon salt

1/3 cup firm butter or margarine

1 egg, beaten

1/2 teaspoon vanilla

4 to 6 tablespoons whipping (heavy) cream

Additional 1 tablespoon whipping (heavy) cream

2 teaspoons white decorator sugar crystals or granulated sugar

1. Heat oven to 400°F. In large bowl, mix flour, 3 tablespoons sugar, the baking powder and salt. Cut in butter, using pastry blender (or pulling 2 table knives through ingredients in opposite directions), until mixture looks like fine crumbs. Stir in egg, vanilla and just enough of the 4 to 6 tablespoons whipping cream so dough leaves side of bowl.

2. Place dough on lightly floured surface; gently roll in flour to coat. Knead lightly 10 times. On ungreased cookie sheet, roll or pat dough into 8-inch circle. Cut into 8 wedges with sharp knife that has been dipped in flour, but do not separate wedges. Brush with 1 tablespoon whipping cream; sprinkle with sugar crystals.

3. Bake 14 to 16 minutes or until light golden brown. Immediately remove from cookie sheet; carefully separate wedges. Serve warm.

1 SCONE: Calories 230 (Calories from Fat 100); Total Fat 11g (Saturated Fat 6g; Trans Fat 0.5g); Cholesterol 55mg; Sodium 360mg; Total Carbohydrate 27g (Dietary Fiber 0g; Sugars 6g); Protein 4g; **% DAILY VALUE**: Vitamin A 8%; Vitamin C 0%; Calcium 10%; Iron 8%; **EXCHANGES:** 2 Starch, 2 Fat; **CARBOHYDRATE CHOICES:** 2

CHOCOLATE CHIP SCONES Stir in 1/2 cup miniature semisweet chocolate chips with the egg, vanilla and whipping cream.

CURRANT SCONES Stir in 1/2 cup currants or raisins with the egg, vanilla and whipping cream.

Left to right: Chocolate Chip Scones and Raspberry–White Chocolate Scones

RASPBERRY–WHITE CHOCOLATE SCONES Substitute almond extract for the vanilla; increase whipping cream to 1/2 cup. Stir in 3/4 cup frozen unsweetened raspberries (do not thaw) and 2/3 cup white vanilla baking chips with the egg, almond extract and whipping cream. Omit kneading step; pat dough into 8-inch circle on ungreased cookie sheet. Continue as directed—except bake 18 to 23 minutes. The berries will bleed slightly into the dough.

holiday inspiration

Not all scones are alike—these just happen to be joyfully good and so easy to make! Scones are similar to biscuits except they're buttery, sweeter and more tender. A pizza cutter works perfectly for cutting the scones before and after baking.

ALMOND-POPPY SEED MUFFINS

prep 10 min   *total time* 30 min   *makes* 12 muffins

1/2 cup sugar

1/3 cup vegetable oil

1 egg

1/2 teaspoon almond extract

1/2 cup sour cream

1/4 cup milk

1 1/3 cups all-purpose flour

1/2 teaspoon baking powder

1/2 teaspoon salt

1/4 teaspoon baking soda

2 tablespoons poppy seed

3 teaspoons sugar

2 tablespoons sliced almonds

1. Heat oven to 375°F. Place paper baking cup in each of 12 regular-size muffin cups, or grease cups with shortening or cooking spray.

2. In large bowl, stir 1/2 cup sugar, the oil, egg and almond extract. Beat in sour cream and milk with spoon until blended. Stir in flour, baking powder, salt, baking soda and poppy seed until well blended. Divide batter evenly among muffin cups. Sprinkle batter with 3 teaspoons sugar and the almonds.

3. Bake 14 to 17 minutes or until toothpick inserted in center comes out clean. Remove from pan to wire rack. Serve warm or cool.

1 MUFFIN: Calories 180 (Calories from Fat 90); Total Fat 10g (Saturated Fat 2.5g; Trans Fat 0g); Cholesterol 25mg; Sodium 160mg; Total Carbohydrate 21g (Dietary Fiber 0g; Sugars 10g); Protein 3g; **% DAILY VALUE:** Vitamin A 0%; Vitamin C 0%; Calcium 6%; Iron 6%; **EXCHANGES:** 1 Starch, 1/2 Other Carbohydrate, 2 Fat; **CARBOHYDRATE CHOICES:** 1 1/2

new twist

Add a gourmet touch by making a glaze with 1/2 cup powdered sugar and 2 to 3 teaspoons milk. Use a small spoon to drizzle the glaze over the muffins. Sprinkle glaze with yellow decorator sugar crystals before it has set, if desired.

make-ahead magic

To make ahead, cover and refrigerate the batter up to 12 hours. Bake at 375°F for 16 to 18 minutes or until golden brown.

BANANA-TOFFEE DROP SCONES

prep 10 min   *total time* 40 min   *makes* 10 scones

2 1/2 cups Original Bisquick mix

1/2 cup toffee bits

1/4 cup sugar

1/4 cup whipping (heavy) cream

1/2 teaspoon vanilla

1 egg

2 medium bananas, mashed (3/4 cup)

1 tablespoon milk

1 tablespoon sugar

1. Heat oven to 425°F. Grease 2 cookie sheets with shortening or cooking spray. In large bowl, stir Bisquick mix, toffee bits, 1/4 cup sugar, the whipping cream, vanilla, egg and bananas until soft dough forms.

2. Drop dough by 10 large tablespoonfuls onto cookie sheets (5 per cookie sheet). Brush tops with milk; sprinkle with 1 tablespoon sugar. Refrigerate second cookie sheet while first cookie sheet bakes.

3. Bake 11 to 13 minutes or until golden brown. Serve warm.

1 SCONE: Calories 240 (Calories from Fat 90); Total Fat 10g (Saturated Fat 4.5g; Trans Fat 0.5g); Cholesterol 35mg; Sodium 480mg; Total Carbohydrate 35g (Dietary Fiber 0g; Sugars 17g); Protein 3g; **% DAILY VALUE:** Vitamin A 2%; Vitamin C 0%; Calcium 6%; Iron 6%; **EXCHANGES:** 1 Starch, 1 1/2 Other Carbohydrate, 2 Fat; **CARBOHYDRATE CHOICES:** 2

BANANA-CHOCOLATE CHIP DROP SCONES

Substitute 1/2 cup miniature semisweet chocolate chips for the toffee bits.

holiday inspiration

White decorator sugar crystals are much, much larger than regular granulated sugar crystals. Use them on top of these muffins for extra sparkle.

new twist

Absolutely heavenly! The whipping cream in these biscuits makes them as tender as can be. For an unexpected winter dessert, serve frozen sweetened strawberries (thawed) over warm biscuits with a generous dollop of softly whipped sweetened whipping cream.

EASY CREAM BISCUITS

prep 10 min   *total time* 25 min
makes about 12 biscuits

1 3/4 cups all-purpose flour
2 1/2 teaspoons baking powder
1/2 teaspoon salt
About 1 1/4 cups whipping (heavy) cream

1. Heat oven to 450°F. In large bowl, mix flour, baking powder and salt. Stir in just enough whipping cream so dough leaves side of bowl and forms a ball. (If dough is too dry, mix in 1 to 2 teaspoons more whipping cream.)

2. Place dough on lightly floured surface; gently roll in flour to coat. Knead lightly 10 times, sprinkling with flour if dough is too sticky. Roll or pat 1/2 inch thick. Cut with floured 2-inch biscuit cutter. On ungreased cookie sheet, place biscuits about 1 inch apart.

3. Bake 10 to 12 minutes or until golden brown. Immediately remove from cookie sheet to wire rack. Serve hot.

1 BISCUIT: Calories 140 (Calories from Fat 70); Total Fat 8g (Saturated Fat 5g; Trans Fat 0g); Cholesterol 30mg; Sodium 210mg; Total Carbohydrate 15g (Dietary Fiber 0g; Sugars 0g); Protein 2g; % DAILY VALUE: Vitamin A 6%; Vitamin C 0%; Calcium 8%; Iron 6%; EXCHANGES: 1 Other Carbohydrate, 1 1/2 Fat; CARBOHYDRATE CHOICES: 1

CINNAMON-RAISIN BISCUITS Stir in 2 tablespoons sugar, 1 teaspoon ground cinnamon and 1/3 cup raisins or currants with the flour. Drizzle Creamy Vanilla Glaze (page 114) over warm biscuits if desired.

CHEESE-GARLIC BISCUITS

prep 10 min *total time* 20 min *makes* 9 biscuits

2 cups Original Bisquick mix
1/2 cup shredded Cheddar cheese (2 oz)
2/3 cup milk
2 tablespoons butter or margarine, melted
1/8 teaspoon garlic powder

1. Heat oven to 450°F. In medium bowl, stir Bisquick mix, cheese and milk until soft dough forms.

2. On ungreased cookie sheet, drop dough by spoonfuls.

3. Bake 8 to 10 minutes or until golden brown. In small bowl, mix butter and garlic powder; brush over warm biscuits.

1 BISCUIT: Calories 160 (Calories from Fat 80); Total Fat 9g (Saturated Fat 3.5g; Trans Fat 1g); Cholesterol 15mg; Sodium 440mg; Total Carbohydrate 17g (Dietary Fiber 0g; Sugars 3g); Protein 4g; **% DAILY VALUE:** Vitamin A 4%; Vitamin C 0%; Calcium 10%; Iron 4%; **EXCHANGES:** 1 Starch, 1 1/2 Fat; **CARBOHYDRATE CHOICES:** 1

holiday inspiration

These warm, moist, cheesy biscuits rank as one of the most requested Betty Crocker recipes. Try some today; they go great with soups, chili, salads and almost anything!

SO-EASY PRALINE PAN BISCUITS

prep 15 min   *total time* 30 min   *makes* 12 biscuits

1/3 cup butter or margarine
1/3 cup packed brown sugar
1/3 cup chopped pecans
2 cups Original Bisquick mix
1/2 cup milk

1. Heat oven to 425°F. In 1-quart saucepan, heat butter and brown sugar over low heat, stirring constantly, until melted. Pour into 9-inch round pan or 8-inch square pan. Sprinkle with pecans.

2. In medium bowl, stir Bisquick mix and milk until dough forms; beat 30 seconds. If dough is too sticky, gradually mix in enough Bisquick mix (up to 1/4 cup) to make dough easy to handle.

3. Place dough on surface dusted with Bisquick mix; gently roll in Bisquick mix to coat. Knead 10 times. Divide dough into 12 equal pieces; gently shape each piece into a ball. Place balls on brown sugar mixture in pan.

4. Bake 12 to 15 minutes or until golden brown. Place heatproof serving plate upside down onto pan; turn plate and pan over. Leave pan over biscuits a few minutes to allow brown sugar mixture to drizzle over biscuits. Cool slightly before serving.

1 BISCUIT: Calories 180 (Calories from Fat 90); Total Fat 10g (Saturated Fat 3.5g; Trans Fat 1g); Cholesterol 15mg; Sodium 330mg; Total Carbohydrate 19g (Dietary Fiber 0g; Sugars 8g); Protein 2g; **% DAILY VALUE:** Vitamin A 4%; Vitamin C 0%; Calcium 6%; Iron 4%; **EXCHANGES:** 1/2 Starch, 1/2 Other Carbohydrate, 2 Fat; **CARBOHYDRATE CHOICES:** 1

holiday inspiration

Kids will love these yummy biscuits with a topping like caramel rolls! Let the kids shape the dough into balls and put them in the pan.

PESTO BISCUITS

prep 15 min *total time* 30 min *makes* 10 biscuits

2 cups all-purpose flour
3 teaspoons baking powder
1/2 teaspoon salt
1/3 cup shortening
1/4 cup basil pesto
About 1/2 cup milk
Finely shredded Parmesan cheese, if desired
Red or green hot pepper (jalapeño) jelly, if desired

1. Heat oven to 450°F. In large bowl, mix flour, baking powder and salt. Cut in shortening and pesto, using pastry blender (or pulling 2 table knives through ingredients in opposite directions), until mixture looks like fine crumbs. Stir in just enough milk so dough leaves side of bowl and forms a ball.

2. Place dough on lightly floured surface. Knead lightly 10 times. Roll or pat 1/2 inch thick. Cut with floured 2 1/2-inch cookie or biscuit cutter. On ungreased cookie sheet, place biscuits about 1 inch apart. Sprinkle with cheese.

3. Bake 10 to 12 minutes or until golden brown. Immediately remove from cookie sheet. Serve warm with pepper jelly.

1 BISCUIT: Calories 190 (Calories from Fat 100); Total Fat 11g (Saturated Fat 2.5g; Trans Fat 1g); Cholesterol 0mg; Sodium 330mg; Total Carbohydrate 20g (Dietary Fiber 0g; Sugars 0g); Protein 4g; **% DAILY VALUE:** Vitamin A 0%; Vitamin C 0%; Calcium 10%; Iron 8%; **EXCHANGES:** 1 1/2 Starch, 2 Fat; **CARBOHYDRATE CHOICES:** 1

holiday inspiration

Butter is easy to jazz up!

- Slice chilled butter 1/4 inch thick, then cut slices with mini cookie cutters. Use cutters with open tops so you can push the butter through. Simple shapes work best (such as stars, hearts, etc.). Put butter on waxed paper; cover and refrigerate until ready to serve. Butter scraps can be softened and reshaped or used in baking.

- To make large butter pats, put a 3-inch cookie cutter on a flat plate; fill with softened butter or margarine, spreading even with top of cutter. Cover and refrigerate until ready to serve. To unmold, run a knife dipped in hot water along the inside of cookie cutter, and remove the cutter.

- Refrigerate butter shapes until ready to serve, or wrap in colorful plastic wrap, tie with a bow and refrigerate until ready to give as a gift with home-made breads.

EASY DROP DANISH

prep 15 min *total time* 30 min *makes* 12 danish

Danish

2 cups Original Bisquick mix

1/4 cup butter or margarine, softened

2 tablespoons granulated sugar

2/3 cup milk

1/4 cup apricot preserves (or other flavor
fruit preserves)

Vanilla Glaze

3/4 cup powdered sugar

1 tablespoon warm water

1/4 teaspoon vanilla

1. Heat oven to 450°F. Lightly grease cookie sheet with shortening or cooking spray. In medium bowl, stir Bisquick mix, butter and sugar until crumbly. Stir in milk until dough forms; beat 15 strokes.

2. Drop dough by rounded tablespoonfuls about 2 inches apart onto cookie sheet. Make a shallow well in center of each with back of spoon; fill each with 1 teaspoon preserves.

3. Bake 10 to 15 minutes or until golden brown.

4. In small bowl, mix all glaze ingredients with spoon until smooth and thin enough to drizzle. Drizzle glaze over warm danish.

1 DANISH: Calories 180 (Calories from Fat 60); Total Fat 7g (Saturated Fat 3g; Trans Fat 0.5g); Cholesterol 10mg; Sodium 320mg; Total Carbohydrate 27g (Dietary Fiber 0g; Sugars 15g); Protein 2g; % DAILY VALUE: Vitamin A 4%; Vitamin C 0%; Calcium 6%; Iron 4%; EXCHANGES: 1 Starch, 1 Other Carbohydrate, 1 Fat; CARBOHYDRATE CHOICES: 2

EASY CHERRY-ALMOND DANISH Substitute cherry preserves for the apricot preserves and almond extract for vanilla in the vanilla glaze. For a nutty crunch, sprinkle the glaze with toasted chopped almonds.

holiday inspiration

Tuck this recipe in your "never-fails" folder. The danish look so pretty and fancy yet are very simple to throw together. Alternate the filling with various types of jam and jelly—they will look especially lovely on a serving tray this way.

GARLIC BREAD WREATH

prep 20 min   *total time* 3 hrs 50 min   *makes* 8 servings

1/4 cup shredded Parmesan cheese (1 oz)

1 loaf (1 lb) frozen white bread dough (from 3-lb package), thawed

1 tablespoon olive or vegetable oil

1 small clove garlic, finely chopped

1. Grease cookie sheet with shortening or cooking spray. Sprinkle 2 tablespoons of the cheese over flat surface. Roll bread dough in cheese into 24-inch rope. Place rope on cookie sheet and form into circle; pinch ends to seal.

2. Make 12 cuts in dough at about 1 1/2-inch intervals from the outer edge of the circle, cutting two-thirds of the way through, using kitchen scissors. Lift and turn every other section of dough toward center of the circle. Cover; let rise in warm place 2 to 3 hours or until double in size. (Dough is ready if indentation remains when touched.)

3. Heat oven to 350°F. Mix oil and garlic; brush over dough. Sprinkle with remaining 2 tablespoons cheese. Bake 25 to 30 minutes or until golden brown.

1 SERVING: Calories 180 (Calories from Fat 40); Total Fat 4.5g (Saturated Fat 1g; Trans Fat 0g); Cholesterol 0mg; Sodium 360mg; Total Carbohydrate 28g (Dietary Fiber 0g; Sugars 0g); Protein 6g; **% DAILY VALUE:** Vitamin A 0%; Vitamin C 0%; Calcium 10%; Iron 10%; **EXCHANGES:** 2 Starch, 1/2 Fat; **CARBOHYDRATE CHOICES:** 2

holiday inspiration

Fill the center of the wreath with one of the following spreads or oil. To create a spot in the center of the wreath to hold the spread, generously grease the outside of a 6-ounce custard cup and place it upside down in the center of the unbaked dough wreath. Bake as directed; cool 5 minutes and remove custard cup with hot pad. To serve, fill another 6-ounce custard cup with one of the butters or flavored spread below and place in the center of the wreath.

- **Basil Butter:** Beat 1/4 cup butter, softened, with 2 tablespoons chopped fresh basil leaves or 2 teaspoons dried basil leaves. Garnish with fresh basil.

- **Sun-Dried Tomato Butter:** Beat 1/4 cup butter, softened, with 2 tablespoons chopped, drained, oil-packed sun-dried tomatoes. Garnish with fresh dill weed.

- **Olive Oil with Fresh Herbs:** Pour olive oil into dish and garnish with fresh rosemary sprigs.

EASY HERB PULL-APART BREAD

prep 10 min   *total time* 4 hrs 45 min   *makes* 12 servings

3 tablespoons butter or margarine
1 teaspoon dried basil leaves
1 teaspoon parsley flakes
1/2 teaspoon dried thyme leaves
2 cloves garlic, finely chopped
24 balls frozen white dinner roll dough (from 3-lb package)

1. Spray 12-cup fluted tube cake pan (do not use 10-cup) with cooking spray. In 1-quart saucepan, heat all ingredients except roll dough over low heat, stirring occasionally, until butter is melted.

2. Place half of the frozen dough balls in pan. Generously brush butter mixture over dough in pan. Layer remaining dough balls in pan. Brush with remaining butter mixture. Cover; let stand in warm place about 4 hours or until double in size.

3. Heat oven to 350°F. Bake 22 to 27 minutes or until bread sounds hollow when tapped and top is deep golden brown. Cool 5 minutes; turn upside down onto serving plate. To serve bread while warm, use a fork to pull the rolls apart. To serve cooled bread, cut it into slices with a serrated knife.

1 SERVING: Calories 250 (Calories from Fat 80); Total Fat 8g (Saturated Fat 3g; Trans Fat 0g); Cholesterol 10mg; Sodium 410mg; Total Carbohydrate 38g (Dietary Fiber 2g; Sugars 5g); Protein 6g; % DAILY VALUE: Vitamin A 2%; Vitamin C 0%; Calcium 10%; Iron 15%; EXCHANGES: 2 1/2 Starch, 1 Fat; CARBOHYDRATE CHOICES: 2 1/2

holiday inspiration

Try this time-saving inspiration. You can cut the rising time of the bread to about 1 hour if you follow the frozen dough package directions for the "speed method."

SAVORY ONION TWIST

prep 15 min   *total time* 9 hrs 5 min   *makes* 1 loaf (16 slices)
see photo on page 148, top

Make-Ahead Potato Roll Dough (page 187)
1 cup shredded Swiss or mozzarella cheese (4 oz)
1/4 cup finely chopped red or green bell pepper
2 tablespoons finely chopped onion
2 tablespoons mayonnaise or salad dressing
1 tablespoon chopped fresh or 1 teaspoon dried cilantro
1/2 teaspoon ground cumin

1. Prepare Make-Ahead Potato Roll Dough through Step 2. Gently push fist into dough to deflate. Divide dough in half; cover and refrigerate half of dough for another use.

2. Grease large cookie sheet with shortening or cooking spray. Roll remaining half of dough on lightly floured surface into 15 × 10–inch rectangle. In small bowl, mix 1/2 cup of the cheese and the remaining ingredients. Spread cheese mixture over dough to within 1/2 inch of edges. Roll up dough, beginning at 15-inch side; pinch edge of dough into roll to seal.

3. Cut roll lengthwise in half. Place halves, filling sides up and side by side, on cookie sheet; twist together gently and loosely. Pinch edges to fasten. Cover; let rise in warm place about 25 minutes or until double in size. (Dough is ready if indentation remains when touched.)

4. Heat oven to 375°F. Bake 20 to 25 minutes or until golden brown. Immediately sprinkle with remaining 1/2 cup cheese. Serve warm.

1 SLICE: Calories 200 (Calories from Fat 70); Total Fat 8g (Saturated Fat 3.5g; Trans Fat 0g); Cholesterol 30mg; Sodium 180mg; Total Carbohydrate 27g (Dietary Fiber 1g; Sugars 5g); Protein 6g; % DAILY VALUE: Vitamin A 8%; Vitamin C 4%; Calcium 8%; Iron 8%; EXCHANGES: 2 Starch, 1 Fat; CARBOHYDRATE CHOICES: 2

holiday inspiration

We think you'll love this twist so much, you'll want to make another one right away. If you prefer, shape the second half of dough into 24 rolls, and place on greased cookie sheet. Cover and let rise in warm place about 1 hour or until double in size. Bake at 400°F for about 15 minutes or until golden brown.

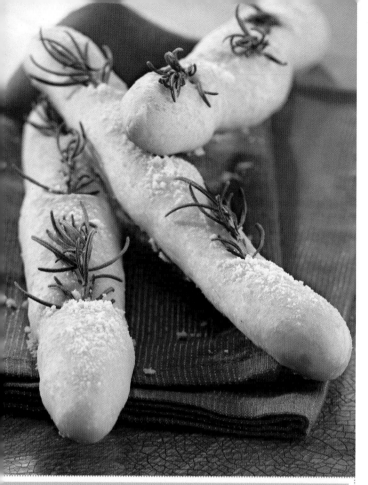

PINE TREE PARMESAN BREADSTICKS

prep 15 min *total time* 1 hr *makes* 12 breadsticks

Cornmeal, if desired
12 balls frozen white dinner roll dough (from 3-lb package), thawed
2 tablespoons olive or vegetable oil
3 or 4 long fresh rosemary sprigs
1 tablespoon grated Parmesan cheese

1. Brush 2 cookie sheets with olive oil; sprinkle with cornmeal. Roll each ball of dough into 9-inch rope. Place ropes about 1/2 inch apart on cookie sheets.

2. Brush 2 tablespoons oil over dough. Break 36 small clusters of rosemary leaves off rosemary sprigs. Using 3 clusters for each breadstick, insert stem end of each cluster 1/4 inch deep lengthwise down center of top of breadstick. Sprinkle cheese over dough. Cover loosely with plastic wrap and let rise in warm place about 30 minutes or until almost double in size.

3. Heat oven to 350°F. Bake 12 to 15 minutes or until light golden brown.

1 BREADSTICK: Calories 140 (Calories from Fat 45); Total Fat 5g (Saturated Fat 1g; Trans Fat 0g); Cholesterol 0mg; Sodium 210mg; Total Carbohydrate 19g (Dietary Fiber 1g; Sugars 2g); Protein 3g; % DAILY VALUE: Vitamin A 0%; Vitamin C 0%; Calcium 6%; Iron 6%; EXCHANGES: 1 Starch, 1 Fat; CARBOHYDRATE CHOICES: 1

holiday inspiration

Rosemary adds its distinctive lemon-pine flavor to these whimsical savory breadsticks. Choose rosemary sprigs with deep green, firm leaves; you can store it in the refrigerator for up to 5 days.

Betty Crocker Christmas Cookbook

FESTIVE FOCACCIA

prep 25 min *total time* 2 hrs 30 min
makes 2 focaccias (12 slices each)

2 1/2 to 3 cups bread flour or all-purpose flour

2 teaspoons sugar

1/4 teaspoon salt

1 package regular or fast-acting dry yeast

1/4 cup olive or vegetable oil

1 cup very warm water (120°F to 130°F)

2 tablespoons olive or vegetable oil

2 medium red bell peppers, cut into 1/4-inch strips

2 small onions, sliced

1 to 2 tablespoons olive or vegetable oil

2 tablespoons chopped fresh herb leaves (such as
    basil, oregano or rosemary)

2 tablespoons shredded Parmesan cheese

1. In large bowl, mix 1 cup of the flour, the sugar, salt and yeast. Add 1/4 cup oil and the warm water. Beat with electric mixer on medium speed 3 minutes, scraping bowl occasionally. Stir in enough remaining flour until dough is soft and leaves side of bowl.

2. Place dough on lightly floured surface. Knead 5 to 10 minutes or until dough is smooth and springy. Grease large bowl with shortening. Place dough in bowl, turning dough to grease all sides. Cover; let rise in warm place 1 hour to 1 hour 30 minutes or until double in size. (Dough is ready if indentation remains when touched.)

3. Heat oven to 425°F. Grease 2 cookie sheets with shortening or cooking spray. Gently push fist into dough to deflate. Divide in half. Shape each half into flattened 12-inch round on cookie sheet. Cover; let rise in warm place 20 minutes.

4. Meanwhile, in 10-inch skillet, heat 2 tablespoons oil over medium heat. Cook bell peppers and onions in oil, stirring occasionally, until tender.

5. Prick centers of focaccias and 1 inch in from edges thoroughly with fork. Brush with 1 to 2 tablespoons oil. Spread bell pepper mixture over focaccias. Sprinkle each with 1 tablespoon herb leaves and cheese. Bake 12 to 15 minutes or until golden brown. Serve warm.

1 SLICE: Calories 100 (Calories from Fat 40); Total Fat 4.5g (Saturated Fat 0.5g; Trans Fat 0g); Cholesterol 0mg; Sodium 35mg; Total Carbohydrate 13g (Dietary Fiber 0g; Sugars 1g); Protein 2g; **% DAILY VALUE:** Vitamin A 10%; Vitamin C 15%; Calcium 0%; Iron 4%; **EXCHANGES:** 1 Starch, 1/2 Fat; **CARBOHYDRATE CHOICES:** 1

new twist

If you're in a pinch, why not use two 1-pound rolls of frozen bread dough for this recipe? Just thaw the dough and follow directions above.

POPOVERS

prep 10 min   *total time* 45 min   *makes* 6 popovers

2 eggs
1 cup all-purpose flour
1 cup milk
1/2 teaspoon salt

1. Heat oven to 450°F. Generously grease 6-cup popover pan with shortening. Heat popover pan in oven 5 minutes.

2. Meanwhile, in medium bowl, beat eggs slightly with fork or wire whisk. Beat in remaining ingredients just until smooth (do not overbeat or popovers may not puff as high). Fill cups about half full.

3. Bake 20 minutes. Reduce oven temperature to 325°F. Bake 10 to 15 minutes longer or until deep golden brown. Immediately remove from cups. Serve hot.

1 POPOVER: Calories 120 (Calories from Fat 25); Total Fat 3g (Saturated Fat 1g; Trans Fat 0g); Cholesterol 75mg; Sodium 240mg; Total Carbohydrate 18g (Dietary Fiber 0g; Sugars 2g); Protein 6g; **% DAILY VALUE:** Vitamin A 4%; Vitamin C 0%; Calcium 6%; Iron 6%; **EXCHANGES:** 1 1/2 Starch, 1/2 Fat; **CARBOHYDRATE CHOICES:** 1

make-ahead magic

Popovers can be baked ahead and reheated. When just out of the oven, pierce each popover with the point of a knife to let the steam out, and cool completely on a wire rack. When it's time to eat, just reheat on an ungreased cookie sheet at 350°F for 5 minutes.

EASY SNOWFLAKE BUNS

prep 15 min   *total time* 3 hrs 40 min   *makes* 12 buns

12 frozen white bread dough rolls (from 3-lb package)
3 tablespoons all-purpose flour
3 tablespoons butter or margarine, softened
3/4 teaspoon hot water

1. Grease bottom and side of 9-inch round pan with shortening or cooking spray. Arrange 8 rolls evenly around outside of pan; place 4 rolls in center. Cover; let thaw and rise in warm place 2 to 3 hours or as directed on package.

2. Heat oven to 350°F. In small bowl, mix flour, butter and hot water. Place in decorating bag with #4 writing tip. Pipe mixture onto centers of each roll in snowflake designs, 1 to 1 1/2 inches in diameter.

3. Bake 20 to 25 minutes or until golden brown. Immediately lift buns from pan (do not turn upside down). Serve warm.

1 BUN: Calories 150 (Calories from Fat 50); Total Fat 6g (Saturated Fat 2g; Trans Fat 0g); Cholesterol 10mg; Sodium 220mg; Total Carbohydrate 21g (Dietary Fiber 1g; Sugars 2g); Protein 3g; **% DAILY VALUE:** Vitamin A 2%; Vitamin C 0%; Calcium 4%; Iron 8%; **EXCHANGES:** 1 1/2 Starch, 1 Fat; **CARBOHYDRATE CHOICES:** 1 1/2

holiday inspiration

Use a small resealable food-storage plastic bag for a quick, disposable decorating bag. Spoon the flour mixture into the bag, then cut off the tip of one of the corners, and pipe the mixture onto the dough.

make-ahead magic

Bake and freeze Easy Snowflake Buns up to 3 months ahead of time. Just before serving, heat the frozen buns in a 350°F oven for 15 to 20 minutes.

Easy Snowflake Buns

GRUYÈRE BREAD RINGS

prep 10 min *total time* 1 hr 10 min *makes* 12 servings

1 cup milk
1/2 cup butter or margarine
1 cup all-purpose flour
4 eggs, slightly beaten
1 cup shredded Gruyère cheese (4 oz)

1. Heat oven to 400°F. Grease large cookie sheet with shortening.

2. In 2-quart saucepan, heat milk and butter to rolling boil. Stir in flour; reduce heat to low. Stir vigorously over low heat about 1 minute or until mixture forms a ball; remove from heat. Beat in eggs all at once; continue beating until smooth. Fold in 2/3 cup of the cheese.

3. Divide dough in half. Onto one end of cookie sheet, drop half of dough by tablespoonfuls to form 4-inch ring (leave room for dough to expand). Repeat with other half of dough on other end of cookie sheet. Smooth dough rings with spatula. Sprinkle with remaining 1/3 cup cheese. Bake 50 to 60 minutes or until puffed and golden.

1 SERVING: Calories 180 (Calories from Fat 120); Total Fat 13g (Saturated Fat 6g; Trans Fat 0.5g); Cholesterol 105mg; Sodium 115mg; Total Carbohydrate 9g (Dietary Fiber 0g; Sugars 1g); Protein 7g; % DAILY VALUE: Vitamin A 10%; Vitamin C 0%; Calcium 15%; Iron 4%; EXCHANGES: 1/2 Starch, 1 High-Fat Meat, 1 Fat; CARBOHYDRATE CHOICES: 1/2

new twist

To make one large ring, drop the dough by tablespoonfuls into an 8-inch ring, and bake 50 to 60 minutes.

holiday inspiration

Gruyère cheese is used in this French classic. It has a rich, sweet, nutty flavor and pale yellow interior with well-spaced medium-size holes. Avoid Gruyère wedges that have a very large number of irregularly shaped or excessively small holes because it may be a sign of poor quality. If you can't find Gruyère substitute Swiss cheese.

OLIVE, BACON *and* CHEDDAR ROLLS

prep 25 min *total time* 40 min *makes* 12 rolls

12 purchased round soft smooth-topped dinner rolls (about 1 to 1 1/2 oz each)*
8 slices bacon
1/4 cup chopped ripe olives, drained (from 4.25-oz can)
1/4 cup finely chopped pimiento-stuffed olives (about 16 olives)
4 medium green onions, finely chopped (1/4 cup)
1/4 cup mayonnaise or salad dressing
1 cup finely shredded Cheddar cheese (4 oz)

1. Heat oven to 350°F. In each roll, cut a pocket from the top down to within 1/2 inch from each side, cutting almost to but not through the bottom; set aside.

2. Line bacon rack or microwavable plate with microwavable paper towels; place bacon on rack. Cover with paper towel. Microwave on High 4 to 6 minutes or until bacon is crisp. Crumble bacon when it is cool enough to handle.

3. In small bowl, mix bacon, olives, onions, mayonnaise and 1/2 cup of the cheese. Fill each pocket with 1 heaping tablespoon bacon mixture. On ungreased cookie sheet, place rolls; sprinkle each roll with 2 teaspoons cheese. Bake 14 to 16 minutes or until filling is hot.

*Do not use cloverleaf rolls for this recipe because the roll sections will separate when the pocket is cut.

1 ROLL: Calories 200 (Calories from Fat 110); Total Fat 12g (Saturated Fat 4g; Trans Fat 0g); Cholesterol 15mg; Sodium 390mg; Total Carbohydrate 15g (Dietary Fiber 1g; Sugars 2g); Protein 7g; % DAILY VALUE: Vitamin A 2%; Vitamin C 0%; Calcium 10%; Iron 6%; EXCHANGES: 1 Starch, 1/2 High-Fat Meat, 1 1/2 Fat; CARBOHYDRATE CHOICES: 1

holiday inspiration

These hearty stuffed rolls would pair nicely with soup, chili or salad—or a steak!

EASY PUFF TWISTS

prep 25 min *total time* 35 min *makes* about 48 twists

2/3 cup grated Parmesan cheese
1 tablespoon paprika
1 package (17.3 oz) frozen puff pastry, thawed
1 egg, slightly beaten

1. Heat oven to 425°F. Line 2 cookie sheets with cooking parchment paper or heavy brown paper. In small bowl, mix cheese and paprika. Roll 1 sheet of pastry on lightly floured surface with floured cloth-covered rolling pin into 12 × 10–inch rectangle.

2. Brush egg over pastry. Sprinkle with 3 table-spoons of the cheese mixture; press gently into pastry. Turn pastry over. Brush egg over other side of pastry. Sprinkle with 3 tablespoons of the cheese mixture; press gently into pastry. Fold pastry lengthwise in half.

3. Cut pastry crosswise into 1/2-inch strips. Unfold strips; roll each end in opposite directions to twist. Place twists on cookie sheet. Bake 7 to 8 minutes or until puffed and golden brown. Remove from cookie sheet to wire rack. Repeat with remaining sheet of pastry, egg and cheese mixture. Serve twists warm or cool.

1 TWIST: Calories 70 (Calories from Fat 40); Total Fat 4.5g (Saturated Fat 1.5g; Trans Fat 0g); Cholesterol 20mg; Sodium 55mg; Total Carbohydrate 5g (Dietary Fiber 0g; Sugars 0g); Protein 1g; % DAILY VALUE: Vitamin A 2%; Vitamin C 0%; Calcium 2%; Iron 2%; EXCHANGES: 1/2 Starch, 1 Fat; CARBOHYDRATE CHOICES: 1/2

CHERRY SWIRL COFFEE CAKE

prep 20 min *total time* 1 hr 5 min *makes* 18 servings
see photo on page 148, bottom

Coffee Cake
1 1/2 cups granulated sugar
1/2 cup butter or margarine, softened
1/2 cup shortening
1 1/2 teaspoons baking powder
1 teaspoon vanilla
1 teaspoon almond extract
4 eggs
3 cups all-purpose flour
1 can (21 oz) cherry pie filling

Glaze
1 cup powdered sugar
1 to 2 tablespoons milk or water

1. Heat oven to 350°F. Generously grease 15 × 10 × 1–inch pan with shortening or cooking spray. In large bowl, beat granulated sugar, butter, shortening, baking powder, vanilla, almond extract and eggs with electric mixer on low speed, scraping bowl constantly. Beat on high speed 3 minutes, scraping bowl occasionally. Stir in flour.

2. Spread two-thirds of the batter in pan. Spread pie filling over batter. Drop remaining batter by tablespoonfuls onto pie filling.

3. Bake about 45 minutes or until toothpick inserted in center comes out clean.

4. In small bowl, mix glaze ingredients with spoon until smooth and thin enough to drizzle. Drizzle glaze over warm coffee cake. Serve warm or let stand until cool.

1 SERVING: Calories 320 (Calories from Fat 110); Total Fat 12g (Saturated Fat 4.5g; Trans Fat 1.5g); Cholesterol 60mg; Sodium 90mg; Total Carbohydrate 48g (Dietary Fiber 1g; Sugars 31g); Protein 4g; % DAILY VALUE: Vitamin A 6%; Vitamin C 0%; Calcium 4%; Iron 8%; EXCHANGES: 1 Starch, 2 Other Carbohydrate, 2 1/2 Fat; CARBOHYDRATE CHOICES: 3

new twist

Garnish the baked coffee cake with sliced almonds, fresh mint and frozen cranberries tossed in sugar.

OVERNIGHT EGGNOG STREUSEL COFFEE CAKE

prep 25 min   *total time* 9 hrs 25 min
makes 15 servings

Streusel Topping

1/3 cup granulated sugar

1 tablespoon all-purpose flour

1 tablespoon butter or margarine, softened

1/2 teaspoon ground nutmeg

1/4 teaspoon ground cinnamon

Coffee Cake

1 cup granulated sugar

1/2 cup butter or margarine, softened

1 cup eggnog

1 container (8 oz) sour cream

1 teaspoon rum extract

2 eggs

2 1/2 cups all-purpose flour

1 1/2 teaspoons baking powder

1/2 teaspoon baking soda

1/2 teaspoon salt

Eggnog Glaze

1/2 cup powdered sugar

1 to 2 tablespoons eggnog

1. Grease bottom only of 13 × 9–inch pan with shortening or cooking spray. In small bowl, mix all topping ingredients with fork until crumbly; set aside.

2. In large bowl, beat 1 cup sugar and 1/2 cup butter with electric mixer on medium speed, or mix with spoon. Beat in 1 cup eggnog, the sour cream, rum extract and eggs until blended. Stir in 2 1/2 cups flour, the baking powder, baking soda and salt. Spread in pan.

3. Sprinkle topping over batter. Cover; refrigerate at least 8 hours. (To bake coffee cake immediately, decrease bake time in step 4 to 30 to 35 minutes.)

4. Heat oven to 350°F. Uncover; bake 35 to 40 minutes or until toothpick inserted in center comes out clean. Cool 20 minutes. In small bowl, mix glaze ingredients until smooth and thin enough to drizzle. Drizzle glaze over coffee cake.

1 SERVING: Calories 290 (Calories from Fat 110); Total Fat 12g (Saturated Fat 6g; Trans Fat 0.5g); Cholesterol 65mg; Sodium 240mg; Total Carbohydrate 41g (Dietary Fiber 0g; Sugars 25g); Protein 4g; % DAILY VALUE: Vitamin A 10%; Vitamin C 0%; Calcium 8%; Iron 6%; EXCHANGES: 1 Starch, 1 1/2 Other Carbohydrate, 2 1/2 Fat; CARBOHYDRATE CHOICES: 3

holiday inspiration

A nod to eggnog! Refrigerated eggnog is preferred to canned eggnog for its excellent dairy flavor and creamy texture. It's amazing, but the flavor of the refrigerated eggnog really won't disappoint you, even if you're used to homemade (see Holiday Eggnog, page 45).

SOUR CREAM COFFEE CAKE

prep 30 min   *total time* 2 hrs   *makes* 16 servings

Brown Sugar Filling

1/2 cup packed brown sugar

1/2 cup finely chopped nuts

1 1/2 teaspoons ground cinnamon

Coffee Cake

3 cups all-purpose or whole wheat flour

1 1/2 teaspoons baking powder

1 1/2 teaspoons baking soda

3/4 teaspoon salt

1 1/2 cups granulated sugar

3/4 cup butter or margarine, softened

1 1/2 teaspoons vanilla

3 eggs

1 1/2 cups sour cream

Glaze

1/2 cup powdered sugar

1/4 teaspoon vanilla

2 to 3 teaspoons milk

1. Heat oven to 350°F. Grease bottom and side of 10 × 4–inch angel food cake pan (tube pan), 12-cup fluted tube cake pan or two 9 × 5–inch loaf pans with shortening or cooking spray.

2. In small bowl, stir all filling ingredients until well mixed; set aside. In large bowl, stir flour, baking powder, baking soda and salt until well mixed; set aside.

3. In another large bowl, beat granulated sugar, butter, 1 1/2 teaspoons vanilla and eggs with electric mixer on medium speed 2 minutes, scraping bowl occasionally. Beat about one-fourth of the flour mixture and sour cream at a time alternately into sugar mixture on low speed until blended.

4. For angel food or fluted tube cake pan, spread one-third of the batter (about 2 cups) in pan, then sprinkle with one-third of the filling; repeat twice. For loaf pans, spread one-fourth of the batter (about 1 1/2 cups) in each pan, then sprinkle each with one-fourth of the filling; repeat once.

5. Bake angel food or fluted tube cake pan about 1 hour, loaf pans about 45 minutes, or until toothpick inserted near center comes out clean. Cool 10 minutes in pan(s) on wire rack. Remove from pan(s) to wire rack. Cool 20 minutes. In small bowl, stir all glaze ingredients until smooth and thin enough to drizzle. Drizzle glaze over coffee cake. Serve warm or cool.

1 SERVING: Calories 360 (Calories from Fat 150); Total Fat 16g (Saturated Fat 8g; Trans Fat 0.5g); Cholesterol 75mg; Sodium 360mg; Total Carbohydrate 49g (Dietary Fiber 1g; Sugars 30g); Protein 5g; % DAILY VALUE: Vitamin A 10%; Vitamin C 0%; Calcium 6%; Iron 8%; EXCHANGES: 1 1/2 Starch, 2 Other Carbohydrate, 3 Fat; CARBOHYDRATE CHOICES: 3

holiday inspiration

The classics never go out of style, so you just can't go wrong with this superb-tasting, moist coffee cake. You may know it by its other names, Jewish Coffee Cake or Jewish Sour Cream Coffee Cake.

CANDY CANE COFFEE CAKES

prep 45 min *total time* 3 hrs

makes 3 coffee cakes (12 servings each)

Coffee Cakes

2 packages regular or fast-acting dry yeast

1/2 cup warm water (105°F to 115°F)

1 1/4 cups buttermilk

2 eggs

5 1/2 to 6 cups bread flour or all-purpose flour

1/2 cup butter or margarine, softened

1/2 cup granulated sugar

2 teaspoons baking powder

2 teaspoons salt

1 1/2 cups cherry-flavored dried cranberries

1 1/2 cups chopped drained maraschino cherries

Glaze

1 cup powdered sugar

1 to 2 tablespoons milk or water

1/4 teaspoon almond extract

Garnish

1/3 cup sliced almonds, toasted (page 110), if desired

1. In large bowl, dissolve yeast in warm water. Add buttermilk, eggs, 2 1/2 cups of the flour, the butter, granulated sugar, baking powder and salt. Beat with electric mixer on low speed 30 seconds, scraping bowl constantly. Beat on medium speed 2 minutes, scraping bowl frequently. Stir in enough remaining flour to make dough easy to handle. (Dough should remain soft and sticky.)

2. Grease 3 cookie sheets with shortening or cooking spray. On lightly floured surface, knead dough about 5 minutes or until smooth and springy. Divide dough into 3 equal parts. Roll one part into 15 × 9–inch rectangle. Place rectangle on cookie sheet.

3. Mix cranberries and cherries. Spread one-third of the cranberry mixture in a strip about 2 1/2 inches wide lengthwise down center of rectangle. Make cuts in dough at 1/2-inch intervals on both 15-inch sides almost to filling. Fold strips over filling, overlapping and crossing in center. Carefully stretch dough until 22 inches long; curve one end to form top of cane. Repeat with remaining 2 parts of dough. Cover; let rise in warm place about 1 hour or until double in size. (Dough is ready if indentation remains when touched.)

4. Heat oven to 375°F. Bake 1 coffee cake at time (refrigerate remaining coffee cakes while others bake). Bake 20 to 25 minutes or until golden brown. Meanwhile, in small bowl, mix all glaze ingredients until smooth and thin enough to drizzle. Drizzle glaze over warm coffee cakes. Decorate with almonds.

1 SERVING: Calories 160 (Calories from Fat 30); Total Fat 3g (Saturated Fat 1.5g; Trans Fat 0g); Cholesterol 20mg; Sodium 190mg; Total Carbohydrate 30g (Dietary Fiber 1g; Sugars 13g); Protein 3g; **% DAILY VALUE:** Vitamin A 2%; Vitamin C 0%; Calcium 4%; Iron 6%; **EXCHANGES:** 1 Starch, 1 Other Carbohydrate, 1/2 Fat; **CARBOHYDRATE CHOICES**

COCOA PECAN RING

prep 25 min *total time* 2 hrs 30 min *makes* 12 servings

Coffee Cake

1 package regular or fast-acting dry yeast

3/4 cup warm water (105°F to 115°F)

1/3 cup unsweetened baking cocoa

1/4 cup granulated sugar

1/4 cup shortening

1/2 teaspoon salt

1 egg

2 1/4 cups all-purpose flour

1/4 cup granulated sugar

1/2 cup finely chopped pecans or walnuts

Glaze

1/2 cup powdered sugar

1/4 teaspoon vanilla

1 to 2 teaspoons milk

Garnish, if desired

Chocolate-dipped blanched almonds

1. In large bowl, dissolve yeast in warm water. Add cocoa, 1/4 cup granulated sugar, the shortening, salt, egg and 1 cup of the flour. Beat with electric mixer on low speed 30 seconds, scraping bowl constantly. Beat on medium speed 2 minutes, scraping bowl occasionally. Stir in remaining flour until smooth. Scrape dough from side of bowl. Cover; let rise in warm place about 1 hour or until double in size.

2. Grease 12-cup fluted tube cake pan with shortening or cooking spray. In small bowl, mix 1/4 cup granulated sugar and the pecans. Stir down dough by beating about 25 strokes. Drop dough by heaping teaspoonfuls into sugar-pecan mixture, coating each ball of dough. Place in pan, making 2 layers of balls. Cover; let rise in warm place about 40 minutes or until double in size.

3. Heat oven to 375°F. Bake about 25 minutes or until golden brown. Place heatproof serving plate upside down onto pan; turn plate and pan over. Carefully remove pan. Cool slightly. In small bowl, mix all glaze ingredients with spoon until smooth and thin enough to drizzle. Drizzle glaze over coffee cake. Garnish with almonds. Serve warm.

1 SERVING: Calories 230 (Calories from Fat 80); Total Fat 9g (Saturated Fat 1.5g; Trans Fat 0.5g); Cholesterol 20mg; Sodium 105mg; Total Carbohydrate 33g (Dietary Fiber 2g; Sugars 13g); Protein 4g; % DAILY VALUE: Vitamin A 0%; Vitamin C 0%; Calcium 0%; Iron 10%; EXCHANGES: 1 Starch, 1 Other Carbohydrate, 2 Fat; CARBOHYDRATE CHOICES: 2

TURTLE PECAN RING Omit glaze and chocolate-dipped blanched almonds. Instead, drizzle with caramel topping and sprinkle with toasted chopped pecans and miniature semisweet chocolate chips.

from the heart

THE CANDY CANE COFFEE CAKES are perfect for gift giving, placed on a decorative plastic platter, wrapped in holiday cellophane and decorated with ribbon. Look for decorative plastic serving pieces and the cellophane in party stores.

SAINT LUCIA CROWN

prep 40 min *total time* 4 hrs 20 min

makes 1 large loaf (32 slices)

Coffee Cake

1/16 to 1/8 teaspoon crushed saffron or 2 or 3 drops yellow food color

1/2 cup warm milk (105°F to 115°F)

2 packages regular or fast-acting dry yeast

1/2 cup warm water (105°F to 115°F)

1/2 cup granulated sugar

1 teaspoon salt

2 eggs, beaten

1/4 cup butter or margarine, softened

4 1/2 to 5 cups bread flour or all-purpose flour

1/2 cup chopped citron or lemon peel

1/4 cup chopped blanched almonds

1 tablespoon grated lemon peel

Glaze

1 cup powdered sugar

1 to 2 tablespoons milk or water

Garnish, if desired

Green and red candied cherries

1. Stir saffron into warm milk. In large bowl, dissolve yeast in warm water. Stir in saffron-milk mixture, granulated sugar, salt, eggs, butter and 2 1/2 cups of the flour. Beat with spoon until smooth. Stir in citron, almonds, lemon peel and enough remaining flour to make dough easy to handle.

2. Place dough on lightly floured surface. Knead about 10 minutes or until smooth and springy. Grease large bowl with shortening. Place dough in bowl, turning dough to grease all sides. Cover; let rise in warm place about 1 hour 30 minutes or until double in size. (Dough is ready if indentation remains when touched.)

3. Grease 2 cookie sheets with shortening or cooking spray. Gently push fist into dough to deflate. Cut off one-third of dough for top braid and reserve. Divide remaining dough into 3 equal parts; roll each part into 25-inch rope. Place ropes close together on cookie sheet. Braid ropes loosely; shape into circle and pinch ends to seal.

4. Divide reserved dough into 3 equal parts; roll each part into 16-inch rope. Place ropes close together on second cookie sheet. Braid ropes loosely; shape into circle and pinch ends to seal. Cover both braids; let rise in warm place about 45 minutes or until double in size.

5. Heat oven to 375°F. Bake 20 to 25 minutes or until golden brown. Remove from cookie sheets to wire rack. Cool completely, about 1 hour.

6. In small bowl, mix glaze ingredients with spoon until smooth and thin enough to drizzle. Drizzle glaze over both braids. Make holes for 5 candles in small braid. Place small braid on large braid. Garnish with cherries. Insert candles.

1 SLICE: Calories 130 (Calories from Fat 25); Total Fat 2.5g (Saturated Fat 1g; Trans Fat 0g); Cholesterol 15mg; Sodium 90mg; Total Carbohydrate 24g (Dietary Fiber 0g; Sugars 9g); Protein 3g; % DAILY VALUE: Vitamin A 0%; Vitamin C 0%; Calcium 0%; Iron 6%; EXCHANGES: 1 Starch, 1/2 Other Carbohydrate, 1/2 Fat; CARBOHYDRATE CHOICES: 1 1/2

SAINT LUCIA BUNS After deflating dough, cut dough into pieces, 2 1/2 inches in diameter. Roll each piece into 12-inch rope; form into tightly coiled S shape. Place a raisin in center of each coil. Place on greased cookie sheet. Brush tops lightly with softened butter or margarine. Cover and let rise in warm place about 45 minutes or until double in size. Bake about 15 minutes or until golden brown. About 1 1/2 dozen buns.

holiday inspiration

Saint Lucia Day is the Swedish holiday celebrated on December 13. Saint Lucia, a beautiful maiden, wore a crown of candles to help light the way when she carried food to Christian martyrs hiding in caves from persecution. Since then, Saint Lucia Day is celebrated by having the oldest daughter be the first to rise and bring buns to all who are sleeping in the household.

JULEKAKE

prep 25 min   *total time* 3 hrs 20 min
makes 1 loaf (16 slices)

1 package regular or fast-acting dry yeast

1/4 cup very warm water (120°F to 130°F)

3/4 cup very warm milk (120°F to 130°F)

1/2 cup sugar

2 tablespoons shortening

1/2 teaspoon salt

1/2 teaspoon ground cardamom

1 egg

1/2 cup raisins

1/3 cup fruitcake mix (mixed candied fruit)

3 1/4 to 3 3/4 cups bread flour or all-purpose flour

1 egg yolk

2 tablespoons water

1. In large bowl, dissolve yeast in warm water. Stir in warm milk, sugar, shortening, salt, cardamom, egg, raisins, fruitcake mix and 1 1/2 cups of the flour. Beat with spoon until smooth. Stir in enough remaining flour to make dough easy to handle.

2. Place dough on lightly floured surface. Knead about 5 minutes or until smooth and springy. Grease large bowl with shortening. Place dough in bowl, turning dough to grease all sides. Cover; let rise in warm place about 1 hour 30 minutes or until double in size. (Dough is ready if indentation remains when touched.)

3. Grease 9-inch round pan with shortening. Gently push fist into dough to deflate. Shape into round loaf. Place in pan. Cover; let rise in warm place about 45 minutes or until double in size.

4. Heat oven to 350°F. In small bowl, beat egg yolk and 2 tablespoons water; brush over dough. Bake 30 to 40 minutes or until golden brown.

1 SLICE: Calories 180 (Calories from Fat 25); Total Fat 3g (Saturated Fat 1g; Trans Fat 0g); Cholesterol 25mg; Sodium 90mg; Total Carbohydrate 35g (Dietary Fiber 1g; Sugars 12g); Protein 4g; % DAILY VALUE: Vitamin A 0%; Vitamin C 0%; Calcium 2%; Iron 8%; EXCHANGES: 1 Starch, 1 1/2 Other Carbohydrate, 1/2 Fat; CARBOHYDRATE CHOICES: 2

holiday inspiration

Candied fruit and cardamom are the signature traditional ingredients in this Norwegian classic. Cardamom (KAR-duh-muhm), a member of the ginger family, has a pungent, warm, spicy and slight lemony-sweet flavor. It's used extensively in Scandinavian and East Indian cooking. Look for ground cardamom in the spices and herbs section of your store.

EASY CARAMEL STICKY ROLLS

prep 10 min   *total time* 35 min   *makes* 6 rolls

1/2 cup packed brown sugar

1/2 cup whipping (heavy) cream

1/4 cup chopped pecans

2 tablespoons granulated sugar

1 teaspoon ground cinnamon

1 can (11 oz) refrigerated soft breadsticks

1. Heat oven to 350°F. In ungreased 8-inch round pan, mix brown sugar and whipping cream. Sprinkle with pecans.

2. In small bowl, mix granulated sugar and cinnamon. Unroll breadstick dough, but do not separate into breadsticks. Sprinkle cinnamon-sugar mixture over dough. Roll up dough from short end; separate at perforations. Place coiled dough in pan.

3. Bake 20 to 25 minutes or until golden brown. Cool 1 minute. Place heatproof serving plate upside down onto pan; turn plate and pan over. Let pan remain 1 minute so caramel can drizzle over rolls.

1 ROLL: Calories 320 (Calories from Fat 110); Total Fat 12g (Saturated Fat 4.5g; Trans Fat 1g); Cholesterol 20mg; Sodium 380mg; Total Carbohydrate 49g (Dietary Fiber 1g; Sugars 26g); Protein 5g; % DAILY VALUE: Vitamin A 4%; Vitamin C 0%; Calcium 4%; Iron 10%; EXCHANGES: 1 1/2 Starch, 2 Other Carbohydrate, 2 Fat; CARBOHYDRATE CHOICES: 3

EASY CARAMEL APPLE STICKY ROLLS Omit the cinnamon-sugar mixture and spread 1/3 cup cinnamon-flavored applesauce over dough.

holiday inspiration

Serve these gooey rolls with a platter of fresh fruit, Canadian-style bacon slices and a pot of fresh-brewed coffee for a fast and fabulous holiday breakfast.

MAKE-AHEAD POTATO ROLL DOUGH

prep 30 min   *total time* 9 hrs 45 min
makes 64 crescent rolls

1 package regular active dry yeast
1 1/2 cups warm water (105°F to 115°F)
1 cup lukewarm unseasoned mashed potatoes
2/3 cup sugar
2/3 cup butter or margarine, softened
1 1/2 teaspoons salt
2 eggs
7 to 7 1/2 cups all-purpose flour

1. In large bowl, dissolve yeast in warm water. Stir in potatoes, sugar, butter, salt, eggs and 3 cups of the flour. Beat with electric mixer on low speed until smooth. Beat on medium speed 1 minute, scraping bowl frequently. Stir in enough remaining flour to make dough easy to handle.

2. Place dough on lightly floured surface; gently roll in flour to coat. Knead about 5 minutes or until dough is smooth and springy. Grease large bowl with shortening. Place dough in bowl, turning dough to grease all sides. Cover bowl tightly with plastic wrap and refrigerate at least 8 hours but no longer than 5 days.

3. Gently push fist into dough to deflate. Divide dough into 4 equal pieces. Use one-fourth of the dough for any dinner roll recipe below.

1 ROLL: Calories 80 (Calories from Fat 20); Total Fat 2.5g (Saturated Fat 1g; Trans Fat 0g); Cholesterol 10mg; Sodium 75mg; Total Carbohydrate 13g (Dietary Fiber 0g; Sugars 2g); Protein 2g; % DAILY VALUE: Vitamin A 0%; Vitamin C 0%; Calcium 0%; Iron 4%; EXCHANGES: 1 Starch, 1/2 Fat; CARBOHYDRATE CHOICES: 1

CRESCENT ROLLS Grease cookie sheet with shortening or cooking spray. Roll one-fourth of potato roll dough into 12-inch circle about 1/4 inch thick on well-floured surface. Spread with softened butter or margarine. Cut circle into 16 wedges. Roll up each wedge, beginning at rounded edge, stretching dough as it is rolled. Place rolls, with points underneath, on cookie sheet and curve slightly. Brush with softened butter or margarine. Cover and let rise in warm place about 1 hour or until dough is double in size. Heat oven to 400°F. Bake 15 minutes. 16 rolls.

FOUR-LEAF CLOVERS Grease bottoms and sides of 8 to 10 regular-size muffin cups with shortening or cooking spray. Shape one-fourth of potato roll dough into 2-inch balls. Place 1 ball in each muffin cup. With kitchen scissors, snip each ball completely in half, then into fourths. Brush with softened butter or margarine. Cover and let rise in warm place about 1 hour or until dough is double in size. Heat oven to 400°F. Bake 15 to 20 minutes. 8 to 10 rolls.

MAKE-AHEAD BROWN-AND-SERVE ROLLS Shape potato roll dough for Crescent Rolls or Four-Leaf Clovers as directed above. Cover and let rise in warm place 1 hour. Heat oven to 275°F. Bake 20 minutes (do not allow to brown). Remove from pans; cool to room temperature. Wrap in foil. Store in refrigerator up to 8 days or in freezer up to 2 months. At serving time, heat oven to 400°F. Bake 8 to 12 minutes or until brown.

MAKE-AHEAD WHOLE WHEAT–POTATO ROLL DOUGH Substitute 3 to 4 cups whole wheat flour for the second addition of all-purpose flour.

holiday inspiration

The next time somebody asks if you would like to bring some bread to a potluck or dinner party, say yes with confidence, and pull out this super do-ahead recipe for light and tender homemade rolls.

JOYFUL DESSERTS

DECADENT CHOCOLATE CAKE
with RASPBERRY SAUCE

prep 40 min   *total time* 2 hrs 20 min   *makes* 12 servings

Cake

1 cup semisweet chocolate chips (6 oz)

1/2 cup butter or margarine

1/2 cup all-purpose flour

4 eggs, separated

1/2 cup sugar

Raspberry Sauce

1 box (10 oz) frozen raspberries, thawed, drained and
    juice reserved

1/4 cup sugar

2 tablespoons cornstarch

1 to 2 tablespoons orange- or raspberry-flavored
    liqueur, if desired

Glaze

1/2 cup semisweet chocolate chips

2 tablespoons butter or margarine

2 tablespoons light corn syrup

Garnish

1/2 cup whipped cream

Fresh raspberries, if desired

1. Heat oven to 325°F. Grease bottom and side of 8 × 2 1/2-inch springform pan or 9 × 1 1/2–inch round pan with shortening. In 2-quart heavy saucepan, melt 1 cup chocolate chips and 1/2 cup butter over medium heat, stirring occasionally; cool 5 minutes. Stir in flour until smooth. Stir in egg yolks until well blended; set aside.

2. In large bowl, beat egg whites with electric mixer on high speed until foamy. Beat in 1/2 cup sugar, 1 tablespoon at a time, until soft peaks form. Gently stir chocolate mixture into egg whites. Spread in pan.

3. Bake springform pan 35 to 40 minutes, round pan 30 to 35 minutes, or until toothpick inserted in center comes out clean (top will appear dry and cracked); cool 10 minutes. Run knife along side of cake to loosen; remove side of springform pan. Turn cake upside down onto wire rack; remove bottom of springform pan and cool completely, about 1 hour.

4. Meanwhile, add enough water to reserved raspberry juice to measure 1 cup. In 1-quart saucepan, mix 1/4 cup sugar and the cornstarch. Stir in juice and thawed raspberries. Heat to boiling over medium heat. Boil and stir 1 minute; strain through strainer or colander to remove seeds. Stir in liqueur; set aside.

5. Place cake on serving plate. In 1-quart saucepan, heat 1/2 cup chocolate chips, 2 tablespoons butter and the corn syrup over medium heat, stirring occasionally, until chips are melted. Spread over top of cake, allowing some to drizzle down side. Place whipped cream in decorating bag fitted with star tip. Pipe a rosette on each serving. Serve cake with sauce. Garnish with fresh raspberries.

1 SERVING: Calories 370 (Calories from Fat 190); Total Fat 21g (Saturated Fat 11g; Trans Fat 0.5g); Cholesterol 110mg; Sodium 95mg; Total Carbohydrate 40g (Dietary Fiber 2g; Sugars 31g); Protein 4g; **% DAILY VALUE:** Vitamin A 10%; Vitamin C 4%; Calcium 2%; Iron 8%; **EXCHANGES:** 1 Starch, 1 1/2 Other Carbohydrate, 4 Fat; **CARBOHYDRATE CHOICES:** 2 1/2

holiday inspiration

Be as creative as you like with the chocolate glaze! Drizzle it over the cake using a fork, or place it in a food-storage plastic bag and squeeze it through a snipped-off corner.

WHITE CHOCOLATE–ALMOND TORTE

prep 40 min *total time* 3 hrs 25 min *makes* 12 servings

Torte

1 cup slivered almonds (6 oz)

1 3/4 cups all-purpose flour

1 teaspoon baking powder

1/4 teaspoon salt

1/2 cup butter or margarine, softened

3/4 cup granulated sugar

3 eggs

1/4 cup milk

1 tablespoon almond-flavored liqueur or 1/2 teaspoon almond extract

1 teaspoon vanilla

6 oz white chocolate baking bars, chopped

White Chocolate Frosting

4 oz white chocolate baking bars, chopped

2 tablespoons boiling water

1 teaspoon vanilla

3/4 cup butter or margarine, softened

2 1/2 cups powdered sugar

1. Heat oven to 325°F. Grease bottom and side of 9- or 10-inch springform pan with shortening; lightly flour. Place almonds on ungreased cookie sheet; bake 4 to 7 minutes, stirring occasionally, until lightly browned. Reserve 2 tablespoons almonds for garnish. Place remaining almonds in food processor or blender. Cover; process until almonds are ground; set aside.

2. In small bowl, mix flour, baking powder and salt; set aside. In large bowl, beat 1/2 cup butter and the granulated sugar with electric mixer on medium speed, scraping bowl occasionally, until fluffy. Add eggs one at a time, beating on high speed after each addition until smooth and blended. Add milk, liqueur, 1 teaspoon vanilla, the flour mixture and ground almonds; beat on medium speed until smooth. Stir in 6 ounces white chocolate. Spread batter in pan.

3. Bake 50 to 55 minutes or until center springs back when lightly touched and top is evenly browned. Cool 15 minutes; remove side of pan. Cool completely, about 1 hour 30 minutes.

4. Meanwhile, in 2-quart saucepan, heat 4 ounces white chocolate and boiling water over low heat, stirring constantly, just until chocolate is melted. Stir in 1 teaspoon vanilla; cool to room temperature. In large bowl, beat 3/4 cup butter on medium speed until fluffy. Gradually beat in cooled white chocolate mixture and powdered sugar until smooth.

5. Run long knife under cake to loosen from pan bottom; transfer to serving plate. Spread frosting over side and top of torte. Garnish with reserved toasted almonds.

1 SERVING: Calories 630 (Calories from Fat 320); Total Fat 36g (Saturated Fat 15g; Trans Fat 1g); Cholesterol 105mg; Sodium 260mg; Total Carbohydrate 69g (Dietary Fiber 2g; Sugars 53g); Protein 8g; **% DAILY VALUE:** Vitamin A 15%; Vitamin C 0%; Calcium 15%; Iron 10%; **EXCHANGES:** 1 1/2 Starch, 3 Other Carbohydrate, 1/2 Medium-Fat Meat, 6 1/2 Fat; **CARBOHYDRATE CHOICES:** 4 1/2

holiday inspiration

Crown the top of this decadent torte with sugared fresh cranberries. Brush cranberries with light corn syrup. Sprinkle with sugar; let stand uncovered until you're ready to add the garnish to the top of the cake.

PEPPERMINT CREAM BROWNIE TORTE

prep 30 min *total time* 2 hrs *makes* 9 servings

Torte
1 box (1 lb 6.5 oz) supreme brownie mix with chocolate syrup pouch

1/4 cup water

1/3 cup vegetable oil

2 eggs

Ganache
1/4 cup whipping (heavy) cream

1/2 cup semisweet chocolate chips

Peppermint Cream
1/2 cup whipping (heavy) cream

4 oz cream cheese (half of 8-oz package), softened

1/4 cup powdered sugar

1/2 teaspoon peppermint extract

Garnish
10 to 12 hard peppermint candies, coarsely crushed

Chocolate Trees, if desired (at right)

1. Heat oven to 350°F. Line 13 × 9–inch pan with 17 × 12–inch sheet of foil. Grease bottom only of foil with shortening. Make brownie mix as directed on box, using water, oil and eggs. Spread batter in pan. Bake as directed. Cool completely in pan on wire rack, about 1 hour.

2. Meanwhile, in 1-quart saucepan, heat 1/4 cup whipping cream over low heat until hot but not boiling; remove from heat. Stir in chocolate chips until melted. Let stand at room temperature about 1 hour or until slightly thickened.

3. In medium bowl, beat 1/2 cup whipping cream with electric mixer on high speed until soft peaks form; set aside. In another medium bowl, beat remaining peppermint cream ingredients on low speed until blended; beat on medium speed until smooth. Fold whipped cream into cream cheese mixture; refrigerate until using.

4. Remove brownies from pan, using foil to lift. Cut brownies crosswise to make 3 equal rectangles. Trim sides if desired. To assemble torte, place 1 brownie rectangle on serving platter; spread with 2/3 cup peppermint cream. Top with second brownie rectangle; spread with ganache. Top with third brownie rectangle; spread with remaining cream. Refrigerate uncovered until serving. Just before serving, sprinkle with candies and arrange Chocolate Trees on top. Store covered in refrigerator.

1 SERVING: Calories 570 (Calories from Fat 240); Total Fat 27g (Saturated Fat 12g; Trans Fat 1.5g); Cholesterol 90mg; Sodium 300mg; Total Carbohydrate 76g (Dietary Fiber 3g; Sugars 57g); Protein 5g; % DAILY VALUE: Vitamin A 10%; Vitamin C 0%; Calcium 8%; Iron 20%; EXCHANGES: 1 Starch, 4 Other Carbohydrate, 5 1/2 Fat; CARBOHYDRATE CHOICES: 5

CHOCOLATE TREES
1 cup semisweet chocolate chips (6 oz)

1 teaspoon shortening

1. Line cookie sheet with a sheet of cooking parchment paper or waxed paper. On paper, draw 1 1/2- to 2-inch tree outlines or trace around 2-inch tree-shaped cookie cutter, leaving 1/2 inch space between each tree. Center toothpick at bottom of and 1/2 inch into each tree outline.

2. In 1-quart saucepan, heat chocolate chips and shortening over low heat, stirring constantly, until chips are melted. Pour chocolate into decorating bag fitted with plain tip; or pour chocolate into resealable food-storage plastic bag and snip off one small corner of bag.

3. Starting at top of each tree outline, pipe chocolate over tree and end of toothpick within tree; fill center with random, squiggly lines. Refrigerate until chocolate hardens. Gently remove trees from paper; refrigerate until serving.

Pipe chocolate over outline of tree and end of toothpick within tree.

holiday inspiration
For a sparkling finish, sprinkle white decorator
sugar crystals over the top of the torte.

MOLTEN CHOCOLATE CAKES

prep 20 min   *total time* 40 min   *makes* 6 servings

Unsweetened baking cocoa
6 oz semisweet baking chocolate, chopped
1/2 cup plus 2 tablespoons butter or margarine
3 whole eggs
3 egg yolks
1 1/2 cups powdered sugar
1/2 cup all-purpose flour
Additional powdered sugar, if desired

1. Heat oven to 450°F. Grease bottoms and sides of six 6-ounce custard cups with shortening; dust with cocoa.*

2. In 2-quart saucepan, melt chocolate and butter over low heat, stirring frequently. Cool slightly.

3. In large bowl, beat whole eggs and egg yolks with wire whisk or hand beater until well blended. Beat in 1 1/2 cups powdered sugar. Beat in melted chocolate mixture and flour. Divide batter evenly among custard cups. Place cups on cookie sheet with sides.

4. Bake 12 to 14 minutes or until sides are set and centers are still soft (tops will be puffed and cracked). Let stand 3 minutes. Run small knife or metal spatula along sides of cakes to loosen. Immediately place heatproof serving plate upside down onto each cup; turn plate and cup over and remove cup. Sprinkle with additional powdered sugar. Serve warm.

*Be sure to grease the custard cups with shortening, dust the cups with cocoa and bake the cakes at the correct oven temperature for the right time. These steps are critical to the success of this recipe. If the centers are too cakelike in texture, bake a few minutes less the next time; if they're too soft, bake a minute or two longer.

1 SERVING: Calories 580 (Calories from Fat 360); Total Fat 40g (Saturated Fat 21g; Trans Fat 1g); Cholesterol 265mg; Sodium 170mg; Total Carbohydrate 46g (Dietary Fiber 5g; Sugars 30g); Protein 9g; % DAILY VALUE: Vitamin A 20%; Vitamin C 0%; Calcium 6%; Iron 15%; EXCHANGES: 1 Starch, 2 Other Carbohydrate, 1 Medium-Fat Meat, 7 Fat; CARBOHYDRATE CHOICES: 3

make-ahead magic

To make ahead, prepare the cake batter and pour into custard cups as directed; cover with plastic wrap and refrigerate up to 24 hours. You may need to bake the cakes 1 to 2 minutes longer.

holiday inspiration

Watch out, these are going to disappear fast! These cakes have a hot, flowing chocolate center that oozes out when you cut into them. Chances are your family wouldn't say no if you wanted to make these for a "trial run" before making them for company.

GOLDEN POUND CAKE

prep 15 min *total time* 3 hrs 10 min *makes* 16 servings

3 cups all-purpose flour
1 teaspoon baking powder
1/4 teaspoon salt
2 3/4 cups sugar
1 1/4 cups butter or margarine, softened
1 teaspoon vanilla
5 eggs
1 cup evaporated milk (from 12-oz can)

1. Heat oven to 325°F. Grease 12-cup fluted tube cake pan or 10 × 4–inch angel food cake pan (tube pan) with shortening (do not use cooking spray); lightly flour. In medium bowl, mix flour, baking powder and salt; set aside.

2. In large bowl, beat sugar, butter, vanilla and eggs with electric mixer on low speed 30 seconds, scraping bowl constantly. Beat on high speed 5 minutes, scraping bowl occasionally. Beat in flour mixture alternately with milk on low speed. Pour into pan.

3. Bake 1 hour 25 minutes to 1 hour 35 minutes or until toothpick inserted in center comes out clean. Cool 20 minutes; remove from pan to wire rack. Cool completely, about 1 hour.

1 SERVING: Calories 390 (Calories from Fat 150); Total Fat 17g (Saturated Fat 8g; Trans Fat 1g); Cholesterol 105mg; Sodium 200mg; Total Carbohydrate 54g (Dietary Fiber 0g; Sugars 36g); Protein 6g; **% DAILY VALUE:** Vitamin A 15%; Vitamin C 0%; Calcium 8%; Iron 8%; **EXCHANGES:** 2 Starch, 1 1/2 Other Carbohydrate, 3 Fat; **CARBOHYDRATE CHOICES:** 3 1/2

ALMOND POUND CAKE Substitute 1 teaspoon almond extract for the vanilla.

LEMON POUND CAKE Substitute 1 teaspoon lemon extract for the vanilla, and fold 2 to 3 teaspoons grated lemon peel into batter.

ORANGE-COCONUT POUND CAKE Fold 1 1/3 cups flaked coconut and 2 to 3 tablespoons shredded orange peel into batter.

TRIPLE-GINGER POUND CAKE Add 1 tablespoon grated gingerroot, 2 teaspoons ground ginger and 1/2 cup finely chopped crystallized ginger with the flour mixture.

holiday inspiration

If you want to send a buttery-sweet treat that will arrive in one piece, this pound cake, with its sturdy texture, is the perfect choice. Once completely cooled, tightly wrap it in several layers of foil. Put the cake in a heavy cardboard box surrounding it with cushioning packing material. As an extra measure of caution, ask the post office to put a fragile sticker on the box.

PEAR-GINGER UPSIDE-DOWN CAKE

prep 25 min   *total time* 1 hr 30 min   *makes* 8 servings

Pear-Ginger Topping

1/4 cup butter or margarine

2/3 cup packed brown sugar

1/2 teaspoon ground ginger

3 pears, peeled, cut into 1/2-inch wedges

1/4 cup finely chopped crystallized ginger

Cake

1 tablespoon all-purpose flour

1/4 cup finely chopped crystallized ginger

1 1/3 cups all-purpose flour

1 teaspoon baking powder

1/4 teaspoon salt

1 cup packed brown sugar

6 tablespoons butter or margarine, softened

2 eggs

1/2 teaspoon vanilla

1/4 cup milk

Ginger Whipped Cream

1 cup whipping (heavy) cream

2 tablespoons granulated sugar

1/4 teaspoon ground ginger

1. Heat oven to 325°F. Grease bottom and sides of 8- or 9-inch square pan with shortening. In 1-quart saucepan, melt 1/4 cup butter over medium heat, stirring occasionally. Stir in 2/3 cup brown sugar. Heat to boiling; remove from heat. Stir in 1/2 teaspoon ground ginger. Pour into pan; spread evenly. Arrange pear wedges on sugar mixture, overlapping tightly and making 2 layers if necessary. Sprinkle 1/4 cup crystallized ginger over pears.

2. In small bowl, toss 1 tablespoon flour and 1/4 cup crystallized ginger to coat; set aside. In another small bowl, mix 1 1/3 cups flour, the baking powder and salt; set aside. In large bowl, beat 1 cup brown sugar and 6 tablespoons butter with electric mixer on medium speed, scraping bowl occasionally, until fluffy. Beat in eggs, one at a time, until smooth. Add vanilla. Gradually beat in flour mixture alternately with milk, beating after each addition until smooth. Stir in ginger-flour mixture. Spread batter over pears in pan.

3. Bake 55 to 65 minutes or until toothpick inserted in center of cake comes out clean. Cool 15 minutes on wire rack. Meanwhile, in chilled medium bowl, beat whipping cream on high speed until it begins to thicken. Gradually add granulated sugar and 1/4 teaspoon ground ginger, beating until soft peaks form.

4. Loosen edges of cake with small knife. Place heatproof plate upside down onto pan; turn plate and pan over. Serve warm with ginger whipped cream.

1 SERVING: Calories 600 (Calories from Fat 250); Total Fat 27g (Saturated Fat 15g; Trans Fat 1g); Cholesterol 135mg; Sodium 290mg; Total Carbohydrate 84g (Dietary Fiber 3g; Sugars 62g); Protein 5g; % DAILY VALUE: Vitamin A 20%; Vitamin C 2%; Calcium 10%; Iron 15%; EXCHANGES: 1 1/2 Starch, 4 Other Carbohydrate, 5 1/2 Fat; CARBOHYDRATE CHOICES: 5 1/2

holiday inspiration

Ginger is one of the hallmark flavors of the season. If you've never tried crystallized ginger you're in for a real treat. Crystallized ginger is fresh gingerroot cooked in a sugar syrup and coated with sugar. Look for it in the spice section of the supermarket or in gourmet food shops. Fresh currants and fresh bay leaves make a splendid seasonal garnish on top of this cake!

CANDY CANE CAKE

prep 15 min *total time* 2 hrs 10 min
makes 16 to 24 servings

Cake
1 box (1 lb 2.25 oz) white cake mix with pudding
1 1/4 cups water
1/3 cup vegetable oil
3 egg whites
1/2 teaspoon red liquid food color
1/2 teaspoon peppermint extract

Glaze
1 cup powdered sugar
1 to 2 tablespoons milk
1/2 teaspoon vanilla or clear vanilla

1. Heat oven to 350°F. Generously grease 10- to 12-cup fluted tube cake pan with shortening or cooking spray; lightly flour. Make cake mix as directed on box, using water, oil and egg whites. Pour about 2 cups batter into pan. Into small bowl, pour about 3/4 cup batter; stir in food color and peppermint extract. Carefully pour pink batter over white batter in pan. Carefully pour remaining white batter over pink batter.

2. Bake 38 to 42 minutes or until toothpick inserted in center comes out clean. Cool 10 minutes. Remove from pan to wire rack or heatproof serving plate. Cool completely, about 1 hour.

3. In small bowl, mix powdered sugar, 1 tablespoon milk and the vanilla. Stir in additional milk, 1 teaspoon at a time, until smooth and consistency of thick syrup. Spread glaze over cake, allowing some to drizzle down side. Store loosely covered at room temperature.

1 SERVING: Calories 210 (Calories from Fat 70); Total Fat 7g (Saturated Fat 2g; Trans Fat 0.5g); Cholesterol 0mg; Sodium 230mg; Total Carbohydrate 33g (Dietary Fiber 0g; Sugars 21g); Protein 2g; **% DAILY VALUE:** Vitamin A 0%; Vitamin C 0%; Calcium 4%; Iron 4%; **EXCHANGES:** 1/2 Starch, 1 1/2 Other Carbohydrate, 1 1/2 Fat; **CARBOHYDRATE CHOICES:** 2

holiday inspiration

- Start with a cake mix and some red food color and you end up with a white-and-red-swirled cake that's perfect for your next potluck. This cake transports very well, so don't forget to pack a knife and spatula for serving.

- To expand on the candy cane theme, fill the open center of the cake with wrapped striped mint candies.

SNOWMAN CAKE

prep 30 min   *total time* 2 hrs 15 min
makes 12 to 16 servings

1 box (1 lb 2.25 oz) white cake mix with pudding
1 1/4 cups water
1/3 cup vegetable oil
3 egg whites
2 candy canes, unwrapped
2 flat-bottom ice-cream cones
Vanilla-flavored candy coating (almond bark), melted
1 container (1 lb) vanilla creamy frosting
1 bag (7 oz) flaked coconut (about 2 2/3 cups)
5 large black gumdrops
1 large orange gumdrop
7 small black gumdrops
2 pretzel rods

1. Heat oven to 350°F. Grease bottoms only of two 8- or 9-inch round pans with shortening or cooking spray. Make cake mix as directed on box, using water, oil and egg whites. Pour into pans.

2. Bake 8-inch rounds 27 to 32 minutes, 9-inch rounds 23 to 28 minutes, or until toothpick inserted in center comes out clean. Cool 10 minutes; remove from pans to wire rack. Cool completely, about 1 hour.

3. Cover large flat tray or piece of cardboard with foil. Attach candy cane to open end of each cone, using melted candy coating, to make ice skates; let stand until set. Arrange cake rounds with sides touching on tray. Frost top and sides of cake with frosting. Sprinkle with coconut, pressing gently so it stays on frosting.

4. Use large black gumdrops for eyes and buttons, large orange gumdrop for nose and small black gumdrops for mouth. Arrange pretzel rods for arms and cones for feet with ice skates. Store loosely covered at room temperature.

1 SERVING: Calories 540 (Calories from Fat 220); Total Fat 25g (Saturated Fat 11g; Trans Fat 3.5g); Cholesterol 0mg; Sodium 480mg; Total Carbohydrate 76g (Dietary Fiber 1g; Sugars 54g); Protein 3g; **% DAILY VALUE:** Vitamin A 0%; Vitamin C 0%; Calcium 6%; Iron 8%; **EXCHANGES:** 1 Starch, 4 Other Carbohydrate, 5 Fat; **CARBOHYDRATE CHOICES:** 5

new twist

Outfit your snowman with earmuffs and a scarf. For earmuffs, place a cream-filled chocolate sandwich cookie on each side of snowman's head, and connect them across the top of the head with black string licorice. For the scarf, any flavor of chewy fruit snack (from 3-foot roll) will work.

NUTCRACKER TORTE *with* RUM CREAM

prep 25 min *total time* 8 hrs *makes* 12 servings

Torte

6 eggs, separated
1/2 cup granulated sugar
2 tablespoons vegetable oil
1 tablespoon rum extract
1/2 cup granulated sugar
1/4 cup all-purpose flour
1 1/4 teaspoons baking powder
1 teaspoon ground cinnamon
1/2 teaspoon ground cloves
1 cup fine graham cracker crumbs (about 12 squares)
1 oz unsweetened baking chocolate, grated
1 cup finely chopped nuts

Rum Cream

2 cups whipping (heavy) cream
1/2 cup powdered sugar
2 teaspoons rum extract
White chocolate curls, if desired

1. Heat oven to 350°F. Line bottoms of two 8- or 9-inch round pans with foil. In large bowl, beat egg whites with electric mixer on high speed until foamy. Beat in 1/2 cup granulated sugar, 1 tablespoon at a time; continue beating until stiff and glossy.

2. In small bowl, beat egg yolks, oil and 1 table-spoon rum extract on low speed until blended. Add 1/2 cup granulated sugar, the flour, baking powder, cinnamon and cloves; beat on medium speed 1 minute. Fold egg yolk mixture into egg whites. Fold in cracker crumbs, chocolate and nuts. Pour into pans.

3. Bake 30 to 35 minutes or until tops spring back when touched lightly. Immediately turn pans upside down, resting rim of each pan on edges of two other upside-down pans. Cool completely, about 1 hour.

4. Loosen edge of each cake layer with knife. Turn each pan upside down and hit sharply on countertop to remove cake; remove foil. Cut each cake horizontally in half for a total of 4 layers. (To cut, mark side of cake with toothpicks and cut with long, thin serrated knife.)

5. In chilled large bowl, beat all rum cream ingredients on high speed until stiff. Fill cake layers and frost top of torte with rum cream. Sprinkle very lightly with additional cinnamon if desired and garnish with white chocolate curls. Refrigerate about 6 hours or until firm (torte will mellow and become moist). Store covered in refrigerator.

1 SERVING: Calories 410 (Calories from Fat 250); Total Fat 28g (Saturated Fat 12g; Trans Fat 0.5g); Cholesterol 160mg; Sodium 135mg; Total Carbohydrate 33g (Dietary Fiber 1g; Sugars 26g); Protein 6g; **% DAILY VALUE:** Vitamin A 15%; Vitamin C 0%; Calcium 8%; Iron 6%; **EXCHANGES:** 1/2 Starch, 1 1/2 Other Carbohydrate, 1/2 High-Fat Meat, 5 Fat; **CARBOHYDRATE CHOICES:** 2

holiday inspiration

Don't let beating up egg whites intimidate you—just follow these tips for success. Cold eggs separate best, making it much easier to cleanly separate the yolks from the whites. If even a speck of yolk or any other type of fat finds its way into egg whites, they will not beat up to the stiff and glossy stage.

BÛCHE DE NOËL

prep 40 min   *total time* 1 hr 25 min   *makes* 10 servings

Cake

3 eggs

1 cup granulated sugar

1/3 cup water

1 teaspoon vanilla

3/4 cup all-purpose flour

1 teaspoon baking powder

1/4 teaspoon salt

Filling

1 cup whipping (heavy) cream

2 tablespoons granulated sugar

1 1/2 teaspoons instant coffee granules or crystals

Chocolate Buttercream Frosting

1/3 cup unsweetened baking cocoa

1/3 cup butter or margarine, softened

2 cups powdered sugar

1 1/2 teaspoons vanilla

1 to 2 tablespoons hot water

Garnish

1/4 cup chopped green pistachio nuts

1. Heat oven to 375°F. Line 15 × 10 × 1-inch pan with foil or waxed paper; grease with shortening or cooking spray. In small bowl, beat eggs with electric mixer on high speed about 5 minutes or until very thick and lemon colored. Pour eggs into large bowl; gradually beat in 1 cup granulated sugar. Beat in 1/3 cup water and the vanilla on low speed. Gradually add flour, baking powder and salt, beating just until batter is smooth. Pour into pan, spreading batter to corners.

2. Bake 12 to 15 minutes or until toothpick inserted in center comes out clean. Immediately loosen cake from edges of pan; invert onto towel generously sprinkled with powdered sugar. Carefully remove foil. Trim off stiff edges of cake if necessary. While hot, carefully roll cake and towel from narrow end. Cool on wire rack at least 30 minutes.

3. In chilled medium bowl, beat all filling ingredients on high speed until stiff. Unroll cake; remove towel. Spread filling over cake. Roll up cake.

4. In medium bowl, beat cocoa and butter on low speed until thoroughly mixed. Beat in powdered sugar until mixed. Beat in vanilla and enough of the hot water until frosting is smooth and spreadable.

5. For tree stump, cut off a 2-inch diagonal slice from one end of cake. Attach stump to one long side using 1 tablespoon frosting. Frost cake with remaining frosting. With tines of fork, make strokes in frosting to look like tree bark. Garnish with nuts.

1 SERVING: Calories 420 (Calories from Fat 170); Total Fat 18g (Saturated Fat 10g; Trans Fat 0.5g); Cholesterol 105mg; Sodium 180mg; Total Carbohydrate 58g (Dietary Fiber 2g; Sugars 47g); Protein 5g; % DAILY VALUE: Vitamin A 10%; Vitamin C 0%; Calcium 6%; Iron 8%; EXCHANGES: 1 Starch, 3 Other Carbohydrate, 3 1/2 Fat; CARBOHYDRATE CHOICES: 4

holiday inspiration

Get rave reviews with this beautiful holiday cake! The translation of this recipe title is "yule log." It's a traditional French Christmas cake shaped and decorated to look like a log. The typical finishing touches include mushroom-shaped baked meringues and "moss" made of chopped pistachio nuts. The time-consuming task of making the mushroom decoration isn't included here, but go ahead and decorate your masterpiece any way you please.

RASPBERRY POKE CAKE

prep 10 min   *total time* 3 hrs 45 min   *makes* 15 servings
see photo on page 188, top

1 box (1 lb 2.25 oz) white cake mix with pudding
1 1/4 cups water
1/3 cup vegetable oil
3 egg whites
1 box (4-serving size) raspberry-flavored gelatin
1 cup boiling water
1/2 cup cold water
2 cups frozen (thawed) whipped topping
Fresh raspberries and mint leaves, if desired

1. Heat oven to 350°F. Grease bottom only of 13 × 9–inch pan with shortening or cooking spray. Make cake mix as directed on box, using water, oil and egg whites. Pour into pan.

2. Bake 28 to 33 minutes or until toothpick inserted in center comes out clean. Cool completely, about 1 hour.

3. Pierce cake every 1/2 inch with fork. In small bowl, stir gelatin and boiling water until smooth; stir in cold water. Pour over cake. Run knife around side of pan to loosen cake. Refrigerate 2 hours. Spread whipped topping over top of cake; garnish with raspberries. Store covered in refrigerator.

1 SERVING: Calories 240 (Calories from Fat 90); Total Fat 10g (Saturated Fat 3.5g; Trans Fat 0.5g); Cholesterol 0mg; Sodium 270mg; Total Carbohydrate 35g (Dietary Fiber 0g; Sugars 22g); Protein 3g; **% DAILY VALUE:** Vitamin A 0%; Vitamin C 0%; Calcium 4%; Iron 4%; **EXCHANGES:** 1/2 Starch, 2 Other Carbohydrate, 2 Fat; **CARBOHYDRATE CHOICES:** 2

STRAWBERRY POKE CAKE Substitute strawberry gelatin for the raspberry gelatin, and garnish the cake with fresh strawberries.

new twist

Tint your whipped topping or whipping cream with green food color so the colors match the spirit of the season! To go all out, garnish with Chocolate Trees (page 194).

CHERRY-ALMOND TORTE

prep 20 min   *total time* 3 hrs 10 min
makes 12 servings

1 box (1 lb) white angel food cake mix
1 1/4 cups cold water
1/2 teaspoon almond extract
1 cup marshmallow creme
1 can (21 oz) cherry pie filling
1/4 cup sliced almonds, toasted (page 110)

1. Move oven rack to lowest position (remove other racks). Heat oven to 350°F. Make cake mix as directed on box, using cold water and adding almond extract with the water. Pour into ungreased 10-inch angel food (tube) cake pan.

2. Bake 37 to 47 minutes or until top is dark golden brown and cracks feel very dry and not sticky. Do not underbake. Immediately turn pan upside down onto glass bottle until cake is completely cool, about 2 hours.

3. Run knife around edges of cake; remove from pan. Cut cake to make 2 layers. (To cut, mark side of cake with toothpicks and cut with long serrated knife.)

4. On serving plate, place bottom layer. Spoon 2/3 cup of the marshmallow creme by heaping teaspoonfuls onto bottom layer. Spoon 1 cup of the pie filling between spoonfuls of marshmallow creme. Sprinkle with half of the almonds. Place other layer on top. Spoon remaining marshmallow creme and pie filling on top of cake, allowing pie filling to drizzle down sides. Sprinkle with remaining almonds. Store covered in refrigerator.

1 SERVING: Calories 240 (Calories from Fat 15); Total Fat 1.5g (Saturated Fat 0g; Trans Fat 0g); Cholesterol 0mg; Sodium 280mg; Total Carbohydrate 51g (Dietary Fiber 1g; Sugars 41g); Protein 4g; **% DAILY VALUE:** Vitamin A 0%; Vitamin C 2%; Calcium 6%; Iron 2%; **EXCHANGES:** 1/2 Starch, 3 Other Carbohydrate, 1/2 Fat; **CARBOHYDRATE CHOICES:** 3 1/2

LEMON-ALMOND TORTE Substitute 1 can (15.75 oz) lemon pie filling for the cherry pie filling.

holiday inspiration

Start with a purchased, round angel food cake instead of making it from the mix and you've got one of the easiest, prettiest desserts around! If you don't want to take the time to cut the cake into layers and fill it, just spoon the marshmallow creme and cherry pie filling on top of cake slices and sprinkle with the almonds.

PUMPKIN PIE

prep 30 min *total time* 3 hrs 45 min *makes* 8 servings

Pastry (page 58)
2 eggs
1/2 cup sugar
1 teaspoon ground cinnamon
1/2 teaspoon salt
1/2 teaspoon ground ginger
1/8 teaspoon ground cloves
1 can (15 oz) pumpkin (not pumpkin pie mix)
1 can (12 oz) evaporated milk
Whipped cream, if desired

1. Heat oven to 425°F. Make pastry, using 9-inch glass pie plate and following Steps 1, 2 and 3 of quiche recipe. Flute edge of pastry in pie plate as desired. Carefully line pastry with a double thickness of foil, gently pressing foil to bottom and side of pastry. Let foil extend over edge to prevent excessive browning. Bake 10 minutes; carefully remove foil and bake 2 to 4 minutes longer or until pastry just begins to brown and has become set. If crust bubbles, gently push bubbles down with back of spoon.

2. Meanwhile, in medium bowl, beat eggs slightly with wire whisk or hand beater. Beat in remaining ingredients except whipped cream.

3. Cover edge of pie crust with 2- to 3-inch strip of foil to prevent excessive browning; remove foil during last 15 minutes of baking. To prevent spilling filling, place pie plate on oven rack. Pour pumpkin mixture into hot pie crust.

4. Bake 15 minutes. Reduce oven temperature to 350°F. Bake about 45 minutes longer or until knife inserted in center comes out clean. Cool on wire rack 2 hours. Serve with whipped cream. After cooling, pie can remain at room temperature up to an additional 4 hours, then should be covered and refrigerated.

1 SERVING: Calories 240 (Calories from Fat 110); Total Fat 12g (Saturated Fat 3g; Trans Fat 1.5g); Cholesterol 55mg; Sodium 310mg; Total Carbohydrate 29g (Dietary Fiber 2g; Sugars 14g); Protein 4g; % DAILY VALUE: Vitamin A 170%; Vitamin C 0%; Calcium 2%; Iron 10%; EXCHANGES: 1 Starch, 1 Other Carbohydrate, 2 1/2 Fat; CARBOHYDRATE CHOICES: 2

PRALINE PUMPKIN PIE Make pie as directed—except decrease second bake time in step 4 to 35 minutes. Mix 1/3 cup packed brown sugar, 1/3 cup chopped pecans and 1 tablespoon butter or margarine, softened; sprinkle over pie. Bake about 10 minutes longer or until knife inserted in center comes out clean.

holiday inspiration

Be sure to use canned pumpkin, not pumpkin pie mix, in this recipe. The mix has sugar and spices already in it, so if you have purchased the pumpkin pie mix, follow the directions on that label.

Left to right: Pecan Pie (page 212) and Pumpkin Pie

CHOCOLATE DREAM TART

prep 10 min   *total time* 1 hr 50 min
makes 12 to 16 servings

1/3 cup butter or margarine, softened

1 cup all-purpose flour

1 egg

1 tablespoon butter or margarine

1 can (14 oz) sweetened condensed milk

1 bag (12 oz) semisweet chocolate chips (2 cups)

1/2 cup chopped walnuts

1 teaspoon vanilla

Unsweetened whipped cream, if desired

1. Heat oven to 400°F. In medium bowl, cut 1/3 cup butter into flour, using pastry blender (or pulling 2 table knives through ingredients in opposite directions), until mixture is crumbly. Stir in egg until dough forms. Press firmly and evenly against bottom and side of ungreased 9-inch tart pan with removable bottom. Bake 12 to 15 minutes or until golden brown; cool on wire rack.

2. Reduce oven temperature to 350°F. In 2-quart saucepan, melt 1 tablespoon butter over low heat. Stir in milk and chocolate chips. Cook over low heat, stirring occasionally, until chocolate is melted. Stir in walnuts and vanilla. Spread in baked crust.

3. Bake about 25 minutes or until edge is set but chocolate appears moist in center. Cool completely in pan on wire rack, about 1 hour. To serve, top each slice with whipped cream.

1 SERVING: Calories 390 (Calories from Fat 190); Total Fat 21g (Saturated Fat 10g; Trans Fat 0g); Cholesterol 45mg; Sodium 90mg; Total Carbohydrate 45g (Dietary Fiber 2g; Sugars 33g); Protein 6g; % DAILY VALUE: Vitamin A 8%; Vitamin C 0%; Calcium 10%; Iron 10%; EXCHANGES: 1 Starch, 2 Other Carbohydrate, 4 Fat; CARBOHYDRATE CHOICES: 3

new twist

To show off this wonderfully rich dessert, garnish with chocolate curls or dip ends of toasted walnut halves into melted chocolate and place on each serving with dollop of whipped cream.

make-ahead magic

To make ahead, tightly cover the completely cooled tart and refrigerate up to 3 days or freeze up to 2 months. About 1 hour before serving, unwrap frozen tart and let stand at room temperature to thaw.

PECAN PIE

prep 30 min   *total time* 1 hr 20 min   *makes* 8 servings
see photo on page 209

Pastry (page 58)
2/3 cup sugar
1/3 cup butter or margarine, melted
1 cup corn syrup
1/2 teaspoon salt
3 eggs
1 cup pecan halves or broken pecans
Whipped cream, if desired
Chopped pecans, if desired

1. Heat oven to 375°F. Make pastry, using 9-inch glass pie plate and following Steps 1, 2 and 3 of quiche recipe. Flute edge of pastry in pie plate as desired.

2. In medium bowl, beat sugar, butter, corn syrup, salt and eggs with wire whisk or hand beater until well blended. Stir in pecan halves. Pour into pastry-lined pie plate.

3. Bake 40 to 50 minutes or until center is set. Serve pie with whipped cream and chopped pecans.

1 SERVING: Calories 530 (Calories from Fat 260); Total Fat 29g (Saturated Fat 8g; Trans Fat 2g); Cholesterol 100mg; Sodium 420mg; Total Carbohydrate 62g (Dietary Fiber 2g; Sugars 33g); Protein 5g; % DAILY VALUE: Vitamin A 8%; Vitamin C 0%; Calcium 2%; Iron 8%; EXCHANGES: 2 Starch, 2 Other Carbohydrate, 5 1/2 Fat; CARBOHYDRATE CHOICES: 4

BRANDY-PECAN PIE Decrease corn syrup to 3/4 cup. Add 1/4 cup brandy to the filling ingredients.

CHOCOLATE-PECAN PIE Melt 2 oz unsweetened baking chocolate with the butter.

CRANBERRY-PECAN PIE Stir in 1 cup dried cranberries with the pecan halves.

HONEY-PECAN PIE Substitute 1/2 cup honey for 1/2 cup of the corn syrup.

ORANGE-PECAN PIE Mix 1 tablespoon grated orange peel with the pastry ingredients. Add 1 tablespoon orange-flavored liqueur to the filling ingredients.

PEANUT–CHOCOLATE CHIP PIE Substitute 1 cup salted peanuts for the pecans. After baking, sprinkle with 1/2 cup semisweet chocolate chips.

new twist

For a pie crust with a twist, braid the edge. Loosely braid three 1/4-inch pastry strips (from trimmed pastry), making the braid long enough to fit along the edge of the pie. Moisten edge of pie and place braid on top, pressing lightly to seal.

make-ahead magic

To make ahead, cool pie completely after baking. Freeze uncovered at least 3 hours. Wrap tightly and freeze up to 1 month. Before serving, unwrap pie and thaw in refrigerator 20 minutes.

FROSTY COFFEE-ALMOND PIE

prep 15 min *total time* 3 hrs 40 min
makes 8 servings

18 creme-filled chocolate sandwich cookies, finely
   crushed (about 1 1/2 cups)
3 tablespoons butter or margarine, melted
1 quart coffee ice cream, slightly softened
1/2 cup sliced almonds, toasted (page 110)
1 cup hot fudge sauce, warmed

1. In small bowl, mix crushed cookies and butter
until well blended. Press on bottom and up side of
ungreased 9-inch glass pie plate. Freeze about
15 minutes or until firm.

2. Carefully spread ice cream evenly in crust.
Sprinkle with almonds. Freeze about 3 hours or
until firm.

3. Remove pie from freezer about 10 minutes
before serving. Serve with hot fudge sauce. Store
covered in freezer.

1 SERVING: Calories 480 (Calories from Fat 210); Total Fat 23g (Saturated
Fat 10g; Trans Fat 2g); Cholesterol 35mg; Sodium 360mg; Total
Carbohydrate 61g (Dietary Fiber 4g; Sugars 42g); Protein 7g; % DAILY
VALUE: Vitamin A 10%; Vitamin C 0%; Calcium 15%; Iron 15%;
EXCHANGES: 2 Starch, 2 Other Carbohydrate, 4 1/2 Fat; CARBOHYDRATE
CHOICES: 4

new twist

Have fun picking the ice cream flavor for this
special treat. Try chocolate, vanilla, strawberry or
any flavor that you like and use a purchased chocolate crumb crust instead of making your own crust.

holiday inspiration

Don't want to worry about forgetting you left the
ice cream on the counter to soften? Just
microwave it on High 15 to 30 seconds.

FLUFFY PEPPERMINT PIE

prep 30 min   *total time* 5 hrs 55 min   *makes* 8 servings

1 1/2 cups thin chocolate wafer cookie crumbs
    (about 24 cookies)

2 tablespoons sugar

1/4 cup butter or margarine, melted

30 large marshmallows

1 can (14 oz) sweetened condensed milk

2 cups whipping (heavy) cream

3 drops red food color

2 teaspoons peppermint extract

1/4 cup crushed hard peppermint candies

1. Spray pie plate with cooking spray. In small bowl, mix cookie crumbs, sugar and butter. Press evenly in bottom and up side of 9-inch glass pie plate.

2. In large microwavable bowl, place marshmallows and milk. Microwave uncovered on High about 3 minutes, stirring once, until marshmallows are melted. Refrigerate about 25 minutes or until mixture mounds slightly when dropped from a spoon.

3. In chilled medium bowl, beat whipping cream, food color and peppermint extract with electric mixer on high speed until stiff. Stir marshmallow mixture until blended; fold into whipped cream. Fold in crushed candies. Mound mixture into crust. Cover; freeze about 5 hours or until frozen. Let stand at room temperature 10 to 15 minutes before cutting. Cover and freeze any remaining pie.

1 **SERVING:** Calories 670 (Calories from Fat 320); Total Fat 35g (Saturated Fat 20g; Trans Fat 2g); Cholesterol 115mg; Sodium 260mg; Total Carbohydrate 81g (Dietary Fiber 0g; Sugars 65g); Protein 7g; **% DAILY VALUE:** Vitamin A 25%; Vitamin C 2%; Calcium 20%; Iron 6%; **EXCHANGES:** 1 1/2 Starch, 4 Other Carbohydrate, 7 Fat; **CARBOHYDRATE CHOICES:** 5 1/2

new twist

Add a final flourish to each serving of pie by sprinkling with additional crushed peppermint candies and adding one whole peppermint candy.

KEY LIME MINI TARTS

prep 10 min   *total time* 1 hr 10 min
makes 5 dozen mini tarts

1 can (14 oz) sweetened condensed milk
1/2 cup Key lime juice
3 drops green food color, if desired
1 container (8 oz) frozen whipped topping, thawed
4 packages (2.1 oz each) frozen mini phyllo dough
  shells
Raspberries, if desired

1. In large bowl, beat milk, lime juice and food color with electric mixer on medium speed until smooth and thickened. Fold in whipped topping.

2. Spoon heaping teaspoonful lime mixture into each phyllo shell. Cover; refrigerate tarts at least 1 hour or until set but no longer than 24 hours. Garnish with raspberries.

1 MINI TART: Calories 45 (Calories from Fat 10); Total Fat 1.5g (Saturated Fat 1g; Trans Fat 0g); Cholesterol 0mg; Sodium 25mg; Total Carbohydrate 7g (Dietary Fiber 0g; Sugars 4g); Protein 0g; **% DAILY VALUE:** Vitamin A 0%; Vitamin C 0%; Calcium 2%; Iron 0%; **EXCHANGES:** 1/2 Other Carbohydrate, 1/2 Fat; **CARBOHYDRATE CHOICES:** 1/2

new twist

If you don't have Key lime juice, substitute 1/2 cup of regular lime juice. You'll need about 2 medium limes.

holiday inspiration

These little phyllo dough shells are slick—what a find! They're always ready to use right from the freezer. There is no need to thaw the phyllo dough shells ahead of time. Just remove them from the freezer when you are ready to fill them, and they will thaw in the refrigerator.

LINDY'S CHEESECAKE

prep 45 min   *total time* 15 hrs   *makes* 16 to 20 servings

Crust

1 cup all-purpose flour

1/2 cup butter or margarine, softened

1/4 cup sugar

1 egg yolk

Cheesecake

5 packages (8 oz each) cream cheese, softened

1 3/4 cups sugar

3 tablespoons all-purpose flour

1 tablespoon grated orange peel, if desired

1 tablespoon grated lemon peel, if desired

1/4 teaspoon salt

5 eggs

2 egg yolks

1/4 whipping (heavy) cream

Garnish

3/4 whipping (heavy) cream

1/3 cup slivered almonds, toasted (page 110), and
lemon or orange peel, if desired

1. Heat oven to 400°F. Lightly grease 9-inch spring-form pan with shortening; remove bottom. In medium bowl, mix all crust ingredients with fork until dough forms; gather into a ball. Press one-third of the dough evenly on bottom of pan. Place on cookie sheet. Bake 8 to 10 minutes or until light golden brown; cool. Assemble bottom and side of pan; secure side. Press remaining dough 2 inches up side of pan.

2. Heat oven to 475°F. In large bowl, beat cream cheese, 1 3/4 cups sugar, 3 tablespoons flour, the orange peel, lemon peel and salt with electric mixer on medium speed about 1 minute or until smooth. Beat in eggs, egg yolks and 1/4 cup whipping cream on low speed until well blended. Pour into crust.

3. Bake 15 minutes. Reduce oven temperature to 200°F. Bake 1 hour longer. Cheesecake may not appear to be done; if a small area in the center seems soft, it will become firm as cheesecake cools. (Do not insert a knife to test for doneness because the hole could cause cheesecake to crack.) Turn off oven; leave cheesecake in oven 30 minutes longer. Remove from oven and cool in pan on wire rack away from drafts 30 minutes.

4. Without releasing or removing side of pan, run metal spatula carefully along side of cheesecake to loosen. Refrigerate uncovered about 3 hours or until chilled; cover and continue refrigerating at least 9 hours but no longer than 48 hours.

5. Run metal spatula along side of cheesecake to loosen again. Remove side of pan; leave cheese-cake on pan bottom to serve. In chilled small bowl, beat 3/4 cup whipping cream with electric mixer on high speed until stiff. Spread whipped cream over top of cheesecake. Decorate with almonds and lemon peel. Store covered in refrigerator.

1 SERVING: Calories 520 (Calories from Fat 350); Total Fat 39g (Saturated Fat 23g; Trans Fat 1g); Cholesterol 220mg; Sodium 310mg; Total Carbohydrate 35g (Dietary Fiber 0g; Sugars 27g); Protein 9g; % DAILY VALUE: Vitamin A 30%; Vitamin C 0%; Calcium 8%; Iron 8%; EXCHANGES: 1/2 Starch, 2 Other Carbohydrate, 1 High-Fat Meat, 6 Fat; CARBOHYDRATE CHOICES: 2

LIGHTER LINDY'S CHEESECAKE For 19 grams of fat and 330 calories per serving, omit crust and Step 1. Move oven rack to lowest position. Lightly grease side only of 9-inch springform pan with shortening. In small bowl, mix 3/4 cup graham cracker crumbs, 2 tablespoons margarine, melted, and 2 tablespoons sugar; press evenly in bottom of pan. Use reduced-fat cream cheese (Neufchâtel); increase flour to 1/4 cup. Substitute 1 1/4 cups fat-free cholesterol-free egg product for the 5 eggs. Omit 1/4 cup whipping cream. Continue as directed in Step 2 except heat oven to 425°F. Omit garnish; serve with fresh fruit if desired.

CHOCOLATE CHIP LINDY'S CHEESECAKE Fold 1 cup miniature semisweet chocolate chips (3 oz) into cheese mixture before pouring into crust. Garnish with caramel topping and toasted pecan halves.

LINDY'S CHEESECAKE WITH FRUIT SKEWERS Thread fresh berries like raspberries, blackberries or blueberries onto short, decorative skewers and insert into each serving. If desired, brush the berries lightly with corn syrup and roll in granulated, colored or decorator's sugar, or sprinkle skewered fruit with powdered sugar before inserting into cheesecake. Add a small sprig of fresh lavender, edible flower or herb if you'd like.

Top to bottom: Lindy's Cheesecake with Fruit Skewers, Lindy's Cheesecake and Chocolate Chip Lindy's Cheesecake

CARAMEL-PECAN BROWNIE DESSERT

prep 20 min   *total time* 5 hrs 20 min   *makes* 12 servings

1 package (1 lb 3.8 oz) fudge brownie mix

1/4 cup water

1/2 cup vegetable oil

2 eggs

1 cup milk chocolate chips

1/2 cup whipping (heavy) cream

20 caramels (from 14-oz bag), unwrapped

1 egg, beaten

1 cup broken pecans

3/4 cup whipping (heavy) cream

2 tablespoons powdered sugar

Cocoa, if desired

1. Heat oven to 350°F (or 325°F for dark or non-stick pan). Grease bottom and side of 10-inch springform pan with shortening. In medium bowl, stir brownie mix, water, oil and 2 eggs until well blended. Stir in chocolate chips. Spread in pan.

2. Bake 50 to 60 minutes or until puffed in center and toothpick inserted near center comes out clean. Cool completely, about 1 hour.

3. Meanwhile, in 1-quart saucepan, heat 1/2 cup whipping cream and the caramels over medium heat, stirring frequently, until caramels are melted. Stir small amount of the hot mixture into beaten egg, then stir egg back into mixture in saucepan. Cook over medium heat 2 to 3 minutes, stirring constantly, until thickened. Stir in pecans. Spread over brownie. Refrigerate uncovered at least 3 hours until chilled.

4. Run metal spatula around side of pan to loosen dessert; remove side of pan. Transfer base to serving plate. In chilled small bowl, beat 3/4 cup whipping cream and the powdered sugar with electric mixer on high speed until stiff peaks form. Spoon whipped cream in 12 dollops around edge of dessert; sprinkle lightly with cocoa. Cut into wedges to serve. Store covered in refrigerator.

1 **SERVING:** Calories 590 (Calories from Fat 310); Total Fat 34g (Saturated Fat 13g; Trans Fat 1g); Cholesterol 90mg; Sodium 240mg; Total Carbohydrate 65g (Dietary Fiber 3g; Sugars 46g); Protein 6g; **% DAILY VALUE:** Vitamin A 10%; Vitamin C 0%; Calcium 10%; Iron 15%; **EXCHANGES:** 2 Starch, 2 1/2 Other Carbohydrate, 6 1/2 Fat; **CARBOHYDRATE CHOICES:** 4

make-ahead magic

Make and refrigerate this dessert up to 24 hours ahead of time. Up to 2 hours before serving, beat the cream with the powdered sugar as directed.

holiday inspiration

- To make each serving look like it came right from the dessert cart, mark the top of the dessert with a knife before adding the whipped cream garnish. That way, you'll know the whipped cream will be centered on each serving.

- Whipped cream topping from an aerosol can works great for this recipe—and saves the time of whipping the cream.

PRALINE PUMPKIN DESSERT

prep 20 min *total time* 1 hr 20 min *makes* 12 servings

1 can (15 oz) pumpkin (not pumpkin pie mix)

1 can (12 oz) evaporated milk

3 eggs

1 cup sugar

4 teaspoons pumpkin pie spice

1 package (1 lb 2.25 oz) golden vanilla cake mix with pudding

1 1/2 cups chopped pecans or walnuts

3/4 cup butter or margarine, melted

Whipped cream, if desired

Additional pumpkin pie spice, if desired

1. Heat oven to 350°F. Grease bottom and sides of 13 × 9–inch pan with shortening or cooking spray. In medium bowl, beat pumpkin, milk, eggs, sugar and 4 teaspoons pumpkin pie spice with wire whisk until smooth. Pour into pan.

2. Sprinkle dry cake mix over pumpkin mixture. Sprinkle with pecans. Pour melted butter evenly over top of dessert.

3. Bake 50 to 60 minutes or until knife inserted in center comes out clean. Cool slightly.

4. To serve, cut dessert into 4 rows by 3 rows. Serve warm or chilled with dollop of whipped cream sprinkled with pumpkin pie spice. Store covered in refrigerator.

1 **SERVING:** Calories 510 (Calories from Fat 240); Total Fat 27g (Saturated Fat 9g; Trans Fat 1.5g); Cholesterol 90mg; Sodium 410mg; Total Carbohydrate 60g (Dietary Fiber 3g; Sugars 42g); Protein 6g; **% DAILY VALUE:** Vitamin A 120%; Vitamin C 0%; Calcium 20%; Iron 10%; **EXCHANGES:** 2 Starch, 2 Other Carbohydrate, 5 Fat; **CARBOHYDRATE CHOICES:** 4

new twist

If you can't find the golden vanilla cake mix, it's okay to use butter recipe yellow cake mix in its place.

make-ahead magic

To make ahead, bake dessert and cool completely. Cover and refrigerate up to 48 hours.

PEANUT BRITTLE BREAD PUDDING

prep 20 min   *total time* 50 min   *makes* 6 servings

Bread Pudding

4 cups soft bread cubes (4 to 5 slices bread)

1/2 cup coarsely broken peanut brittle

1 egg

1/2 cup milk

1/2 cup packed brown sugar

1/4 cup butter or margarine, melted

Hot Buttered Rum Sauce

1/2 cup packed brown sugar

1/2 cup butter or margarine, softened

2/3 cup whipping (heavy) cream

1/4 cup rum or 3 tablespoons water plus
   2 teaspoons rum extract

Whipped cream, if desired

1. Heat oven to 350°F. Grease 1-quart casserole with shortening or cooking spray. Place 2 cups of the bread cubes in casserole. Sprinkle with half of the peanut brittle; repeat with remaining bread cubes and peanut brittle.

2. In small bowl, beat egg. Stir in milk, 1/2 cup brown sugar and 1/4 cup butter; pour over bread mixture.

3. Bake uncovered 25 to 30 minutes or until golden brown.

4. Meanwhile, in 2-quart saucepan, mix all sauce ingredients. Heat to boiling over high heat, stirring constantly. Boil 3 to 4 minutes, stirring constantly, until slightly thickened. Serve warm bread pudding with warm sauce and whipped cream. Store sauce covered in refrigerator up to 1 week. Sauce may separate during storage; stir before serving.

1 SERVING: Calories 570 (Calories from Fat 340); Total Fat 38g (Saturated Fat 19g; Trans Fat 2g); Cholesterol 135mg; Sodium 310mg; Total Carbohydrate 53g (Dietary Fiber 0g; Sugars 42g); Protein 5g; **% DAILY VALUE:** Vitamin A 25%; Vitamin C 0%; Calcium 10%; Iron 8%; **EXCHANGES:** 1 Starch, 2 1/2 Other Carbohydrate, 7 1/2 Fat; **CARBOHYDRATE CHOICES:** 3 1/2

new twist

- Warm their hearts with this homey dessert. Instead of making the rum sauce, drizzle purchased chocolate syrup over warm pudding, and sprinkle with extra crushed peanut brittle.

- Pour on the decadence! This wonderful rum sauce is also delicious served on ice cream or drizzled over Golden Pound Cake (page 197). Stir in toasted pecans or chopped toffee bits for a crunchy topping.

BettyCrocker.com

CREAMY RICE PUDDING *with* BRANDIED CHERRY SAUCE

prep 15 min *total time* 4 hrs 50 min *makes* 8 servings
see photo on page 188, bottom

Rice Pudding

4 cups milk

3/4 cup uncooked regular long-grain rice

1/3 cup sugar

1/4 teaspoon salt

2 eggs, beaten

1 cup whipping (heavy) cream

1 teaspoon vanilla

Brandied Cherry Sauce

1/2 cup sugar

1 tablespoon cornstarch

1/4 cup orange juice

1 1/2 cups frozen unsweetened tart red cherries
(from 1-lb bag)

2 tablespoons brandy or orange juice

1. In 2-quart saucepan, heat milk, rice, 1/3 cup sugar and the salt to boiling over medium-high heat. Reduce heat to medium-low. Simmer uncovered 40 to 45 minutes, stirring frequently, until rice is tender and mixture is thickened.

2. Stir a small amount of the hot rice mixture into eggs, then stir eggs back into mixture in saucepan. Continue cooking over medium heat about 3 minutes, stirring constantly, until heated through. Cool 45 minutes, stirring occasionally.

3. In chilled large serving bowl, beat whipping cream and vanilla with electric mixer on high speed until thickened. Fold in cooled rice mixture. Cover; refrigerate at least 3 hours until well chilled (or serve immediately).

4. In 1-quart saucepan, mix 1/2 cup sugar and the cornstarch. Stir in orange juice and frozen cherries. Heat over medium-high heat, stirring frequently, until mixture boils and thickens slightly. Stir in brandy. Serve sauce warm or chilled with pudding.

1 SERVING: Calories 370 (Calories from Fat 140); Total Fat 15g (Saturated Fat 9g; Trans Fat 0g); Cholesterol 105mg; Sodium 160mg; Total Carbohydrate 50g (Dietary Fiber 0g; Sugars 34g); Protein 8g; % DAILY VALUE: Vitamin A 15%; Vitamin C 4%; Calcium 15%; Iron 6%; EXCHANGES: 1 Starch, 2 Other Carbohydrate, 1/2 Low-Fat Milk, 2 1/2 Fat; CARBOHYDRATE CHOICES: 3

make-ahead magic

To make ahead, spoon pudding into individual serving dishes; cover and refrigerate up to 24 hours. Refrigerate the sauce in a covered container.

holiday inspiration

For dreamiest, creamiest pudding, the rice should just barely bubble as it cooks. The milk may evaporate during cooking, so you may have to stir in a little more to keep the saucy consistency.

CHRISTMAS STEAMED PUDDING

prep 15 min *total time* 2 hrs 20 min *makes* 8 servings

1 cup boiling water

1 cup chopped raisins

2 tablespoons butter or margarine

1 1/2 cups all-purpose flour

1/2 cup sugar

1 teaspoon baking soda

1 teaspoon salt

1/2 cup molasses

1 egg

Creamy Sauce (at right)

or

Rum Hard Sauce (at right)

1. Generously grease 6-cup mold with shortening. In small bowl, pour boiling water over raisins; stir in butter until melted. In medium bowl, mix flour, sugar, baking soda and salt. Stir in raisin mixture, molasses and egg. Pour into mold.

2. Cover mold tightly with foil. Place mold on rack in 4-quart Dutch oven or steamer. Pour enough boiling water into Dutch oven until halfway up mold. Cover Dutch oven. Keep water boiling over low heat about 2 hours or until toothpick inserted in center of pudding comes out clean.

3. Meanwhile, make Creamy Sauce or Rum Hard Sauce.

4. Remove mold from Dutch oven. Let stand 5 minutes; unmold. Serve warm pudding with sauce.

1 SERVING: Calories 480 (Calories from Fat 190); Total Fat 21g (Saturated Fat 11g; Trans Fat 1g); Cholesterol 85mg; Sodium 570mg; Total Carbohydrate 68g (Dietary Fiber 1g; Sugars 42g); Protein 4g; % DAILY VALUE: Vitamin A 15%; Vitamin C 0%; Calcium 8%; Iron 15%; EXCHANGES: 1 1/2 Starch, 3 Other Carbohydrate, 4 Fat; CARBOHYDRATE CHOICES: 4 1/2

CREAMY SAUCE

1/2 cup powdered sugar

1/2 cup butter or margarine, softened

1/2 cup whipping (heavy) cream

In 1-quart saucepan, mix powdered sugar and butter until smooth and creamy. Stir in whipping cream. Heat to boiling, stirring occasionally. Serve warm.

RUM HARD SAUCE

1/2 cup butter or margarine, softened

1 cup powdered sugar

1 tablespoon rum or 2 teaspoons rum extract

In small bowl, beat butter with electric mixer on high speed about 5 minutes or until smooth. Gradually beat in powdered sugar and rum. Cover; refrigerate 1 hour.

holiday inspiration

- A custom still observed in parts of England is to have every family member take a turn stirring the batter, always in a clockwise direction, while making a secret wish.

- Surround the pudding with beautiful sugared fruits. Brush small fruits (such as grapes, cranberries, kumquats) with light corn syrup. Sprinkle with sugar; let stand uncovered until you're ready to add the garnish to the platter.

CRANBERRY-APPLE DUMPLINGS *with* CRIMSON SAUCE

prep 30 min   *total time* 1 hr   *makes* 6 servings

Crimson Sauce

1 can (16 oz) whole berry cranberry sauce

1/4 cup orange juice or water

2 tablespoons red cinnamon candies

Pastry

2 cups all-purpose flour

1 teaspoon salt

2/3 cup plus 2 tablespoons shortening

4 to 6 tablespoons cold water

Dumplings

4 small cooking apples (about 3 inches in diameter), peeled, cored

4 teaspoons sugar

1 egg, slightly beaten

Additional sugar, if desired

1. Heat oven to 400°F. Lightly grease 15 × 10 × 1–inch pan or large cookie sheet with shortening. In 1-quart saucepan, heat cranberry sauce, orange juice and cinnamon candies over medium heat, stirring occasionally, until hot and candies are melted; set aside.

2. In medium bowl, mix flour and salt. Cut in shortening, using pastry blender (or pulling two table knives through ingredients in opposite directions), until particles are size of small peas. Sprinkle with cold water, 1 tablespoon at a time, tossing with fork until all flour is moistened and pastry almost leaves side of bowl (1 to 2 teaspoons more water can be added if necessary). Roll pastry into rectangle, 10 × 8 inches. Cut pastry into four 4-inch squares, using pastry cutter or knife. Cut leaves from remaining 2-inch piece of pastry, using small leaf-shape cutter or knife.

3. Place apple on each pastry square. Spoon 1 tablespoon sauce into center of each apple. Sprinkle each apple with 1 teaspoon of the sugar. Moisten corners of pastry squares. Bring 2 opposite corners of pastry up over apple; pinch to seal. Repeat with remaining corners; pinch edges of pastry to seal. Decorate with pastry leaves. Place dumplings in pan. Brush with egg; sprinkle with additional sugar.

4. Bake about 30 minutes or until crust is golden brown and apples are tender. Serve warm with remaining sauce.

1 SERVING: Calories 610 (Calories from Fat 260); Total Fat 29g (Saturated Fat 7g; Trans Fat 4.5g); Cholesterol 35mg; Sodium 430mg; Total Carbohydrate 82g (Dietary Fiber 4g; Sugars 45g); Protein 6g; % DAILY VALUE: Vitamin A 2%; Vitamin C 8%; Calcium 0%; Iron 15%; EXCHANGES: 2 Starch, 1 Fruit, 2 1/2 Other Carbohydrate, 5 1/2 Fat; CARBOHYDRATE CHOICES: 5 1/2

new twist

Garnish each dumpling with fresh mint leaves and a fresh cranberry. Also try sprinkling powdered sugar over entire dessert plate before placing the dumpling on top.

WINTER POACHED PEARS

prep 10 min   *total time* 1 hr 5 min   *makes* 4 servings

4 firm ripe pears

2 cups water

3 tea bags red zesty herbal tea flavored with hibiscus, rosehips and lemongrass

2 cups cranberry-raspberry juice

2 tablespoons red cinnamon candies

1. Peel pears, leaving stems intact; set aside. In 3-quart saucepan, heat water to boiling; remove from heat. Add tea bags; let steep 10 minutes. Squeeze tea from tea bags; discard bags. Stir juice and candies into tea. Heat over medium heat, stirring occasionally, until candies are melted.

2. Arrange pears upright and close together in saucepan. Heat to boiling; reduce heat. Cover; simmer about 20 minutes, spooning sauce over pears occasionally, until pears are tender when pierced with tip of sharp knife.

3. Remove pears from syrup. Cook syrup over medium-high heat about 25 minutes, stirring constantly, until thickened. Serve sauce over pears.

1 SERVING: Calories 220 (Calories from Fat 5); Total Fat 0.5g (Saturated Fat 0g; Trans Fat 0g); Cholesterol 0mg; Sodium 5mg; Total Carbohydrate 52g (Dietary Fiber 5g; Sugars 42g); Protein 0g; % DAILY VALUE: Vitamin A 2%; Vitamin C 30%; Calcium 2%; Iron 4%; EXCHANGES: 1 Fruit, 2 1/2 Other Carbohydrate; CARBOHYDRATE CHOICES: 3 1/2

holiday inspiration

- To prevent the pears from falling over, try this trick: Cut a very thin slice from the bottom of each pear to make a flat surface, and they won't topple over on the serving plates.

- These rosy red pears are the perfect ending to any holiday meal, and they're not laden with fat and calories. Serve with fat-free vanilla ice cream, and garnish with fresh raspberries and mint leaves.

RASPBERRY TRIFLE

prep 25 min   *total time* 3 hrs 25 min   *makes* 10 servings

1/2 cup sugar

3 tablespoons cornstarch

1/4 teaspoon salt

3 cups milk

1/2 cup dry sherry or white wine, or 1/3 cup orange juice plus 2 tablespoons sherry flavoring

3 egg yolks, beaten

3 tablespoons butter or margarine

1 tablespoon vanilla

2 packages (3 oz each) ladyfingers

1/2 cup raspberry preserves

3 cups fresh raspberries or 2 boxes (10 oz each) frozen raspberries, thawed, drained

1 cup whipping (heavy) cream

2 tablespoons sugar

2 tablespoons slivered almonds, toasted (page 110)

Additional fresh raspberries, if desired

Fresh mint leaves, if desired

1. In 3-quart saucepan, mix 1/2 cup sugar, the cornstarch and salt. Gradually stir in milk and sherry. Heat to boiling over medium heat, stirring constantly. Boil and stir 1 minute. Gradually stir at least half of the hot mixture into egg yolks, then stir back into hot mixture in saucepan. Boil and stir 1 minute; remove from heat. Stir in butter and vanilla. Cover; refrigerate at least 3 hours but no longer than 24 hours.

2. Split ladyfingers horizontally in half; spread each half with raspberry preserves. In 2-quart serving bowl, layer one-fourth of the ladyfingers, cut sides up, 1 1/2 cups of the raspberries and half of the chilled pudding. Repeat layers once with one-fourth of ladyfingers, remaining 1 1/2 cups raspberries and remaining pudding. Arrange remaining ladyfingers around edge of bowl in upright position with cut sides toward center. (It may be necessary to gently ease ladyfingers down into pudding about 1 inch so they remain upright.)

3. In chilled medium bowl, beat whipping cream and 2 tablespoons sugar with electric mixer on high speed until stiff; spread over dessert. Sprinkle with almonds. Cover; refrigerate until serving time. Garnish with additional raspberries and mint leaves. Cover and refrigerate any remaining dessert.

1 SERVING: Calories 370 (Calories from Fat 160); Total Fat 18g (Saturated Fat 9g; Trans Fat 1g); Cholesterol 115mg; Sodium 180mg; Total Carbohydrate 48g (Dietary Fiber 3g; Sugars 36g); Protein 6g; % DAILY VALUE: Vitamin A 15%; Vitamin C 20%; Calcium 10%; Iron 6%; EXCHANGES: 1/2 Starch, 2 1/2 Other Carbohydrate, 1/2 Low-Fat Milk, 3 Fat; CARBOHYDRATE CHOICES: 3

holiday inspiration

Ladyfingers are delicate little sponge cake cookies
with oval-shaped ends. Look for ladyfingers in the
bakery section next to the shortcake cups or in the
freezer section next to the pie crusts, cakes and pies.

EASY TIRAMISÙ DESSERT

prep 15 min   *total time* 1 hr 15 min   *makes* 12 servings

1 package (10.75 oz) frozen pound cake, thawed and cut into 9 slices, or 9 slices Golden Pound Cake (page 197)

3/4 cup strong-brewed coffee (room temperature)

1 cup sugar

1/2 cup chocolate-flavored syrup

1 package (8 oz) mascarpone cheese or cream cheese, softened

2 cups whipping (heavy) cream

2 bars (1.4 oz each) chocolate-covered toffee candy, chopped

1. In bottom of 11 × 7–inch glass baking dish, arrange cake slices, cutting slices if necessary to cover bottom of dish. Drizzle coffee over cake.

2. In large bowl, beat sugar, chocolate syrup and cheese with electric mixer on medium speed until smooth. Add whipping cream. Beat on medium speed until light and fluffy. Spread over cake. Sprinkle with candy.

3. Cover; refrigerate at least 1 hour but no longer than 24 hours to set dessert and blend flavors.

1 SERVING: Calories 460 (Calories from Fat 280); Total Fat 31g (Saturated Fat 18g; Trans Fat 1.5g); Cholesterol 105mg; Sodium 125mg; Total Carbohydrate 43g (Dietary Fiber 0g; Sugars 34g); Protein 4g; **% DAILY VALUE:** Vitamin A 20%; Vitamin C 0%; Calcium 6%; Iron 6%; **EXCHANGES:** 1 Starch, 2 Other Carbohydrate, 6 Fat; **CARBOHYDRATE CHOICES:** 3

holiday inspiration

- Start a new tradition by hosting a Dessert Open House. Ask guests to bring a favorite dessert to share, and make sure this tiramisù treat is on the menu! Here are a few tips to help you set the table and set the mood:

- You may want to consider using your dining table as well as two or three smaller tables. This lets guests gather and mingle in more than one area.

- Create an atmosphere. Use lots of twinkling lights and candles. Have a warm fire in the fireplace to welcome guests.

- Nuts and cheeses are perfect alongside decadent desserts. Check out your deli for cheeses such as Camembert, Liederkranz, Brie, Stilton, blue and Cheddar. Serve with platters of fresh apple and pear slices.

- For coffee lovers, serve this dessert with freshly brewed Italian roast coffee and an assortment of fun coffee toppings like whipped cream, chocolate shavings, raw sugar, ground cinnamon and flavored liqueurs (such as almond, hazelnut, orange or coffee).

WINTER FRUIT KABOBS *with* PEACH GLAZE

prep 35 min *total time* 35 min *makes* 16 kabobs

Fruit Kabobs

6 cups bite-size pieces assorted fresh fruit (pineapple, pears, apples, kiwifruit, strawberries)

2 cups grapes

Peach Glaze

3/4 cup peach or apricot preserves

2 tablespoons butter or margarine

2 tablespoons orange-flavored liqueur or orange juice

1/4 teaspoon ground cinnamon

1. On each of sixteen 8-inch skewers, thread 4 to 6 pieces of fruit, including grapes. Place skewers on large cookie sheet; set aside.

2. In 1-quart saucepan, heat preserves, butter, liqueur and cinnamon over medium-high heat, stirring frequently, until butter is melted. Brush about 1/4 to 1/3 cup of preserves mixture over kabobs; reserve remaining preserves mixture.

3. Set oven control to broil. Broil kabobs with tops 4 to 6 inches from heat 2 minutes or until fruit is hot and glaze is bubbly. Serve warm or cold with remaining preserves mixture.

1 KABOB: Calories 110 (Calories from Fat 15); Total Fat 2g (Saturated Fat 1g; Trans Fat 0g); Cholesterol 0mg; Sodium 15mg; Total Carbohydrate 22g (Dietary Fiber 2g; Sugars 16g); Protein 0g; **% DAILY VALUE:** Vitamin A 2%; Vitamin C 6%; Calcium 0%; Iron 0%; **EXCHANGES:** 1/2 Fruit, 1 Other Carbohydrate; **CARBOHYDRATE CHOICES:** 1 1/2

holiday inspiration

- Always soak bamboo skewers in water at least 30 minutes before using to prevent burning.

- It might be more expensive, but buying already cut-up fruit is a trade-off if you want to save time.

BettyCrocker.com

MERRY BERRY FROZEN SOUFFLÉ

prep 15 min   *total time* 8 hrs 45 min   *makes* 6 servings

Soufflé
4 egg whites
1/4 teaspoon salt
1/3 cup water
3/4 cup sugar
1 can (16 oz) whole berry cranberry sauce
2 cups frozen (thawed) whipped topping

Candied Cranberries
1/2 cup water
3/4 cup sugar
1/2 cup fresh cranberries

1. In large bowl, beat egg whites and salt with electric mixer on high speed until soft peaks form; set aside. In 1-quart saucepan, heat 1/3 cup water and 3/4 cup sugar to boiling over medium-high heat, stirring frequently, until sugar is dissolved. Cook over medium heat to 245°F on candy thermometer or until small amount of mixture dropped into cup of very cold water forms a firm ball.

2. Slowly beat sugar mixture into egg whites on low speed. Beat on medium speed about 8 minutes or until mixture cools to room temperature.

3. Fold cranberry sauce and whipped topping into egg white mixture. Spoon into 6 individual soufflé dishes, about 1 1/4 cups each; smooth tops. Cover with plastic wrap; freeze at least 8 hours but no longer than 24 hours.

4. Line cookie sheet with waxed paper. Heat 1/2 cup water and 1/2 cup of the sugar to boiling in 1-quart saucepan over medium-high heat, stirring frequently, until sugar is dissolved. Cook over medium-high heat to 234°F on candy thermometer or until small amount of mixture dropped into cup of very cold water forms a soft ball that flattens when removed from water. Remove from heat; stir in cranberries. Let stand about 2 minutes or until cranberries are softened. Remove cranberries with slotted spoon to cookie sheet. Place remaining 1/4 cup sugar on plate; roll cranberries in sugar to coat. (Cranberries can be prepared up to 6 hours before using; keep refrigerated.)

5. Let soufflé stand at room temperature 30 minutes before serving. Garnish with Candied Cranberries.

1 SERVING: Calories 400 (Calories from Fat 40); Total Fat 4.5g (Saturated Fat 4g; Trans Fat 0g); Cholesterol 0mg; Sodium 160mg; Total Carbohydrate 87g (Dietary Fiber 2g; Sugars 82g); Protein 3g; **% DAILY VALUE:** Vitamin A 0%; Vitamin C 4%; Calcium 0%; Iron 0%; **EXCHANGES:** 1 Fruit, 5 Other Carbohydrate, 1 Fat; **CARBOHYDRATE CHOICES:** 6

holiday inspiration

Don't worry if you don't have individual soufflé dishes. Just spoon entire recipe into a freezer-proof 2 1/2-quart glass serving bowl or soufflé dish. To serve, scoop soufflé onto dessert plates dusted with baking cocoa, and offer chocolate syrup on the side.

MILK CHOCOLATE FONDUE

prep 15 min *total time* 15 min

makes 8 servings (1/4 cup fondue and 6 dippers each)

2/3 cup half-and-half

12 oz milk chocolate or 1 bag (11.5 oz) milk chocolate chips (2 cups)

2 tablespoons orange-flavored liqueur, kirsch, brandy or half-and-half

Dippers (pound cake cubes, strawberries, pineapple chunks, apple slices, marshmallows)

1. In heavy 2-quart saucepan, heat half-and-half and chocolate over low heat, stirring constantly, until chocolate is melted and mixture is smooth; remove from heat. Stir in liqueur. Pour into fondue pot or chafing dish.

2. Spear dippers with fondue forks; dip into fondue. (If fondue becomes too thick, stir in a small amount of half-and-half.)

1 SERVING: Calories 360 (Calories from Fat 180); Total Fat 20g (Saturated Fat 11g; Trans Fat 0.5g); Cholesterol 35mg; Sodium 55mg; Total Carbohydrate 42g (Dietary Fiber 3g; Sugars 34g); Protein 5g; **% DAILY VALUE:** Vitamin A 4%; Vitamin C 50%; Calcium 10%; Iron 6%; **EXCHANGES:** 1 Fruit, 2 Other Carbohydrate, 4 Fat; **CARBOHYDRATE CHOICES:** 3

new twist

If dark chocolate is your passion, substitute semisweet chocolate chips or bittersweet baking chocolate for the milk chocolate in this recipe. Try using cubes of Chocolate-Pistachio Bread (page 154), Cranberry Bread (page 152), Pumpkin Bread (page 152) or Zucchini Bread (page 152) as dippers too!

250

265

GIFTS *to* GIVE

CREAMY CHOCOLATE MARBLE FUDGE

prep 40 min *total time* 3 hrs 40 min
makes 8 dozen candies

6 cups sugar

1 can (12 oz) evaporated milk

1 cup butter or margarine

1 package (8 oz) cream cheese, softened

2 jars (7 oz each) marshmallow creme or 1 bag
   (10.5 oz) miniature marshmallows

1 tablespoon vanilla

1 bag (12 oz) white vanilla baking chips (2 cups)

1 cup milk chocolate chips (6 oz)

1 cup semisweet chocolate chips (6 oz)

2 tablespoons unsweetened baking cocoa

1/2 cup chopped nuts, if desired

1. Butter bottom and sides of 13 × 9-inch pan or line with foil, leaving 1 inch of foil overhanging at 2 opposite sides of pan. In 6-quart Dutch oven, heat sugar, milk, butter and cream cheese to boiling over medium-high heat; cook 6 to 8 minutes, stirring constantly. Reduce heat to medium. Cook about 10 minutes, stirring occasionally, to 225°F on candy thermometer; remove from heat.

2. Quickly stir in marshmallow creme and vanilla. Pour 4 cups hot marshmallow mixture over white baking chips in large bowl; stir to mix. Into remaining marshmallow mixture, stir milk chocolate chips, semisweet chocolate chips, cocoa and nuts.

3. Pour one-third of the white mixture into pan, spreading evenly. Quickly pour one-third of the chocolate mixture over top, spreading evenly. Repeat twice. Swirl knife greased with butter through mixtures for marbled design. Cool until set.

4. Refrigerate uncovered about 3 hours or until set. Cut into 12 rows by 8 rows with knife greased with butter. Store covered in refrigerator.

1 CANDY: Calories 130 (Calories from Fat 45); Total Fat 5g (Saturated Fat 3g; Trans Fat 0g); Cholesterol 10mg; Sodium 35mg; Total Carbohydrate 21g (Dietary Fiber 0g; Sugars 20g); Protein 0g; **% DAILY VALUE:** Vitamin A 2%; Vitamin C 0%; Calcium 2%; Iron 0%; **EXCHANGES:** 1 1/2 Other Carbohydrate, 1 Fat; **CARBOHYDRATE CHOICES:** 1 1/2

holiday inspiration

To easily scoop the marshmallow creme out of the jars, lightly spray a rubber spatula with cooking spray. The sticky marshmallow won't stick quite as much!

DELUXE CHRISTMAS FUDGE

prep 20 min *total time* 2 hrs 20 min

makes 6 dozen candies

1 1/2 bags (12-oz size) semisweet chocolate chips (3 cups)

2 cups miniature marshmallows or 16 large marshmallows, cut in half

1 can (14 oz) sweetened condensed milk

1 teaspoon vanilla

1 cup pistachio nuts

1/2 cup chopped candied cherries

1/4 cup white vanilla baking chips, melted, if desired

1. Line 9-inch square pan with foil, leaving 1 inch of foil overhanging at two opposite sides of pan. Grease foil with butter.

2. In 8-cup microwavable measuring cup, place chocolate chips, marshmallows and milk. Microwave uncovered on High 3 to 5 minutes, stirring every minute, until marshmallows and chips are melted and can be stirred smooth.

3. Stir in vanilla, nuts and cherries. Immediately pour into pan. Drizzle with melted white baking chips. Refrigerate about 2 hours or until firm. Remove fudge from pan, using foil edges to lift. Cut into 9 rows by 8 rows, or cut into diamond shapes.

1 CANDY: Calories 80 (Calories from Fat 30); Total Fat 3.5g (Saturated Fat 1.5g; Trans Fat 0g); Cholesterol 0mg; Sodium 10mg; Total Carbohydrate 10g (Dietary Fiber 0g; Sugars 8g); Protein 1g; **% DAILY VALUE:** Vitamin A 0%; Vitamin C 0%; Calcium 2%; Iron 0%; **EXCHANGES:** 1/2 Other Carbohydrate, 1 Fat; **CARBOHYDRATE CHOICES:** 1/2

HAZELNUT FUDGE Omit cherries; substitute hazelnuts for the pistachios and add 2 tablespoons hazelnut liqueur.

from the heart

LOOKING FOR A NEW WAY TO GIVE FUDGE AS A GIFT? Try these fun ideas.

• COOKIE CUTTER FUDGE: Choose cutters that are at least 1/2 inch deep and have simple shapes, like mittens or trees. It's difficult to remove the fudge from cutters with small, intricate designs. Place each cutter on a 5-inch piece of foil. Seal foil tightly around outside of each cutter; arrange on cookie sheet. Lightly spray the inside of each cutter with cooking spray. Pour fudge mixture into cutters, filling to the top. Refrigerate uncovered about 2 hours or until firm. Carefully remove foil. Leave in cutters, or gently press the fudge out.

• MINI FUDGE BITES: Place decorative miniature paper liners in cups of miniature muffin pan. Fill each cup with fudge mixture; top each with pistachio nuts, candied cherries or white baking chips, pressing down gently. Refrigerate as directed.

• PERSONALIZED FUDGE: Cut firm fudge into desired shapes. On the top of the fudge shapes, write a name or holiday greeting with any color of decorating icing or gel from a tube. Or, drizzle white chocolate into desired shapes onto waxed paper and let stand until set.

Top to bottom: Cookie Cutter Fudge, Deluxe Christmas Fudge, and Mini Fudge Bites

Toffee (top and bottom) and Maple-Nut Brittle (middle; recipe on page 244)

TOFFEE

prep 35 min   *total time* 1 hr 35 min
makes about 3 dozen candies

1 cup sugar
1 cup butter or margarine
1/4 cup water
1/2 cup semisweet chocolate chips
1/2 cup finely chopped pecans

1. In heavy 2-quart saucepan, heat sugar, butter and water to boiling, stirring constantly; reduce heat to medium. Cook about 13 minutes, stirring constantly, to 300°F on candy thermometer or until small amount of mixture dropped into cup of very cold water separates into hard, brittle threads. (Watch carefully so mixture does not burn.)

2. Immediately pour toffee onto ungreased large cookie sheet. If necessary, quickly spread mixture to 1/4-inch thickness. Sprinkle with chocolate chips; let stand about 1 minute or until chips are completely softened. Spread softened chocolate evenly over toffee. Sprinkle with pecans.

3. Let stand at room temperature about 1 hour, or refrigerate if desired, until firm. Break into bite-size pieces. Store in airtight container.

1 CANDY: Calories 90 (Calories from Fat 60); Total Fat 7g (Saturated Fat 3g; Trans Fat 0g); Cholesterol 15mg; Sodium 35mg; Total Carbohydrate 7g (Dietary Fiber 0g; Sugars 7g); Protein 0g; **% DAILY VALUE:** Vitamin A 4%; Vitamin C 0%; Calcium 0%; Iron 0%; **EXCHANGES:** 1/2 Other Carbohydrate, 1 1/2 Fat; **CARBOHYDRATE CHOICES:** 1/2

from the heart

PACKAGING GIFTS FOR THE HOLIDAYS can be as fun as making them. Look for interesting containers like oversized coffee mugs or decorative boxes with lids (found in party stores), and fill with Toffee. Separate the layers with colored tissue paper or plastic wrap.

MAPLE-NUT BRITTLE

prep 30 min   *total time* 1 hr 30 min
makes about 3 dozen candies
see photo on page 242

1 cup packed brown sugar
1/2 cup maple-flavored syrup
1 can (about 12 oz) lightly salted mixed nuts (2 cups)
1 tablespoon butter or margarine
1 teaspoon baking soda

1. Heat oven to 200°F. Generously butter large cookie sheet; keep warm in oven.

2. In 8-cup microwavable measure, mix brown sugar and maple syrup. Microwave uncovered on High 5 minutes.

3. Stir in nuts. Microwave uncovered on High 5 to 7 minutes or until syrup is bubbling and nuts are toasted—syrup will be very hot.

4. Stir in butter. Microwave uncovered on High 1 minute. Quickly and thoroughly stir in baking soda until mixture is light and foamy. Pour onto cookie sheet; quickly spread candy.

5. Cool 30 to 60 minutes or until hardened. Break into pieces. Store candy in airtight container at room temperature up to 2 weeks.

1 CANDY: Calories 90 (Calories from Fat 45); Total Fat 5g (Saturated Fat 1g; Trans Fat 0g); Cholesterol 0mg; Sodium 60mg; Total Carbohydrate 11g (Dietary Fiber 0g; Sugars 8g); Protein 1g; % DAILY VALUE: Vitamin A 0%; Vitamin C 0%; Calcium 0%; Iron 2%; EXCHANGES: 1 Other Carbohydrate, 1 Fat; CARBOHYDRATE CHOICES: 1

new twist

If you're not fond of mixed nuts, feel free to use an equal amount of your favorite nut. Out of maple syrup? Use corn syrup instead.

holiday inspiration

For a festive touch, drizzle melted semisweet chocolate or white vanilla baking chips in a zigzag pattern over the nut brittle.

CARAMELS

prep 45 min   *total time* 2 hrs 45 min   *makes* 64 candies

2 cups sugar
1/2 cup butter or margarine
2 cups whipping (heavy) cream
3/4 cup light corn syrup

1. Butter bottom and sides of 8- or 9-inch square glass baking dish.

2. In heavy 3-quart saucepan, heat all ingredients to boiling over medium heat, stirring constantly. Boil uncovered about 35 minutes, stirring frequently, to 245°F on candy thermometer or until small amount of mixture dropped into cup of very cold water forms a firm ball that holds its shape until pressed. Immediately spread in baking dish. Cool completely, about 2 hours.

3. Cut into 1-inch squares. Wrap individually in waxed paper or plastic wrap; store wrapped candies in airtight container.

1 CANDY: Calories 80 (Calories from Fat 40); Total Fat 4g (Saturated Fat 2.5g; Trans Fat 0g); Cholesterol 15mg; Sodium 15mg; Total Carbohydrate 9g (Dietary Fiber 0g; Sugars 8g); Protein 0g; % DAILY VALUE: Vitamin A 4%; Vitamin C 0%; Calcium 0%; Iron 0%; EXCHANGES: 1/2 Other Carbohydrate, 1 Fat; CARBOHYDRATE CHOICES: 1/2

CHOCOLATE CARAMELS Heat 2 oz unsweetened baking chocolate with the sugar mixture.

holiday inspiration

Cut little rectangles of waxed paper ahead of time, so when you're ready to wrap, you're ready to go! Here's another secret—cutting the caramels with kitchen scissors is quicker and easier than using a knife.

DIVINITY

prep 55 min *total time* 4 hrs 55 min
makes about 4 dozen candies

2 2/3 cups sugar
2/3 cup light corn syrup
1/2 cup water
2 egg whites
1 teaspoon vanilla
2/3 cup coarsely chopped nuts

1. Line cookie sheet with waxed paper. In 2-quart saucepan, cook sugar, corn syrup and water (use 1 tablespoon less water on humid days) over low heat, stirring constantly, until sugar is dissolved. Cook without stirring to 260°F on candy thermometer or until small amount of mixture dropped into cup of very cold water forms a hard ball that holds its shape but is pliable.

2. In medium bowl, beat egg whites with electric mixer on high speed until stiff peaks form. (For best results, use electric stand mixer, not a portable handheld mixer because total beating time is about 6 minutes and mixture is thick.) Continue beating on medium speed while pouring hot syrup in a thin stream into egg whites. Add vanilla. Beat until mixture holds its shape and becomes slightly dull. (If mixture becomes too stiff for mixer, continue beating with wooden spoon.) Fold in nuts.

3. Quickly drop mixture from buttered spoon onto waxed paper. Let stand at room temperature at least 4 hours, but no longer than 12 hours, until candies feel firm and dry to the touch. Store in airtight container at room temperature.

1 CANDY: Calories 70 (Calories from Fat 10); Total Fat 1g (Saturated Fat 0g; Trans Fat 0g); Cholesterol 0mg; Sodium 10mg; Total Carbohydrate 15g (Dietary Fiber 0g; Sugars 13g); Protein 0g; % DAILY VALUE: Vitamin A 0%; Vitamin C 0%; Calcium 0%; Iron 0%; EXCHANGES: 1 Other Carbohydrate; CARBOHYDRATE CHOICES: 1

CHERRY-ALMOND DIVINITY Substitute 1/2 cup chopped candied cherries for the nuts and almond extract for the vanilla.

CHOCOLATE-MINT DIVINITY Substitute 1/2 cup semisweet chocolate chips for the nuts and 1/4 teaspoon mint or peppermint extract for the vanilla. Add 2 drops green food color with the extract.

PEPPERMINT DIVINITY Substitute 1/2 cup crushed hard peppermint candies for the nuts. If desired, add 2 or 3 drops red food color with the vanilla.

make-ahead magic

To make ahead, store candies in airtight container and freeze up to 2 months.

holiday inspiration

Did you ever say, "Why didn't I think of that?" Then try this! When Divinity has lost its gloss and is ready for dropping onto waxed paper, spoon it quickly into a 1-quart resealable plastic bag. Snip off one corner of the bag to make a 1/2-inch-diameter hole. Squeeze out Divinity, forming swirls with peaks, onto waxed paper-covered cookie sheet.

Betty Crocker Christmas Cookbook

LUSCIOUS CHOCOLATE TRUFFLES

prep 20 min *total time* 1 hr 25 min
makes about 2 dozen candies

1 bag (12 oz) semisweet chocolate chips (2 cups)
2 tablespoons butter or margarine
1/4 cup whipping (heavy) cream
2 tablespoons liqueur (almond, cherry, coffee, hazelnut, Irish cream, orange, raspberry, etc.), if desired
1 tablespoon shortening
Finely chopped nuts, if desired
1/4 cup powdered sugar or cocoa, if desired
1/2 teaspoon milk, if desired

1. Line cookie sheet with foil. In heavy 2-quart saucepan, melt 1 cup of the chocolate chips over low heat, stirring constantly; remove from heat. Stir in butter. Stir in whipping cream and liqueur. Refrigerate 10 to 15 minutes, stirring frequently, just until thick enough to hold a shape.

2. Drop mixture by teaspoonfuls onto foil. Shape into balls. (If mixture is too sticky, refrigerate until firm enough to shape.) Freeze 30 minutes.

3. In 1-quart saucepan, heat shortening and remaining 1 cup chocolate chips over low heat, stirring constantly, until chocolate is melted and mixture is smooth; remove from heat. Using fork, dip truffles, one at a time, into chocolate. Return to foil-covered cookie sheet. Immediately sprinkle some of the truffles with nuts, powdered sugar or cocoa. Refrigerate about 10 minutes or until coating is set.

4. In small bowl, stir powdered sugar and milk until smooth; drizzle over some of the truffles. Refrigerate just until set. Store in airtight container in refrigerator. Serve truffles at room temperature by removing from refrigerator about 30 minutes before serving.

1 CANDY: Calories 100 (Calories from Fat 60); Total Fat 7g (Saturated Fat 3.5g; Trans Fat 0g); Cholesterol 5mg; Sodium 10mg; Total Carbohydrate 9g (Dietary Fiber 0g; Sugars 8g); Protein 0g; % DAILY VALUE: Vitamin A 0%; Vitamin C 0%; Calcium 0%; Iron 2%; EXCHANGES: 1/2 Other Carbohydrate, 1 1/2 Fat; CARBOHYDRATE CHOICES: 1/2

MILK CHOCOLATE TRUFFLES Substitute 1 cup milk chocolate chips for the 1 cup of semisweet chocolate chips in Step 1.

TOFFEE TRUFFLES Stir 3 tablespoons chopped chocolate-covered English toffee candy into whipping cream mixture. Sprinkle truffles with additional chopped candy instead of nuts as directed in Step 3.

WHITE AND DARK CHOCOLATE TRUFFLES Stir 3 tablespoons chopped white chocolate baking bar into whipping cream mixture. Drizzle with melted white chocolate instead of powdered sugar mixture as directed in Step 4, if desired.

from the heart

FOR THE ULTIMATE IN DECADENT GIFTS, put together a montage of all four flavors! Keep in mind that recipients will be begging you to make these again next year, so mark this page with one of those easy-to-remove little notes with the sticky strip.

CAPPUCCINO-PECAN NUGGETS

prep 50 min *total time* 2 hrs
makes 3 dozen candies
see photo on page 236, top

1/4 cup packed brown sugar

1 tablespoon instant espresso coffee granules

2/3 cup sweetened condensed milk

12 oz vanilla-flavored candy coating (almond bark), chopped

12 vanilla or chocolate caramels

1/4 cup semisweet chocolate chips

1 tablespoon whipping (heavy) cream

72 large pecan halves (about 1 1/2 cups)

10 to 12 oz milk chocolate, semisweet or bittersweet baking chocolate, chopped

3 tablespoons shortening

Finely chopped pecans, instant espresso coffee granules or unsweetened baking cocoa, if desired

1. Line 8- or 9-inch square pan with foil, leaving 1 inch of foil overhanging at two opposite sides of pan; spray foil with cooking spray.

2. In 8-cup microwavable measuring cup, mix brown sugar and 1 tablespoon coffee granules. Stir in milk. Microwave uncovered on High 2 to 3 minutes, stirring every minute, until boiling. Stir in candy coating until melted. Pour into pan. Refrigerate uncovered about 30 minutes or until firm. Remove mixture from pan, using foil edges to lift. Cut into 6 rows by 6 rows.

3. In 2-cup microwavable measuring cup, place caramels, chocolate chips and whipping cream. Microwave uncovered on Medium (50%) 1 minute 30 seconds to 2 minutes 30 seconds, stirring every minute, until mixture is almost melted. Stir until smooth. Refrigerate uncovered about 15 minutes, stirring once or twice, until mixture holds its shape and is cool enough to handle.

4. Line cookie sheet with waxed paper. For each nugget, roll 1/2 teaspoon caramel-chocolate mixture into ball. Press 2 pecan halves on ball in sandwich shape, flattening ball slightly between bottom sides of pecan halves. Flatten slightly and shape 1 square coffee mixture evenly around pecan cluster; roll between hands to form ball. Place on cookie sheet. Refrigerate about 15 minutes or until firm.

5. Line cookie sheet with foil. In microwavable 4-cup measuring cup or bowl, place milk chocolate and shortening. Microwave uncovered on Medium (50%) 3 to 4 minutes, stirring every minute, until chocolate is almost melted. Stir until smooth.

6. Dip 1 nugget at a time into chocolate, using fork, until coated. Place on foil-lined cookie sheet. Immediately sprinkle some of the nuggets with finely chopped pecans, coffee or cocoa. Drizzle some of the nuggets with remaining melted chocolate if desired. Refrigerate about 10 minutes or just until set. Serve at room temperature. Store in airtight container at room temperature.

1 CANDY: Calories 180 (Calories from Fat 100); Total Fat 11g (Saturated Fat 4.5g; Trans Fat 0g); Cholesterol 0mg; Sodium 30mg; Total Carbohydrate 19g (Dietary Fiber 0g; Sugars 17g); Protein 2g; **% DAILY VALUE:** Vitamin A 0%; Vitamin C 0%; Calcium 6%; Iron 0%; **EXCHANGES:** 1 1/2 Other Carbohydrate, 2 Fat; **CARBOHYDRATE CHOICES:** 1

new twist

Create dramatic chocolate drizzles in a couple of ways:

- Dip fork or small tableware-type spoon into melted chocolate, allowing the first large drop of chocolate to drip back into the bowl. Then, using back-and-forth motions, drizzle chocolate over cookies, bars or candies.

- Spoon melted chocolate into a decorating bag with a writing tip, and squeeze out the chocolate. Or spoon melted chocolate into a small, resealable food-storage plastic bag, snip off a very tiny piece of one corner of the bag and gently squeeze out the melted chocolate.

CHOCOLATE-COVERED PEANUT BUTTER CANDIES

prep 25 min *total time* 2 hrs 25 min *makes* 64 candies

Candies

1/2 cup creamy peanut butter

1/4 cup butter or margarine, softened

1/4 cup chopped peanuts

1/2 teaspoon vanilla

2 cups powdered sugar

1 bag (12 oz) semisweet chocolate chips (2 cups)

1 tablespoon plus 1 teaspoon shortening

Peanut Butter Icing

1/2 cup powdered sugar

2 tablespoons creamy peanut butter

About 1 tablespoon milk

1. Line 8- or 9-inch square pan with foil, leaving 1 inch of foil overhanging at two opposite sides of pan. Grease foil with butter.

2. In medium bowl, mix 1/2 cup peanut butter, the butter, peanuts and vanilla. Stir in 2 cups powdered sugar, 1/2 cup at a time, until stiff dough forms. (Work in powdered sugar with hands if necessary.) If dough is crumbly, work in additional 1 tablespoon peanut butter. Pat mixture in pan. Cover; refrigerate about 1 hour or until firm. Remove from pan, using foil edges to lift. Cut into 8 rows by 8 rows.

3. Line cookie sheet with waxed paper. In 1-quart saucepan, melt chocolate chips and shortening over low heat, stirring constantly. Dip peanut butter squares, one at a time, into chocolate mixture (see holiday inspirations, below). Place on waxed paper. Refrigerate uncovered about 30 minutes or until firm.

4. In small bowl, mix 1/2 cup powdered sugar and 2 tablespoons peanut butter. Beat in milk with wire whisk until smooth. Stir in additional milk, if necessary, 1 teaspoon at a time, until thin enough to drizzle.

5. Drizzle icing over tops of chocolate-covered squares. Refrigerate uncovered about 30 minutes or until firm. Store candies loosely covered in refrigerator.

1 CANDY: Calories 80 (Calories from Fat 35); Total Fat 4g (Saturated Fat 1.5g; Trans Fat 0g); Cholesterol 0mg; Sodium 15mg; Total Carbohydrate 9g (Dietary Fiber 0g; Sugars 8g); Protein 1g; **% DAILY VALUE:** Vitamin A 0%; Vitamin C 0%; Calcium 0%; Iron 0%; **EXCHANGES:** 1/2 Other Carbohydrate, 1 Fat; **CARBOHYDRATE CHOICES:** 1/2

holiday inspiration

To make dipping the candies easy, here are some handy tips:

• Using a dry fork, dip one candy at a time completely into the melted chocolate. Lift up and draw the fork across the side of the pan or bowl to remove excess chocolate.

• Using another fork, push the candy off the dipping fork onto a cookie sheet covered with waxed paper. Refrigerate candies 30 minutes or just until coating has hardened.

CRUNCHY PEANUT CLUSTERS

prep 15 min   *total time* 1 hr 15 min
makes about 6 1/2 dozen candies

1 package (24 oz) vanilla-flavored candy coating
    (almond bark), broken into pieces
2/3 cup creamy peanut butter
4 cups Cheerios® cereal
2 cups miniature marshmallows
2 cups dry-roasted peanuts

1. In 4-quart saucepan, melt candy coating over medium heat, stirring frequently. Stir in peanut butter until mixture is smooth. Add remaining ingredients, stirring until completely coated.

2. On waxed paper or cookie sheet, drop mixture by heaping teaspoonfuls. Let stand about 1 hour or until firm. Store tightly covered.

1 CANDY: Calories 100 (Calories from Fat 50); Total Fat 6g (Saturated Fat 2g; Trans Fat 0g); Cholesterol 0mg; Sodium 60mg; Total Carbohydrate 8g (Dietary Fiber 0g; Sugars 7g); Protein 2g; % DAILY VALUE: Vitamin A 0%; Vitamin C 0%; Calcium 2%; Iron 4%; EXCHANGES: 1/2 Starch, 1 Fat; CARBOHYDRATE CHOICES: 1/2

holiday inspiration

Add holiday sparkle by sprinkling the clusters with red and green colored sugar right after they're all formed and before they get firm. Vanilla-flavored candy coating, also called almond bark, confectionery coating or summer coating, is mainly used for candy making. The most common types of candy coating you'll find in grocery stores are vanilla and chocolate; specialty stores, such as cake decorating shops, may carry coating in pastel colors. You can add food color to the vanilla variety after it's melted.

PEPPERMINT BARK

prep 15 min *total time* 1 hr 15 min
makes about 16 candies

1 package (16 oz) vanilla-flavored candy coating
  (almond bark), broken into pieces
24 hard peppermint candies

1. Line cookie sheet with waxed paper, foil or cooking parchment paper. In 8-cup microwavable measure or 2-quart microwavable casserole, place candy coating. Microwave uncovered on High 2 to 3 minutes, stirring every 30 seconds, until almost melted. Stir until smooth.

2. Place peppermint candies in heavy food-storage plastic bag; crush with rolling pin or bottom of small heavy saucepan. Pour crushed candies into wire strainer. Shake strainer over melted coating until all of the tiniest candy pieces fall into the coating; reserve the larger candy pieces. Stir coating to mix evenly.

3. Spread coating evenly on waxed paper. Sprinkle evenly with remaining candy pieces. Let stand about 1 hour or until cool and hardened. Break into pieces.

1 CANDY: Calories 190 (Calories from Fat 80); Total Fat 9g (Saturated Fat 6g; Trans Fat 0g); Cholesterol 0mg; Sodium 30mg; Total Carbohydrate 24g (Dietary Fiber 0g; Sugars 25g); Protein 2g; **% DAILY VALUE:** Vitamin A 0%; Vitamin C 0%; Calcium 6%; Iron 0%; **EXCHANGES:** 1 1/2 Other Carbohydrate, 2 Fat; **CARBOHYDRATE CHOICES:** 1 1/2

holiday inspiration

Several brands of candy coating are available. The white color varies from a cream or almond color to a more white color. And when melted, some are thinner than others. Watch carefully while melting and make a note of the brand you prefer to work with.

new twist

Let your imagination run wild! Leave out the crushed peppermint candy, and try some of the following combinations:

- Chocolate-covered coffee beans and chopped hazelnuts

- Dried cranberries and chopped almonds

- Crushed red and green ring-shaped hard candies

- Chopped candied pineapple and macadamia nuts

- Red and green plain or mint candy-coated chocolate candies

BettyCrocker.com

RUM BALLS

prep 20 min *total time* 5 days 20 min
makes about 5 dozen candies

1 package (9 oz) thin chocolate wafer cookies,
  finely crushed (about 2 cups)
2 cups finely chopped almonds, pecans or walnuts
2 cups powdered sugar
1/4 cup light rum
1/4 cup light corn syrup
1/2 cup powdered sugar

1. In large bowl, mix crushed cookies, almonds and 2 cups powdered sugar. Stir in rum and corn syrup. Shape mixture into 1-inch balls.

2. In small bowl, place 1/2 cup powdered sugar. Roll balls in sugar. Cover tightly and refrigerate at least 5 days before serving to blend flavors.

1 CANDY: Calories 70 (Calories from Fat 25); Total Fat 3g (Saturated Fat 0g; Trans Fat 0g); Cholesterol 0mg; Sodium 25mg; Total Carbohydrate 10g (Dietary Fiber 0g; Sugars 7g); Protein 1g; **% DAILY VALUE:** Vitamin A 0%; Vitamin C 0%; Calcium 0%; Iron 2%; **EXCHANGES:** 1/2 Other Carbohydrate, 1/2 Fat; **CARBOHYDRATE CHOICES:** 1/2

BOURBON BALLS Substitute 1/4 cup bourbon for the rum.

BRANDY BALLS Substitute 1/4 cup brandy for the rum.

TOASTED NUT–RUM BALLS Toast the nuts (see page 110) before chopping.

holiday inspiration

For a clever, amusing way to show off these favorites, place individual balls in shot glasses—or put more in champagne or martini glasses.

CHOCOLATE-COVERED CARAMEL CORN

prep 20 min *total time* 3 hrs 50 min
makes about 18 cups snack

12 cups popped popcorn*

3 cups unblanched whole almonds, pecan halves or walnut halves

1/2 cup butter or margarine

1 cup packed brown sugar

1/4 cup light corn syrup

1/2 teaspoon salt*

1/2 teaspoon baking soda

1/2 cup semisweet chocolate chips, milk chocolate chips or white vanilla baking chips

1. Heat oven to 200°F. Remove any unpopped kernels from popcorn. In very large roasting pan or very large bowl, place popcorn and nuts, or divide popcorn and nuts between 2 ungreased 13 × 9–inch pans.

2. In 2-quart saucepan, melt butter over medium heat. Stir in brown sugar, corn syrup and salt. Heat to boiling, stirring occasionally. Continue cooking 5 minutes without stirring; remove from heat. Stir in baking soda until foamy.

3. Pour sugar mixture over popcorn mixture; toss until evenly coated. If using bowl, transfer mixture to 2 ungreased 13 × 9–inch pans. Bake 1 hour, stirring every 15 minutes. Spread on foil or cooking parchment paper. Cool completely, about 30 minutes.

4. In medium bowl, place 3 cups popcorn mixture. In 1-quart saucepan, melt chocolate chips over low heat, stirring constantly. Drizzle chocolate evenly over 3 cups popcorn mixture; toss gently to thoroughly coat popcorn. Spread in single layer on foil or cooking parchment paper. Cool about 2 hours or until chocolate is firm. Add chocolate-covered popcorn mixture to remaining popcorn mixture; toss gently to combine. Store tightly covered.

*Omit salt if using salted microwave popcorn or bags of popped popcorn containing salt.

1 CUP: Calories 330 (Calories from Fat 200); Total Fat 22g (Saturated Fat 5g; Trans Fat 0g); Cholesterol 15mg; Sodium 150mg; Total Carbohydrate 27g (Dietary Fiber 4g; Sugars 17g); Protein 6g; % DAILY VALUE: Vitamin A 4%; Vitamin C 0%; Calcium 8%; Iron 8%; EXCHANGES: 1 Starch, 1 Other Carbohydrate, 1/2 High-Fat Meat, 3 1/2 Fat; CARBO-HYDRATE CHOICES: 2

new twist

If you want two or three kinds of chocolate in your mixture, make separate batches of each type of chocolate-covered popcorn mixture, following the directions in Step 4. If you make two kinds of chocolate-covered popcorn mixture, you will have 12 cups of plain caramel corn left; if you choose three kinds of chocolate-covered popcorn, you'll have 9 cups of plain caramel corn left.

holiday inspiration

You'll want to gobble up this popcorn just as soon as possible, so to get there even faster, look for bags of popped plain white popcorn in the snacks and chips aisle of your supermarket.

DECADENT FUDGE SAUCE

prep 10 min *total time* 10 min
makes about 3 cups sauce

1 can (12 oz) evaporated milk
1 bag (12 oz) semisweet chocolate chips (2 cups)
1/2 cup sugar
1 tablespoon butter or margarine
2 teaspoons orange-flavored liqueur or 1 teaspoon
     orange extract, if desired

1. In 2-quart saucepan, heat milk, chocolate chips and sugar to boiling over medium heat, stirring constantly; remove from heat.

2. Stir in butter and liqueur until sauce is smooth and creamy. Serve warm. Store covered in refrigerator up to 4 weeks. Reheat slightly before serving if desired.

1 TABLESPOON: Calories 60 (Calories from Fat 25); Total Fat 2.5g (Saturated Fat 1.5g; Trans Fat 0g); Cholesterol 0mg; Sodium 10mg; Total Carbohydrate 7g (Dietary Fiber 0g; Sugars 7g); Protein 0g; % DAILY VALUE: Vitamin A 0%; Vitamin C 0%; Calcium 2%; Iron 0%; EXCHANGES: 1/2 Other Carbohydrate, 1/2 Fat; CARBOHYDRATE CHOICES: 1/2

CLASSIC FUDGE SAUCE Omit the liqueur and add 1 teaspoon vanilla.

IRISH CREAM FUDGE SAUCE Substitute 2 tablespoons Irish cream liqueur for the orange liqueur.

RASPBERRY–CHOCOLATE FUDGE SAUCE Substitute 2 tablespoons raspberry-flavored liqueur for the orange liqueur.

from the heart

CHOCOLATE LOVERS WOULD ADORE A JAR OF THIS SAUCE along with some Luscious Chocolate Truffles (page 248) and Chocolate-Covered Caramel Corn (page 257). Tuck them all into a basket or other decorative container.

Top to bottom: White Chocolate Almond Sauce,
Hot Buttered Rum Sauce and Divine Caramel Sauce

new twist

Don't limit this sauce to ice cream! Serve it with
fresh fruit or over pieces of Golden Pound Cake
(page 197) or unfrosted chocolate cake.

WHITE CHOCOLATE–ALMOND SAUCE

prep 15 min   *total time* 15 min
makes about 2 3/4 cups sauce

2 tablespoons butter or margarine
1 cup slivered almonds
1 cup whipping (heavy) cream
1 bag (12 oz) white vanilla baking chips (2 cups)
1 tablespoon amaretto or 1/4 teaspoon almond extract

1. In 3-quart saucepan, heat butter and almonds
over medium heat 6 to 8 minutes, stirring frequently, until almonds are medium brown; remove
from heat.

2. Stir in whipping cream until well blended (mixture will spatter). Stir in baking chips. Heat over
low heat, stirring frequently, until chips are melted.
Stir in amaretto. Or, to microwave, place butter and
almonds in 8-cup microwavable measuring cup.
Microwave uncovered on High 3 to 4 minutes, stirring every minute, until almonds begin to brown.
Stir in whipping cream until well blended. Stir in
baking chips. Microwave uncovered about 1 minute
or until chips can be stirred smooth. Stir in
amaretto.

3. Serve warm or cold. Stir before serving. Store
covered in refrigerator up to 4 weeks.

1 TABLESPOON: Calories 80 (Calories from Fat 50); Total Fat 6g
(Saturated Fat 3g; Trans Fat 0g); Cholesterol 10mg; Sodium 20mg;
Total Carbohydrate 5g (Dietary Fiber 0g; Sugars 5g); Protein 1g; % DAILY
VALUE: Vitamin A 0%; Vitamin C 0%; Calcium 0%; Iron 0%; EXCHANGES:
1/2 Other Carbohydrate, 1 Fat; CARBOHYDRATE CHOICES: 1/2

HOT BUTTERED RUM SAUCE

prep 10 min *total time* 10 min
makes about 1 1/2 cups sauce

1/2 cup packed brown sugar

1/2 cup butter or margarine, softened

2/3 cup whipping (heavy) cream

1/4 cup rum or 3 tablespoons water plus
    2 teaspoons rum extract

In 2-quart saucepan, mix all ingredients. Heat to boiling over high heat, stirring constantly. Boil 3 to 4 minutes, stirring constantly, until slightly thickened. Serve warm. Store covered in refrigerator up to 1 week. Sauce may separate during storage; stir before serving.

1 TABLESPOON: Calories 80 (Calories from Fat 60); Total Fat 6g (Saturated Fat 3.5g; Trans Fat 0g); Cholesterol 20mg; Sodium 30mg; Total Carbohydrate 5g (Dietary Fiber 0g; Sugars 5g); Protein 0g; % DAILY VALUE: Vitamin A 4%; Vitamin C 0%; Calcium 0%; Iron 0%; EXCHANGES: 1/2 Other Carbohydrate, 1 Fat; CARBOHYDRATE CHOICES: 1/2

new twist

Dark rum will give the sauce a richer, more complex flavor. Also try spiced rum or coconut-flavored rum!

DIVINE CARAMEL SAUCE

prep 15 min *total time* 45 min
makes about 2 1/2 cups sauce

1 cup light corn syrup

1 1/4 cups packed brown sugar

1/4 cup butter or margarine

1 cup whipping (heavy) cream

1. In 2-quart saucepan, heat corn syrup, brown sugar and butter to boiling over low heat, stirring constantly. Boil 5 minutes, stirring occasionally.

2. Stir in whipping cream; heat to boiling. Cool about 30 minutes. Serve warm. Store covered in refrigerator up to 2 months. Reheat slightly before serving if desired.

1 TABLESPOON: Calories 80 (Calories from Fat 30); Total Fat 3.5g (Saturated Fat 2g; Trans Fat 0g); Cholesterol 10mg; Sodium 25mg; Total Carbohydrate 13g (Dietary Fiber 0g; Sugars 10g); Protein 0g; % DAILY VALUE: Vitamin A 2%; Vitamin C 0%; Calcium 0%; Iron 0%; EXCHANGES: 1 Other Carbohydrate, 1/2 Fat; CARBOHYDRATE CHOICES: 1

DIVINE TOASTED PECAN–CARAMEL SAUCE Add 1 cup chopped toasted pecans after cooling in Step 2.

from the heart

FILL BASKET WITH JARS of White Chocolate–Almond Sauce, Decadent Fudge Sauce (page 258) and Lemon Curd (page 262). Some gift recipients may want a copy of the recipes; others would prefer a coupon good for a free refill!

THE DIVINE CARAMEL SAUCE IS SO UTTERLY MAGNIFICENT AND DELICIOUS, you may find it hard to part with, but it's a great gift pairing with Golden Pound Cake (page 197).

MIXED-BERRY JAM

prep 25 min *total time* 24 hrs 25 min
makes about 5 half-pints jam

1 cup crushed strawberries (1 pint whole berries)
1 cup crushed raspberries (1 pint whole berries)
4 cups sugar
1/2 teaspoon grated lemon peel
1 tablespoon lemon juice
1 pouch (3 oz) liquid fruit pectin

1. In large glass or plastic bowl, mix berries and sugar. Let stand at room temperature about 10 minutes, stirring occasionally, until sugar is dissolved.

2. Stir in lemon peel, lemon juice and pectin. Stir 3 to 5 minutes or until slightly thickened.

3. Spoon mixture into freezer containers, leaving 1/2-inch headspace. Seal immediately. Let stand at room temperature until set, about 24 hours. Refrigerate up to 3 weeks, or freeze up to 1 year (thaw in refrigerator or at room temperature before serving). Use as a spread or in desserts.

1 TABLESPOON: Calories 45 (Calories from Fat 0); Total Fat 0g (Saturated Fat 0g; Trans Fat 0g); Cholesterol 0mg; Sodium 0mg; Total Carbohydrate 11g (Dietary Fiber 0g; Sugars 11g); Protein 0g; % DAILY VALUE: Vitamin A 0%; Vitamin C 2%; Calcium 0%; Iron 0%; EXCHANGES: 1 Other Carbohydrate; CARBOHYDRATE CHOICES: 1

new twist

If fresh berries aren't available, frozen berries, thawed and drained, are a good substitute.

LEMON CURD

prep 25 min *total time* 25 min
makes about 2 cups curd

1 cup sugar
1 tablespoon finely shredded lemon peel
1 cup lemon juice (5 large lemons)
3 tablespoons firm butter or margarine, cut up
3 eggs, slightly beaten

1. In heavy 1 1/2-quart saucepan, mix sugar, lemon peel and lemon juice with wire whisk.

2. Stir in butter and eggs. Cook over medium heat about 8 minutes, stirring constantly, until mixture thickens and coats back of spoon (do not boil). Immediately pour into one 1-pint container or two 1-cup containers.

3. Store covered in refrigerator up to 2 months.

1 TABLESPOON: Calories 45 (Calories from Fat 15); Total Fat 1.5g (Saturated Fat 0.5g; Trans Fat 0g); Cholesterol 25mg; Sodium 15mg; Total Carbohydrate 7g (Dietary Fiber 0g; Sugars 6g); Protein 0g; % DAILY VALUE: Vitamin A 0%; Vitamin C 0%; Calcium 0%; Iron 0%; EXCHANGES: 1/2 Other Carbohydrate, 1/2 Fat; CARBOHYDRATE CHOICES: 1/2

KEY LIME CURD Substitute lime peel for the lemon peel and Key lime juice for the lemon juice.

new twist

This is a tart, refreshing custard. It makes a tasty spread for Scones (page 160), crumpets or English muffins.

To: PAUL
From: VAL

Left to right: Mixed-Berry Jam and
Lemon Curd

STRAWBERRY FRUIT DIP

prep 5 min *total time* 1 hr 5 min

makes about 1 cup dip

1 bag (16 oz) frozen unsweetened whole strawberries,
   thawed, drained
1/2 cup seedless strawberry spreadable fruit

1. In blender or food processor, cover and blend
strawberries until smooth. Pour into medium bowl.
Stir in spreadable fruit.

2. Cover; refrigerate about 1 hour or until chilled.
Serve with cut-up fresh fruit.

1 TABLESPOON: Calories 35 (Calories from Fat 0); Total Fat 0g (Saturated
Fat 0g; Trans Fat 0g); Cholesterol 0mg; Sodium 0mg; Total Carbohydrate 8g (Dietary Fiber 1g; Sugars 7g); Protein 0g; **% DAILY VALUE:**
Vitamin A 0%; Vitamin C 15%; Calcium 0%; Iron 0%; **EXCHANGES:**
1/2 Other Carbohydrate; **CARBOHYDRATE CHOICES:** 1/2

HUMMUS *and* OLIVE TAPENADE SPREAD

prep 5 min *total time* 5 min

makes about 2 2/3 cups spread

see photo on page 236, bottom

2 containers (7 oz each) regular or roasted red
  pepper hummus

1 can (4.25 oz) chopped ripe olives, drained

2 tablespoons Greek vinaigrette or zesty Italian
  dressing

1/8 teaspoon garlic powder

Chopped fresh parsley and red bell pepper, if desired

1. Spread hummus on 8- to 10-inch serving plate.

2. In small bowl, mix olives, vinaigrette and
garlic powder. Spread over hummus, leaving about
2-inch border of hummus around edge. Sprinkle
with parsley.

1 **TABLESPOON:** Calories 25 (Calories from Fat 10); Total Fat 1.5g
(Saturated Fat 0g; Trans Fat 0g); Cholesterol 0mg; Sodium 65mg; Total
Carbohydrate 2g (Dietary Fiber 0g; Sugars 0g); Protein 0g; **% DAILY
VALUE:** Vitamin A 0%; Vitamin C 0%; Calcium 0%; Iron 2%; **EXCHANGES:**
1/2 Fat; **CARBOHYDRATE CHOICES:** 0

new twist

Three-fourths cup chopped pitted Kalamata olives
can be substituted for the ripe olives. Look for
already-pitted Kalamata olives to save a little time.

from the heart

VEGETARIANS WOULD LOVE TO RECEIVE THIS HUMMUS SPREAD AS A GIFT. Package the
olive mixture separately, and arrange it in a container with the purchased hummus, a pretty plate and pita
bread or pita chips. On the gift card, include a note about how to layer the hummus and olive mixture and
suggest serving it with the pita bread or chips.

HEALTHIER FOOD GIFTS ARE OFTEN GREATLY APPRECIATED. On the gift card for the
Strawberry Fruit Dip, suggest that it be served with fresh fruit or angel food cake squares dippers or that it
can be served over frozen yogurt or sorbet.

CONFETTI CHOCOLATE-OATMEAL COOKIE MIX

prep 10 min *total time* 10 min
makes about 3 dozen cookies

1 cup sugar
3/4 cup all-purpose flour
1/3 cup unsweetened baking cocoa
1/2 teaspoon baking soda
1/4 teaspoon salt
1 1/2 cups quick-cooking or old-fashioned oats
1 cup miniature candy-coated milk chocolate
   baking bits

1. In medium bowl, mix sugar, flour, cocoa, baking soda and salt. Place in 1-quart food-safe jar; tap lightly to pack. Top with oats and baking bits. Cover tightly. Wrap as desired.

2. Give with gift card that reads: Heat oven to 350°F. To make cookies, place contents of jar, 1/2 cup softened butter or margarine, 2 tablespoons water, 1/2 teaspoon vanilla and 1 egg in large bowl. Stir 30 seconds with spoon or until mixed. Spoon dough by rounded teaspoonfuls 2 inches apart onto ungreased cookie sheet. Bake 10 to 12 minutes or until edges are set. Cool 5 minutes. Remove from cookie sheet to wire rack; cool.

1 COOKIE: Calories 100 (Calories from Fat 40); Total Fat 4.5g (Saturated Fat 2g; Trans Fat 0g); Cholesterol 15mg; Sodium 55mg; Total Carbohydrate 14g (Dietary Fiber 0g; Sugars 9g); Protein 1g; % DAILY VALUE: Vitamin A 2%; Vitamin C 0%; Calcium 0%; Iron 2%; EXCHANGES: 1/2 Starch, 1/2 Other Carbohydrate, 1 Fat; CARBOHYDRATE CHOICES: 1

SPICY MOCHA MIX

prep 10 min *total time* 10 min
makes 24 servings (about 1 cup each)

1/2 cup sugar
1/4 cup instant coffee granules or crystals
1/4 cup unsweetened baking cocoa
1 teaspoon ground nutmeg
1/2 teaspoon ground cinnamon

1. In small bowl, stir all ingredients until completely mixed. Store in tightly covered container at room temperature up to 6 months.

2. Give with gift card that reads: For each serving, place 2 to 3 teaspoons mix in cup or mug and fill with 2/3 cup boiling water; stir. Top with whipped cream and grated chocolate if desired. For 6 servings, place 1/4 to 1/3 cup mix in heatproof container and add 4 cups boiling water.

1 SERVING: Calories 20 (Calories from Fat 0); Total Fat 0g (Saturated Fat 0g; Trans Fat 0g); Cholesterol 0mg; Sodium 0mg; Total Carbohydrate 5g (Dietary Fiber 0g; Sugars 4g); Protein 0g; % DAILY VALUE: Vitamin A 0%; Vitamin C 0%; Calcium 0%; Iron 0%; EXCHANGES: Free; CARBOHYDRATE CHOICES: 1/2

DOUBLE-CHOCOLATE MOCHA MIX Omit nutmeg and cinnamon. Add 1 cup milk chocolate, semisweet chocolate or white vanilla baking chips with the ingredients in Step 1.

from the heart

FOR A "BAKE-IT-EASY" COOKIE MIX GIFT, LAYER THE SUGAR MIXTURE, OATS AND BAKING BITS in a brightly colored 2-quart plastic mixing bowl. Place a serving plate for the cookies on top of the mixing bowl. Wrap bowl with cellophane, and tie with ribbon, spoon and gift card.

ANY BUSY FRIEND WILL LOVE A "PAMPERING PACKAGE." Fill a basket with a large holiday mug, a jar of Spicy Mocha Mix or Double-Chocolate Mocha Mix, a package of chocolate-covered graham crackers or biscotti, and a new book off the best-seller list.

Left to right: Chai Mix and Gingersnaps (page 126)

CHAI MIX

prep 10 min *total time* 10 min
makes 8 servings (about 2 cups each)

1 cup instant nonfat dry milk
1/2 cup vanilla-flavored instant creamer (dry)
1/4 cup plus 2 tablespoons powdered sugar
1/2 cup unsweetened instant tea (dry)
2 teaspoons ground cinnamon
1 teaspoon ground cardamom
1/2 teaspoon ground cloves

1. In small bowl, mix dry milk, creamer and pow-dered sugar. In another small bowl, mix remaining ingredients. Into 16-ounce jar, alternately spoon milk and tea mixtures, packing lightly.

2. Give with gift card that reads: For each serv-ing, place 1/4 cup Chai Mix in cup or mug. Fill with 1 cup very hot water. For creamier chai, use half milk and half water.

1 SERVING: Calories 110 (Calories from Fat 30); Total Fat 3.5g (Saturated Fat 3g; Trans Fat 0g); Cholesterol 0mg; Sodium 65mg; Total Carbohydrate 17g (Dietary Fiber 0g; Sugars 15g); Protein 4g; % DAILY VALUE: Vitamin A 4%; Vitamin C 0%; Calcium 10%; Iron 2%; EXCHANGES: 1 Other Carbohydrate, 1/2 Skim Milk, 1/2 Fat; CARBOHYDRATE CHOICES: 1

from the heart

CHAI IS THE HINDI WORD FOR TEA MADE WITH MILK AND SPICES such as cardamom, cinnamon, cloves, ginger, nutmeg and pepper. Give a jar of the Chai Mix with a lovely mug and cinnamon sticks for stirring.

SWEDISH NUTS

prep 10 min   *total time* 40 min
makes 8 servings (about 1/4 cup each)

1 egg white, slightly beaten
2 cups pecan or walnut halves
1/3 cup sugar
2 teaspoons ground cardamom

1. Heat oven to 300°F. Grease 15 × 10 × 1-inch pan with shortening or cooking spray. In medium bowl, mix egg white and pecan halves until pecans are coated and sticky.

2. In small bowl, mix sugar and cardamom; sprinkle over pecans. Stir until pecans are completely coated. Spread pecans in single layer in pan.

3. Bake about 30 minutes or until toasted. Cool completely, or serve slightly warm. Store tightly covered up to 3 weeks.

1 SERVING: Calories 220 (Calories from Fat 160); Total Fat 18g (Saturated Fat 1.5g; Trans Fat 0g); Cholesterol 0mg; Sodium 5mg; Total Carbohydrate 12g (Dietary Fiber 3g; Sugars 9g); Protein 3g; **% DAILY VALUE:** Vitamin A 0%; Vitamin C 0%; Calcium 0%; Iron 4%; **EXCHANGES:** 1/2 Other Carbohydrate, 1/2 High-Fat Meat, 3 Fat; **CARBOHYDRATE CHOICES:** 1

new twist

Ground cinnamon can be substituted for the cardamom; both spices are perfect for the holidays.

from the heart

UNIQUE FOOD GIFTS ARE SUCH A NICE SURPRISE. A bag of these nuts along with an excellent blue cheese, bottled vinaigrette dressing and fresh pears is the start of a spectacular salad. All that's needed is the greens.

EASY FESTIVE PEPPERMINT MARSHMALLOWS

prep 15 min *total time* 8 hrs 15 min
makes about 40 marshmallows

Powdered sugar
2 1/2 tablespoons unflavored gelatin
1/2 cup cold water
1 1/2 cups granulated sugar
1 cup corn syrup
1/4 teaspoon salt
1/2 cup water
1 teaspoon peppermint extract

1. Generously dust 11 × 7–inch glass baking dish with powdered sugar. In large bowl, sprinkle gelatin on 1/2 cup cold water to soften; set aside.

2. In 2-quart saucepan, heat granulated sugar, corn syrup, salt and 1/2 cup water over low heat, stirring constantly, until sugar is dissolved. Heat to boiling; cook without stirring to 250°F on candy thermometer or until small amount of mixture dropped into cup of very cold water forms a ball that holds its shape but is pliable; remove from heat.

3. Slowly pour syrup into softened gelatin while beating with electric mixer on high speed. Beat on high speed until mixture is white and has almost tripled in volume. Add peppermint extract; beat on high speed 1 minute. Pour into pan. Sprinkle with powdered sugar, patting lightly with hands. Let stand uncovered at least 8 hours.

4. Place cutting board upside down on dish of marshmallows; turn board and dish over to remove marshmallow mixture. Cut into shapes with miniature cookie cutters or knife dipped in water to keep from sticking. Store in airtight container at room temperature up to 3 weeks.

1 MARSHMALLOW: Calories 60 (Calories from Fat 0); Total Fat 0g (Saturated Fat 0g; Trans Fat 0g); Cholesterol 0mg; Sodium 25mg; Total Carbohydrate 14g (Dietary Fiber 0g; Sugars 11g); Protein 0g; **% DAILY VALUE:** Vitamin A 0%; Vitamin C 0%; Calcium 0%; Iron 0%; **EXCHANGES:** 1 Other Carbohydrate; **CARBOHYDRATE CHOICES:** 1

EASY FESTIVE ALMOND MARSHMALLOWS
Substitute almond extract for the peppermint.

EASY FESTIVE STRAWBERRY MARSHMALLOWS
Substitute strawberry for the peppermint extract.

EASY FESTIVE VANILLA MARSHMALLOWS
Substitute vanilla extract for the peppermint.

from the heart

PACKAGE A COLLECTION OF MARSHMALLOWS IN A PLASTIC BAG, and tie with curly ribbon. Place bags of marshmallows in oversized mugs along with packages of gourmet cocoa.

TEX-MEX PARTY NUTS

prep 10 min   *total time* 1 hr 20 min
makes 9 servings (about 1/4 cup each)

1 can (9.5 to 11.5 oz) salted mixed nuts
1 tablespoon butter or margarine, melted
2 teaspoons chili powder
1/2 teaspoon garlic powder
1/2 teaspoon onion powder
1/4 teaspoon ground cinnamon
1/4 teaspoon ground red pepper (cayenne)
2 tablespoons sugar

1. Heat oven to 300°F. In medium bowl, mix nuts and butter until nuts are coated. In small bowl, mix remaining ingredients except sugar; sprinkle over nuts. Stir until nuts are completely coated. Spread in single layer in 15 × 10 × 1–inch pan.

2. Bake uncovered about 10 minutes or until nuts are toasted. Return to medium bowl. While nuts are still hot, sprinkle with sugar and toss to coat.

3. Cool completely, about 1 hour. Store in airtight container at room temperature up to 3 weeks.

1 SERVING: Calories 220 (Calories from Fat 160); Total Fat 18g (Saturated Fat 3.5g; Trans Fat 0g); Cholesterol 0mg; Sodium 210mg; Total Carbohydrate 10g (Dietary Fiber 3g; Sugars 4g); Protein 5g; **% DAILY VALUE:** Vitamin A 6%; Vitamin C 0%; Calcium 4%; Iron 6%; **EXCHANGES:** 1/2 Other Carbohydrate, 1/2 High-Fat Meat, 3 Fat; **CARBOHYDRATE CHOICES:** 1/2

from the heart

FOR ALL OF YOUR BEER AFICIONADO FRIENDS, put together a gift bag of their favorite beer or a new specialty beer and a bag of these spicy nuts—they're perfect together!

new twist

Instead of the ham shanks, 2-pound ham hocks or
1 ham bone can be used.

Top to bottom: Santa's Soup Mix
and Santa's Soup

SANTA'S SOUP MIX

prep 10 min *total time* 10 min
makes 6 servings (about 1 1/2 cups each)

2 cups mixed dried beans (1/3 cup each yellow split
    peas, green split peas, lima beans, pinto beans,
    kidney beans and great northern beans)
1/4 cup dried minced onion
2 teaspoons chicken bouillon granules
1/4 teaspoon ground cumin
1/4 teaspoon garlic powder

1. In 1-pint glass jar, layer all ingredients. Store tightly covered at room temperature up to 2 months.

2. Give with gift card that includes Santa's Soup recipe.

SANTA'S SOUP

8 cups water
Santa's Soup Mix
2 medium carrots, chopped (1 cup)
2 medium stalks celery, chopped (1 cup)
2 lb smoked ham shanks

In 4-quart Dutch oven, heat water and Santa's Soup Mix to boiling. Boil 2 minutes; remove from heat. Cover; let stand 1 hour. Stir in carrots and celery. Add ham shanks. Heat to boiling; reduce heat. Cover; simmer about 2 hours or until beans are tender. Skim fat if necessary. Remove ham shanks; remove ham from bone. Trim excess fat from ham. Cut ham into 1/2-inch pieces. Stir ham into soup; heat until hot.

1 SERVING: Calories 310 (Calories from Fat 60); Total Fat 7g (Saturated Fat 2.5g; Trans Fat 0g); Cholesterol 20mg; Sodium 570mg; Total Carbohydrate 43g (Dietary Fiber 12g; Sugars 5g); Protein 19g; **% DAILY VALUE:** Vitamin A 80%; Vitamin C 6%; Calcium 10%; Iron 25%; **EXCHANGES:** 3 Starch, 1 1/2 Lean Meat; **CARBOHYDRATE CHOICES:** 3

from the heart

PACKAGE THIS HEARTWARMING SOUP MIX IN A PRETTY GLASS JAR, and include soup bowls or large mugs and a copy of Santa's Soup recipe.

306

320

SANTA'S WORKSHOP

CHRISTMAS SNACK MIX

prep 10 min   *total time* 10 min
makes 16 cups snack

1 jar (1 lb) dry-roasted peanuts
2 bags (14 oz each) red and green candy-coated
    chocolate candies
2 bags (14 oz each) red and green candy-coated
    chocolate-covered peanuts
1 bag (14 oz) chocolate-covered peanuts
1 jar (7 oz) wheat germ nuts snack

In large container, mix all ingredients. Store in
covered container up to 1 month.

1/4 CUP: Calories 230 (Calories from Fat 120); Total Fat 14g (Saturated
Fat 4.5g; Trans Fat 0g); Cholesterol 0mg; Sodium 95mg; Total
Carbohydrate 21g (Dietary Fiber 2g; Sugars 17g); Protein 5g; % DAILY
VALUE: Vitamin A 0%; Vitamin C 0%; Calcium 4%; Iron 4%; EXCHANGES:
1/2 Starch, 1 Other Carbohydrate, 1/2 High-Fat Meat, 2 Fat; CARBO-
HYDRATE CHOICES: 1 1/2

new twist

Make this snack mix all year long, using red and
white candies for Valentine's Day, pastel-colored
candies for Easter and autumn-colored candies for
Halloween.

MUDDY BUDDIES

prep 10 min   *total time* 10 min   *makes* 9 cups snack

9 cups Chex® cereal (any variety)
1 cup semisweet chocolate chips (6 oz)
1/2 cup peanut butter
1/4 cup butter or margarine
1 teaspoon vanilla
1 1/2 cups powdered sugar

1. Measure cereal into large bowl; set aside.

2. In 1-quart microwavable bowl, microwave
chocolate chips, peanut butter and butter uncovered on High 1 minute; stir. Microwave 30 seconds
longer or until mixture can be stirred smooth. Stir
in vanilla.

3. Pour chocolate mixture over cereal in bowl,
stirring until evenly coated. Pour into 2-gallon
food-storage plastic bag; add powdered sugar.
Seal bag; shake until well coated. Spread on waxed
paper to cool. Store in airtight container in refrigerator up to 2 weeks.

1/4 CUP: Calories 100 (Calories from Fat 40); Total Fat 4.5g (Saturated
Fat 2g; Trans Fat 0g); Cholesterol 0mg; Sodium 80mg; Total
Carbohydrate 14g (Dietary Fiber 0g; Sugars 8g); Protein 2g; % DAILY
VALUE: Vitamin A 2%; Vitamin C 0%; Calcium 2%; Iron 10%;
EXCHANGES: 1/2 Starch, 1/2 Other Carbohydrate, 1 Fat; CARBOHYDRATE
CHOICES: 1

STOVE-TOP DIRECTIONS Measure cereal into large
bowl; set aside. In 1-quart saucepan, heat chocolate chips, peanut butter and butter over low heat,
stirring frequently, until melted. Remove from
heat; stir in vanilla. Continue as directed in Step 3.

holiday inspiration

- This yummy snack is perfect for adults to give to
  kids or for one kid to give to another! Kids can
  help by shaking the cereal mixture in the bag; then
  let them pick out a gift container and decorate it.

- To slim this delicious mix down just a bit,
  decrease chocolate chips to 3/4 cup and omit
  butter and vanilla.

Top to bottom: Christmas Snack Mix,
Muddy Buddies and Teddy Bear Snack Toss
(page 286)

NO-BAKE PEANUT BUTTER SQUARES

prep 20 min *total time* 50 min *makes* 36 squares

1 1/2 cups powdered sugar

1 cup graham cracker crumbs (about 12 squares)

1/2 cup butter or margarine

1/2 cup peanut butter

1 cup semisweet chocolate chips or white vanilla baking chips (6 oz)

Candy decorations, if desired

1. In medium bowl, mix powdered sugar and cracker crumbs. In 1-quart saucepan, heat butter and peanut butter over low heat, stirring occasionally, until melted. Stir into crumb mixture. Press in ungreased 8-inch square pan.

2. In 1-quart saucepan, melt chocolate chips over low heat, stirring frequently. Spread over crumb mixture. Immediately sprinkle with candy decorations. Refrigerate about 30 minutes or until firm.

3. Cut into 6 rows by 6 rows. (To cut diamond shapes, first cut straight parallel lines 1 to 1 1/2 inches apart down the length of the pan. Second, cut diagonal lines 1 to 1 1/2 inches apart across the straight cuts.) Store loosely covered in refrigerator.

1 SQUARE: Calories 100 (Calories from Fat 50); Total Fat 6g (Saturated Fat 2.5g; Trans Fat 0g); Cholesterol 5mg; Sodium 45mg; Total Carbohydrate 10g (Dietary Fiber 0g; Sugars 9g); Protein 1g; % DAILY VALUE: Vitamin A 0%; Vitamin C 0%; Calcium 0%; Iron 0%; EXCHANGES: 1/2 Other Carbohydrate, 1 1/2 Fat; CARBOHYDRATE CHOICES: 1/2

PEANUT BUTTER BONBONS Line a cookie sheet with waxed paper or plastic wrap. Instead of pressing crumb mixture into pan, shape it into 1-inch balls. Heat chocolate chips or white vanilla baking chips with 1 tablespoon shortening until melted as directed in step 2. Dip the balls into melted chocolate, using tongs, to coat, and place on waxed paper. Decorate with candies if desired, then refrigerate the bonbons until firm.

from the heart

CREATE A PEANUT LOVER'S BASKET by filling a decorative container or box with whole peanuts in the shell and nestle the candies in another container in the peanuts.

DOUBLE-FROSTED CHOCOLATE SANDWICH COOKIES

prep 45 min *total time* 1 hr 15 min
makes 3 dozen cookies

1 bag (12 oz) white vanilla baking chips
4 teaspoons shortening
1 package (14 oz) creme-filled chocolate
    sandwich cookies
1 bag (10 oz) mint-flavored chocolate chips
Candy decorations, colored glitter sugars or
    decorator sugar crystals

1. Line cookie sheet with waxed paper. In small microwavable bowl, microwave white baking chips and 2 teaspoons of the shortening uncovered on Medium (50%) 4 to 5 minutes or until mixture can be stirred smooth. Dip 18 of the cookies, one at a time, into white chip mixture; place on waxed paper. Refrigerate 5 to 10 minutes or until coating is set.

2. Meanwhile, in small microwavable bowl, microwave mint chocolate chips and remaining 2 teaspoons shortening uncovered on Medium (50%) 4 to 5 minutes or until mixture can be stirred smooth. Dip remaining cookies, one at a time, into chocolate mixture; place on waxed paper. Refrigerate 5 to 10 minutes or until coating is set.

3. Drizzle remaining melted chocolate mixture (reheat slightly if mixture has hardened) over tops of white-coated cookies; sprinkle with candy decorations. Drizzle remaining melted white mixture (reheat slightly if mixture has hardened) over tops of chocolate-coated cookies; sprinkle with candy decorations. Let stand about 10 minutes or until set.

1 COOKIE: Calories 150 (Calories from Fat 70); Total Fat 8g (Saturated Fat 4g; Trans Fat 0.5g); Cholesterol 0mg; Sodium 85mg; Total Carbohydrate 18g (Dietary Fiber 1g; Sugars 14g); Protein 2g; **% DAILY VALUE:** Vitamin A 0%; Vitamin C 0%; Calcium 2%; Iron 4%; **EXCHANGES:** 1/2 Starch, 1/2 Other Carbohydrate, 1 1/2 Fat; **CARBOHYDRATE CHOICES:** 1

holiday inspiration

This is a fun inside activity for kids on a cold wintry day—try these tips to make cookie dipping easy to clean up. Let the fun begin!

- Cover work surface with butcher's paper or a vinyl tablecloth.

- Create at least two work stations with all the "fixin's" so everyone has enough space to create their masterpieces.

- Everyone, put on your apron! If aprons aren't available, large dish towels work just fine.

- Keep moistened cloths ready for sticky fingers and spills.

- Find fun boxes or decorative cellophane bags for packaging up the goodies!

PEPPERMINT WANDS

prep 25 min *total time* 40 min *makes* 16 candy canes

1/2 cup semisweet chocolate chips or white vanilla
baking chips

2 teaspoons shortening

16 peppermint sticks or candy canes, about
6 inches long

Crushed hard peppermint candies, miniature chocolate
chips, candy decorations, colored glitter sugars or
decorator sugar crystals, if desired

1. Line cookie sheet with waxed paper. In heavy
1-quart saucepan, melt chocolate chips and shortening over lowest possible heat, stirring constantly.

2. Tip saucepan so chocolate runs to one side.
Dip 1 candy cane at a time into chocolate, coating
about one-third to one-half of each cane with
chocolate. Place on waxed paper. Let stand about
2 minutes or until chocolate is partially dry.

3. Roll chocolate-dipped ends in crushed peppermint candies. Place on waxed paper. Let stand
about 10 minutes or until chocolate is dry. Store
loosely covered at room temperature up to 2 weeks.

1 CANDY CANE: Calories 90 (Calories from Fat 20); Total Fat 2g (Saturated
Fat 1g; Trans Fat 0g); Cholesterol 0mg; Sodium 5mg; Total
Carbohydrate 18g (Dietary Fiber 0g; Sugars 18g); Protein 0g; % DAILY
VALUE: Vitamin A 0%; Vitamin C 0%; Calcium 0%; Iron 0%; EXCHANGES:
1 Other Carbohydrate, 1/2 Fat; CARBOHYDRATE CHOICES: 1

holiday inspiration

- Dip wands first into dark chocolate, then after
  dark chocolate has set, dip into white chocolate,
  leaving a some of the dark chocolate showing. Or,
  drizzle melted chocolate in a zigzag design over
  wands.

- Why not try using mint chocolate chips? And to
  make these more quickly, zap the chocolate in the
  microwave to melt. Place chocolate chips and
  shortening in 2-cup microwavable measuring cup.
  Microwave uncovered on Medium (50%) about
  3 minutes or until chips are softened; stir until
  smooth. Continue as directed.

CHOCOLATE SPOONS

prep 25 min *total time* 35 min *makes* 18 to 24 spoons

1 cup semisweet chocolate chips, white vanilla baking
chips or mint-flavored chocolate chips (6 oz)

18 to 24 red plastic spoons

Candy decorations, crushed hard peppermint candies,
miniature candy-coated chocolate chips or decorator sugar crystals, if desired

1. Line cookie sheet with waxed paper. In heavy
1-quart saucepan, melt chocolate chips over lowest possible heat, stirring constantly.

2. Tip saucepan so chocolate runs to one side.
Dip bowl portion of each spoon into chocolate.
Sprinkle with candy decorations. Place on waxed
paper. Let stand about 10 minutes or until chocolate is dry.

3. Wrap spoons in plastic wrap or cellophane.

1 SPOON: Calories 50 (Calories from Fat 25); Total Fat 3g (Saturated Fat
1.5g; Trans Fat 0g); Cholesterol 0mg; Sodium 0mg; Total Carbohydrate
6g (Dietary Fiber 0g; Sugars 5g); Protein 0g; % DAILY VALUE: Vitamin A
0%; Vitamin C 0%; Calcium 0%; Iron 0%; EXCHANGES: 1/2 Other
Carbohydrate, 1/2 Fat; CARBOHYDRATE CHOICES: 1/2

holiday inspiration

Get the whole family involved with this fun recipe:

- Delegate dipping, sprinkling and wrapping to
  different people or teams.

- Double-dipping is encouraged for spoons. Dip
  first into dark chocolate, then after dark chocolate has set, dip into white chocolate, leaving
  some of the dark chocolate showing. Or, drizzle
  melted chocolate in a zigzag design over spoons.

- For a larger gift, put several wrapped chocolate
  spoons in holiday mugs. Include pouches of
  cocoa mix or special coffees.

- Keep a basket of chocolate spoons, each wrapped
  and tied with ribbon, by your entryway. As guests
  leave, surprise them with a sweet treat.

Peppermint Wands
and Chocolate Spoons

TEDDY BEAR SNACK TOSS

prep 10 min *total time* 10 min

makes about 6 cups snack

see photo on page 279

2 cups teddy bear-shaped graham snacks

2 cups Honey Nut Cheerios® cereal

1 cup honey-roasted peanuts or 2 cups
  chocolate-covered peanuts

1/2 cup raisins

In large bowl, mix all ingredients. Store in tightly
covered container up to 2 weeks.

1/4 CUP: Calories 80 (Calories from Fat 35); Total Fat 4g (Saturated Fat
0.5g; Trans Fat 0g); Cholesterol 0mg; Sodium 70mg; Total
Carbohydrate 10g (Dietary Fiber 0g; Sugars 5g); Protein 2g; % DAILY
VALUE: Vitamin A 0%; Vitamin C 0%; Calcium 0%; Iron 4%; EXCHANGES:
1/2 Starch, 1 Fat; CARBOHYDRATE CHOICES: 1/2

holiday inspiration

Dry snacks, like nuts, popcorn, mints and other
hard candies, are perfect mates for unusual containers. Look for unusual items around your house
to serve your holiday nibbles in. If you need to,
line containers with plastic wrap to keep the food
clean and to keep the food from staining the container. Hint: Use a holiday napkin to hide the
plastic wrap before filling the container.

- The creamer and sugar bowl from the silver
  service you usually never put out.

- Wire or wooden baskets and boxes used in the
  home office.

- Bric-a-brac vases and containers

- Ice bucket or champagne bucket

- Soup tureen

- Fondue pot

- Seasonal-themed cookie jar

- Boxes wrapped with holiday gift wrap

- Canning or jelly jars tied with raffia or ribbon

CHOCOLATE-MARSHMALLOW DIP

prep 5 min *total time* 5 min *makes* 1 1/2 cups dip

1 jar (7 oz) marshmallow creme

1 container (4 oz) snack-size chocolate pudding

Crushed hard peppermint candies, if desired

Assorted holiday cookies, if desired

Assorted fruits, if desired

Small pretzel twists, if desired

1. Stir marshmallow creme until smooth. Just
before serving, in small bowl, layer marshmallow
creme and pudding. Garnish with crushed candies
and pretzel twist.

2. Serve dip with cookies, fruits and pretzels.

1/4 CUP: Calories 130 (Calories from Fat 10); Total Fat 1g (Saturated Fat
0g; Trans Fat 0g); Cholesterol 0mg; Sodium 40mg; Total Carbohydrate
30g (Dietary Fiber 0g; Sugars 26g); Protein 0g; % DAILY VALUE: Vitamin
A 0%; Vitamin C 0%; Calcium 0%; Iron 0%; EXCHANGES: 2 Other
Carbohydrate; CARBOHYDRATE CHOICES: 2

holiday inspiration

Kids love this dynamite dip. For fun serving ideas:

- Layer this dip in a soda fountain-style sundae
  glass to show off the layers. For a festive finish,
  top with candy decorations, miniature candy-
  coated chocolate candies or chopped peanuts.

- Skewer banana chunks, strawberries, kiwifruit
  pieces, grapes and pineapple chunks on 4-inch
  drinking straws for funky fruit dippers.

- If you're concerned about double-dippers, use
  individual clear serving dishes, and dip without
  fear.

CHRISTMAS PEANUT BUTTER FONDUE

prep 15 min   *total time* 15 min
makes 6 servings (1/4 cup fondue and 6 dippers each)

2/3 cup packed brown sugar
1/4 cup half-and-half
1 tablespoon honey
3/4 cup creamy peanut butter
Dippers (apple slices, pound cake stars, marshmallows)

1. In 2-quart saucepan, heat brown sugar, half-and-half and honey to boiling over medium heat, stirring occasionally. Stir in peanut butter until smooth. Pour into fondue pot or individual serving bowls.

2. Spear dippers with fondue forks; dip into fondue.

1 SERVING: Calories 460 (Calories from Fat 200); Total Fat 22g (Saturated Fat 6g; Trans Fat 0.5g); Cholesterol 20mg; Sodium 180mg; Total Carbohydrate 57g (Dietary Fiber 3g; Sugars 45g); Protein 10g; % DAILY VALUE: Vitamin A 0%; Vitamin C 4%; Calcium 6%; Iron 8%; EXCHANGES: 1 Starch, 3 Other Carbohydrate, 1 High-Fat Meat, 2 1/2 Fat; CARBOHYDRATE CHOICES: 4

holiday inspiration

Have the Christmas Peanut Butter Fondue ready, and invite the neighbor kids to a holiday party. Activities could include building a Christmas Cottage (page 323) or cookie decorating.

To make fondue even more fun, use sugar-cone sundae cups for individual-size fondues, and consider these dippers:

• Purchased pound cake cut into cubes or seasonal shapes

• Animal crackers or graham cracker squares

• Marshmallows

• Strawberries, grapes, pineapple chunks, banana slices, apple slices and pear slices

• Small plain or chocolate-covered pretzel twists

Betty Crocker Christmas Cookbook

NORTH POLE STRAWBERRY SMOOTHIE

prep 5 min   *total time* 5 min   *makes* 2 servings

1 box (10 oz) frozen strawberries in syrup, partially thawed, undrained

1/4 cup water

2 cups vanilla frozen yogurt

2 tablespoons vanilla reduced-fat yogurt

1 strawberry-flavored or peppermint candy cane, about 6 inches long, finely crushed

White decorator sugar crystals, if desired

Green and red decorating gel, if desired

1. In blender, cover and blend strawberries and water on medium-high speed until slushy. Blend on medium speed until smooth. Pour into 2-cup measuring cup.

2. Wash and dry blender. In blender, cover and blend frozen yogurt and reduced-fat yogurt on medium speed until smooth.

3. Place sugar crystals on small plate. Pipe decorating gel around rim of two 12-ounce glasses. Dip rims into sugar crystals.

4. Carefully pour yogurt mixture and strawberries at the same time into glasses, creating a half-and-half design. Serve with large drinking straws if desired.

1 SERVING: Calories 510 (Calories from Fat 35); Total Fat 4g (Saturated Fat 2.5g; Trans Fat 0g); Cholesterol 15mg; Sodium 170mg; Total Carbohydrate 108g (Dietary Fiber 4g; Sugars 91g); Protein 12g; % DAILY VALUE: Vitamin A 6%; Vitamin C 100%; Calcium 40%; Iron 6%; EXCHANGES: 6 Other Carbohydrate, 1 1/2 Skim Milk, 1/2 Fat; CARBO-HYDRATE CHOICES: 7

holiday inspiration

Host a Santa's Breakfast for the neighborhood kids!

- Send out invitations immediately after Thanksgiving.

- Limit the party to six guests, plus a couple of helpful parents.

- Enlist a Santa (the earlier the better) to join the kids for breakfast.

- Have a small wrapped gift at each place setting or in Santa's sack to be given out.

"LOLLIPOP" COOKIES

prep 15 min *total time* 3 hrs

makes about 2 dozen cookies

1 box (15.6 oz) Rice Chex or 1 box (1 lb)
    Corn Chex cereal

1 bag (16 oz) large marshmallows (about 64)

1/4 cup butter or margarine

About 24 wooden sticks with rounded ends or
    cookie sticks, if desired

Creamy Vanilla Glaze, if desired (page 114)

Candy-coated chocolate candies, if desired

1. Butter 15 × 10 × 1–inch pan.

2. In large microwavable bowl, microwave marshmallows and butter on High 2 to 3 minutes, stirring every minute, until mixture is smooth. Stir in cereal. Using buttered back of spoon or hands, press firmly in pan. Cool 2 to 3 hours before cutting into shapes.

3. Cut into shapes with 2 1/2- to 3-inch holiday cutters (such as snowmen, stars, Christmas trees, etc.) that have been lightly sprayed with cooking spray; insert wooden stick about 1 inch into bottom of each shape; re-shape cut-outs as needed. Decorate with glaze and candies.

1 COOKIE: Calories 170 (Calories from Fat 40); Total Fat 4g (Saturated Fat 2g; Trans Fat 0g); Cholesterol 10mg; Sodium 200mg; Total Carbohydrate 31g (Dietary Fiber 0g; Sugars 12g); Protein 2g; % DAILY VALUE: Vitamin A 10%; Vitamin C 4%; Calcium 6%; Iron 30%; EXCHANGES: 1 Starch, 1 Other Carbohydrate, 1/2 Fat; CARBOHYDRATE CHOICES: 2

FAST-TRACK SNACK SQUARES Follow recipe as directed—except after pressing cereal mixture in pan, melt 1/4 cup butter and 1 bag (12 oz) semisweet chocolate chips (2 cups) in microwavable bowl uncovered on High 1 minute 30 seconds, stirring every 30 seconds. Spread evenly over cereal mixture. Refrigerate 1 to 2 hours or until set. Cut into 24 squares.

holiday inspiration

Look for wooden sticks with rounded ends in the baking aisle with the paper baking cups and disposable pans or in bags of caramels. The cookie sticks can be found in the cake-decorating or candy-making section of craft or party stores. Also check sources on the Internet. Another option is to ask the meat department for the round wooden sticks used to make corn dogs (also called Pronto Pups).

SOFT NO-ROLL SUGAR COOKIES

prep 1 hr 20 min *total time* 3 hrs 20 min
makes about 3 1/2 dozen cookies

1 cup granulated sugar
1 cup powdered sugar
1 cup butter or margarine, softened
3/4 cup vegetable oil
2 tablespoons milk
1 tablespoon vanilla
2 eggs
4 1/4 cups all-purpose flour
1 teaspoon baking soda
1 teaspoon cream of tartar
1/2 teaspoon salt
1/2 cup Rainbow Dust (at right) or granulated sugar

1. In large bowl, beat granulated sugar, powdered sugar, butter, oil, milk, vanilla and eggs with electric mixer on medium speed, or mix with spoon. Stir in flour, baking soda, cream of tartar and salt. Cover; refrigerate about 2 hours or until firm.

2. Heat oven to 350°F. Place Rainbow Dust in small bowl. Shape dough into 1 1/2-inch balls. Roll balls in Rainbow Dust. On ungreased cookie sheet, place balls about 3 inches apart. Press bottom of drinking glass on each ball until about 1/4 inch thick. Sprinkle each cookie with a little additional Rainbow Dust.

3. Bake 13 to 15 minutes or until set and edges just begin to turn brown. Immediately remove from cookie sheet to wire rack.

1 COOKIE: Calories 160 (Calories from Fat 80); Total Fat 9g (Saturated Fat 3g; Trans Fat 0g); Cholesterol 20mg; Sodium 90mg; Total Carbohydrate 20g (Dietary Fiber 0g; Sugars 10g); Protein 2g; **% DAILY VALUE:** Vitamin A 4%; Vitamin C 0%; Calcium 0%; Iron 4%; **EXCHANGES:** 1/2 Starch, 1 Other Carbohydrate, 1 1/2 Fat; **CARBOHYDRATE CHOICES:** 1

RAINBOW DUST (COLORED SUGAR)

1/2 granulated cup sugar
Food colors (see chart below)

Place sugar in resealable food-storage plastic bag. Choose a color from the chart, and add food colors to sugar in bag. Seal bag. Squeeze sugar in bag until it becomes colored. Store sugar in sealed bag or bottle with tight-fitting lid.

Color	Number of Drops of Liquid Food Color
Orange	2 drops yellow and 2 drops red
Peach	4 drops yellow and 1 drop red
Yellow	4 drops yellow
Pale yellow	2 drops yellow
Green	8 drops green
Lime green	3 drops yellow and 1 drop green
Blue	5 drops blue
Turquoise blue	3 drops blue and 1 drop green
Baby blue	2 drops blue
Purple	3 drops red and 2 drops blue
Red	10 drops red
Rose	5 drops red and 1 drop blue
Pink	1 drop red

holiday inspiration

For gift giving, match the packaging and tissue paper used to separate layers of cookies to the colors of Rainbow Dust you used.

Betty Crocker Christmas Cookbook

HIDDEN TREASURE COOKIES

prep 1 hr 15 min   *total time* 1 hr 45 min
makes about 4 dozen cookies

1/2 cup powdered sugar
1 cup butter or margarine, softened
1 teaspoon vanilla
2 1/4 cups all-purpose flour
1/2 cup finely chopped nuts
1/4 teaspoon salt
12 caramels, each cut into 4 pieces
Additional powdered sugar

1. Heat oven to 400°F. In large bowl, mix 1/2 cup powdered sugar, the butter and vanilla. Stir in flour, nuts and salt until dough holds together.

2. Mold portions of dough around pieces of caramels to form 1-inch balls. On ungreased cookie sheet, place balls about 1 inch apart.

3. Bake 10 to 12 minutes or until set but not brown. In small bowl, place additional powdered sugar. Roll cookies in powdered sugar while warm. Cool completely on wire rack, about 30 minutes. Roll in powdered sugar again.

1 COOKIE: Calories 90 (Calories from Fat 45); Total Fat 5g (Saturated Fat 2g; Trans Fat 0g); Cholesterol 10mg; Sodium 45mg; Total Carbohydrate 10g (Dietary Fiber 0g; Sugars 4g); Protein 0g; **% DAILY VALUE:** Vitamin A 2%; Vitamin C 0%; Calcium 0%; Iron 0%; **EXCHANGES:** 1/2 Other Carbohydrate, 1 Fat; **CARBOHYDRATE CHOICES:** 1/2

new twist

Ahoy Matey! Vary the treasures in your cookies! Instead of caramels, try these enticing ideas:

- Candied cherries
- Malted milk balls
- Chocolate-covered raisins
- Gummy fruit candies

LEMON STAMPERS

prep 1 hr 10 min *total time* 3 hrs 40 min
makes about 5 dozen cookies

1 cup butter or margarine, softened
1 package (3 oz) cream cheese, softened
1/2 cup sugar
1 tablespoon grated lemon peel
2 cups all-purpose flour

1. In large bowl, beat butter and cream cheese with electric mixer on medium speed, or mix with spoon. Stir in sugar and lemon peel. Gradually stir in flour. Cover; refrigerate about 2 hours or until firm.

2. Heat oven to 375°F. Shape dough into 1-inch balls. On ungreased cookie sheet, place balls about 2 inches apart. "Stamp" balls to about 1/4-inch thickness using a potato masher, the bottom of a glass, the bumpy side of a meat mallet, the end of an empty spool of thread or a cookie press, dipping first into additional sugar.

3. Bake 7 to 9 minutes or until set but not brown. Remove from cookie sheet to wire rack. Cool completely, about 30 minutes.

1 COOKIE: Calories 50 (Calories from Fat 30); Total Fat 3.5g (Saturated Fat 2g; Trans Fat 0g); Cholesterol 10mg; Sodium 25mg; Total Carbohydrate 5g (Dietary Fiber 0g; Sugars 2g); Protein 0g; % DAILY VALUE: Vitamin A 2%; Vitamin C 0%; Calcium 0%; Iron 0%; EXCHANGES: 1/2 Other Carbohydrate, 1/2 Fat; CARBOHYDRATE CHOICES: 1/2

new twist

- Here's a tip to remember when shaping dough into balls: Use a level tablespoon of dough to create a perfect 1-inch ball.

- For bright-topped cookies, sprinkle with Rainbow Dust (page 292) before baking.

JOLLY SANTA COOKIES

prep 30 min *total time* 1 hr 20 min
makes about 1 1/2 dozen cookies

1/2 cup butter or margarine, softened
1 cup granulated sugar
1 teaspoon grated lemon peel
1 egg
2 tablespoons milk
2 cups all-purpose flour
1 teaspoon baking powder
1/2 teaspoon baking soda
1/2 teaspoon salt
1 cup plus 2 tablespoons vanilla creamy frosting
    (from 1-lb container)
3 tablespoons red sugar
18 miniature marshmallows
36 currants or semisweet chocolate chips
18 red cinnamon candies
3/4 cup shredded coconut

1. Heat oven to 400°F. In large bowl, beat butter, granulated sugar and lemon peel with electric mixer on medium speed, or mix with spoon. Stir in egg and milk. Stir in flour, baking powder, baking soda and salt.

2. Onto ungreased cookie sheet, drop dough by rounded tablespoonfuls about 3 inches apart. Press bottom of drinking glass on each until about 1/4 inch and 3 inches in diameter. Bake 8 to 10 minutes or until light golden brown. Immediately remove from cookie sheet to wire rack. Cool completely, about 30 minutes.

3. Spread frosting on cookie (frost and decorate each cookie before starting another). Over top third of cookie, sprinkle red sugar for hat; press on miniature marshmallow for tassel. Into center third of cookie, press 2 currants for eyes and 1 cinnamon candy for nose. Over bottom third of cookie, sprinkle coconut for beard.

1 COOKIE: Calories 260 (Calories from Fat 90); Total Fat 10g (Saturated Fat 7g; Trans Fat 0g); Cholesterol 25mg; Sodium 180mg; Total Carbohydrate 42g (Dietary Fiber 0g; Sugars 30g); Protein 2g; % DAILY VALUE: Vitamin A 4%; Vitamin C 0%; Calcium 2%; Iron 4%; EXCHANGES: 3 Other Carbohydrate, 2 Fat; CARBOHYDRATE CHOICES: 3

holiday inspiration

These absolutely adorable cookies will be enjoyed by "kids" of all ages. Let little hands press on the marshmallows, currants and cinnamon candies.

Betty Crocker.com

REINDEER PEANUT BUTTER POPS

prep 55 min *total time* 3 hrs 25 min
makes about 28 cookies

1/2 cup granulated sugar

1/2 cup packed brown sugar

1/2 cup creamy peanut butter

1/2 cup butter or margarine, softened

1 egg

1 1/2 cups all-purpose flour

3/4 teaspoon baking soda

1/2 teaspoon baking powder

About 28 wooden sticks with rounded ends
   or cookie sticks, if desired

About 56 small pretzel twists

1 oz semisweet baking chocolate

1/2 teaspoon shortening

About 56 candy-coated chocolate candies

About 28 red candy-coated chocolate candies
   or red cinnamon candies

1. In large bowl, beat granulated sugar, brown sugar, peanut butter, butter and egg with electric mixer on medium speed, or mix with spoon. Stir in flour, baking soda and baking powder.

2. Wrap dough in plastic wrap, leaving ends open. Roll dough into log, about 7 inches long. Pinch along top of log and plastic to form one corner of triangle. Roll log over; pinch again to form second corner. Roll log over; pinch again to form third corner. Straighten sides of log to form a triangular-shaped log. Close ends of plastic wrap; refrigerate at least 2 hours.

3. Heat oven to 375°F. Unwrap log; cut into 1/4-inch slices. Insert 1 inch of wooden stick into a corner of each cookie. On ungreased cookie sheet, place slices about 2 inches apart. Reshape cookies if necessary. Insert 2 pretzels into top of each cookie slice for antlers. Bake 6 to 8 minutes or until edges are firm. Cool 1 minute; remove from cookie sheet to wire rack. Cool completely, about 30 minutes.

4. Line plate with waxed paper. In small microwavable bowl, microwave chocolate and shortening uncovered on Medium (50%) 3 to 4 minutes, stirring

after 2 minutes, until mixture is smooth. Dip half of each candy-coated chocolate candy into melted chocolate, using tweezers to hold candy; let dry on waxed paper. Attach chocolate-dipped and cinnamon candies to cookies using melted chocolate mixture (reheat if necessary) for eyes and nose of reindeers. Store in airtight container.

1 COOKIE: Calories 140 (Calories from Fat 60); Total Fat 7g (Saturated Fat 2.5g; Trans Fat 0g); Cholesterol 15mg; Sodium 130mg; Total Carbohydrate 17g (Dietary Fiber 0g; Sugars 10g); Protein 2g; **% DAILY VALUE:** Vitamin A 2%; Vitamin C 0%; Calcium 0%; Iron 4%; **EXCHANGES:** 1 Other Carbohydrate, 1 1/2 Fat; **CARBOHYDRATE CHOICES:** 1

holiday inspiration

Look for wooden sticks with rounded ends in the baking aisle with the paper baking cups and disposable pans or in bags of caramels. The cookie sticks can be found in the cake-decorating or candy-making section of craft or party stores. Also check sources on the Internet. Another option is to ask the meat department for the round wooden sticks used to make corn dogs (also called Pronto Pups).

CHRISTMAS COOKIE PACKAGES

prep 2 hrs 10 min *total time* 3 hrs 40 min
makes about 5 dozen cookies

1 1/2 cups powdered sugar

1 cup butter or margarine, softened

1 teaspoon vanilla

1/2 teaspoon almond extract

1 egg

2 1/2 cups all-purpose flour

1 teaspoon baking soda

1 teaspoon cream of tartar

Decorating icings (any color from 4.25-oz tubes)

Snowflake or star candy decors, if desired

Edible glitter, if desired

1. In large bowl, mix powdered sugar, butter, vanilla, almond extract and egg with spoon. Stir in flour, baking soda and cream of tartar. Cover; refrigerate about 2 hours or until firm.

2. Heat oven to 375°F. Lightly grease cookie sheet with shortening or cooking spray. Divide dough in half. Roll half of dough at a time on lightly floured surface to 1/4-inch thickness. Cut into 2-inch squares. Place on cookie sheet.

3. Bake 7 to 8 minutes or until edges are light brown. Remove from cookie sheet to wire rack. Cool completely, about 30 minutes.

4. Decorate tops of each package with icings to form ribbon and bow; arrange with candies and sprinkle with glitter.

1 COOKIE: Calories 100 (Calories from Fat 40); Total Fat 4.5g (Saturated Fat 2.5g; Trans Fat 0g); Cholesterol 10mg; Sodium 45mg; Total Carbohydrate 14g (Dietary Fiber 0g; Sugars 9g); Protein 0g; % DAILY VALUE: Vitamin A 2%; Vitamin C 0%; Calcium 0%; Iron 0%; EXCHANGES: 1 Other Carbohydrate, 1 Fat; CARBOHYDRATE CHOICES: 1

holiday inspiration

If you forget to remove your cookies from the cookie sheets in time and the cookies seem to stick, pop the whole sheet back in the hot oven for a minute or two. The heat should soften the cookies slightly, making them easier to remove.

WINTERLAND CRITTERS

makes about 30 cookies

For All Critters

1 package (20 oz) vanilla-flavored candy coating
(almond bark)

1 package (16 oz) Vienna-style creme-filled
sandwich cookies

Make 10 of Each of These Variations

Penguins (at right)

Reindeer (page 301)

Santas (page 301)

1. Line cookie sheet with waxed paper. In 4-cup microwavable measuring cup, microwave 6 squares of candy coating uncovered on High 1 minute; stir. Microwave 1 to 2 minutes longer, stirring well every 30 seconds, until smooth. Candy coating will be used to coat cookies and to attach candies to cookies. Add squares of coating as needed, microwaving 10 to 15 seconds at a time and stirring until smooth.

2. Follow directions for decorating about ten each of Penguins, Reindeer and Santas.

PENGUINS

Black string licorice, cut into 3-inch lengths for body and about 1/2-inch pieces for eyes

Candy corn, cut crosswise in half (discard large ends)

White fudge or yogurt-covered small pretzel twists

Any color of chewy fruit snack in 3-foot rolls (from 4.5-oz box) or red string licorice, cut into 7-inch strips

Assorted large and small gumdrops

1. Dip one cookie at a time into candy coating to cover completely. Place on waxed paper on cookie sheet. Immediately place 3-inch lengths of licorice on cookie to form outline of penguin; insert 1/2-inch pieces of licorice into coating for eyes. Insert candy corn pieces into coating for beaks. Let stand about 20 minutes until coating is completely set.

2. Attach pretzel to end of cookie, using candy coating, for feet. Let stand until coating is set.

3. Cut 6 × 1/2–inch strip of fruit snack roll for scarf; tie scarf around neck of penguin. For earmuffs, flatten 2 small gumdrops for ends of earmuffs; cut 2 × 1/4–inch strip of fruit snack roll for headband of earmuffs. For hat, cut triangle shape from fruit snack roll. Attach to penguin, using candy coating. Let stand until coating is set.

REINDEER

Small pretzel twists

Assorted candy decorations or miniature
chocolate chips

Whole almonds

Any color of chewy fruit snack in 3-foot rolls
(from 4.5-oz box)

1. Dip each end of cookie into candy coating, leaving middle of cookie uncoated. Place on waxed paper on cookie sheet. Attach pretzel to end of cookie, using candy coating, for hooves. Let stand about 20 minutes or until coating is set.

2. Break off end of rounded tips of pretzel to resemble antlers. Dip cookie top into melted coating; immediately attach antlers.

3. Attach candies for eyes, using melted coating. Attach almond for nose, using melted coating. Add red candy to end of almond if desired. Cut 3 × 1/8–inch strip of fruit snack roll for collar; attach collar around reindeer neck, using coating. Attach candies to collar if desired. Let stand until coating is set.

SANTAS

Red sugar

White fudge or yogurt-covered small pretzel twists

Santa face candy decorations

Any color of chewy fruit snack in 3-foot rolls (from
4.5-oz box)

Large red and green gumdrops

Assorted candies and jelly beans

1. Dip one cookie at a time into candy coating to cover completely; immediately sprinkle with red sugar. Place on waxed paper on cookie sheet. Attach pretzel to end of cookie, using coating, for feet. Let stand about 20 minutes or until coating is set.

2. Dip cookie top into melted coating; sprinkle with red sugar. Attach Santa face to front of cookie, using extra coating if needed.

3. Cut 3 × 1/8–inch strip of fruit snack roll for belt; attach belt around Santa, using coating. Cut large red gumdrop into fourths; attach 2 of the pieces to each cookie, using coating, for arms. Attach candies to end of arms for mittens. Attach other candies for decorations if desired.

4. Attach large green gumdrop to Santa's back, using coating, for Santa's toy bag. Let stand until coating is set.

CHRISTMAS MICE
SHORTBREAD

prep 30 min *total time* 1 hr 30 min
makes 15 cookies

15 maraschino cherries with stems, drained
2/3 cup white vanilla baking chips or chocolate chips
1/2 teaspoon vegetable oil
1 package (5.3 oz) shortbread triangles
30 sliced almonds
15 white vanilla baking chips or chocolate chips
Shredded coconut, if desired
15 small red candies

1. Cover work area with piece of waxed paper about 18 inches long. Dry cherries with paper towels.

2. In 6-ounce custard cup, microwave 2/3 cup chips and the oil uncovered on High 1 minute to 1 minute 10 seconds or until chips are softened; stir until smooth.

3. Hold 1 cherry by stem (mouse tail), and dip into melted chips, covering completely. Immediately place on shortbread triangle, with tail at 45-degree angle. Place 2 of the sliced almonds against front of cherry to form mouse ears. Repeat with remaining cherries, shortbread and almonds.

4. Using the remaining melted chips as glue and a toothpick to spread the melted chips, attach the flat side of a whole chip (flat side back) to the base of the almonds to form the mouse head. Using melted chips as glue, attach a few shreds of coconut for the whiskers and a red candy for the nose.

5. Let cool without moving 50 to 60 minutes or until melted chip mixture is firm and completely set. Store in cool place up to 1 week.

1 COOKIE: Calories 110 (Calories from Fat 50); Total Fat 5g (Saturated Fat 2.5g; Trans Fat 0.5g); Cholesterol 0mg; Sodium 55mg; Total Carbohydrate 13g (Dietary Fiber 0g; Sugars 10g); Protein 1g; % DAILY VALUE: Vitamin A 0%; Vitamin C 0%; Calcium 2%; Iron 0%; EXCHANGES: 1 Other Carbohydrate, 1 Fat; CARBOHYDRATE CHOICES: 1

holiday inspiration

The shortbread cookies resemble a wedge of cheese, but you can use other purchased or home-made flat-surfaced cookies for the base of your mice decorations. A merry mouse can add the final touch to your holiday food platters. Kids will have fun placing mice on a saucer next to Grandma and Grandpa's cups of coffee or on a plate of cookies for Santa.

HOLIDAY FUN DOUGH

1 1/4 cups Original Bisquick mix
1/4 cup salt
1 teaspoon cream of tartar
1 cup water
1 teaspoon liquid or paste food color*

1. In 4-cup microwavable measuring cup, stir Bisquick mix, salt and cream of tartar until mixed; set aside. In liquid measuring cup, mix water and food color.

2. Stir a small amount of colored water at a time into dry mixture until all water is added. Microwave uncovered on High 1 minute. Scrape mixture from side of cup and stir.

3. Microwave uncovered 2 to 3 minutes longer, stirring every minute, until mixture almost forms a ball. Let dough stand uncovered about 3 minutes.

4. Remove dough from measuring cup, using spoon. Knead dough in your hands or on the counter about 1 minute or until smooth. (If dough is sticky, add 1 to 2 tablespoons Bisquick mix.) Cool about 15 minutes. Use dough to make fun shapes. Store in tightly covered container in refrigerator up to 1 month. Dough is not edible.

*If using paste food color, knead it into dough after removing the dough from the measuring cup as directed in Step 4. Paste food color will give you deeper, more vivid color than liquid food color.

holiday inspiration

This easy and colorful dough will provide hours of playtime fun. But remember—this isn't for nibbling! Divide the dough as desired before adding food color or make several batches of this recipe, varying the colors of each batch—kids love it!

SQUIGGLE PAINT

makes 1/2 cup paint

1/4 cup all-purpose flour
1/4 cup salt
1/4 cup water ·
2 tablespoons tempera powder (any color)
Glitter, confetti or other nonedible decorations

1. In medium bowl, stir flour, salt, water and tempera powder until well mixed. Pour paint into plastic squeeze bottle with screw-on top.* Repeat this step with different tempera powders to make more colors, if desired.

2. Squeeze designs onto paper or cardboard. Immediately sprinkle glitter or confetti over paint; let dry. Store paint in a covered container at room temperature up to 5 days. Paint is not edible; for decoration only.

*Save squeeze bottles from honey, mustard, ketchup and other products.

new twist

If you prefer not to make "paint" from scratch, check out craft stores for fun products like puff paint. Place the kids' finished masterpieces in inexpensive frames and give as gifts to grand-parents, aunties and uncles!

MERRY TREE WREATH

makes 1 wreath
see photo on page 276, top

Artificial round pine wreath, 30 inches in diameter
Wire cutter
14 dogwood sticks, 9 inches long
2 or 3 pieces florist wire, 16 inches long
Pliers
Hot-glue gun with glue sticks
7 jingle bells, 1 1/4 inches in diameter
7 round ornaments, 3/4 inches in diameter
5 round ornaments, 2 inches in diameter
5 round ornaments, 1 1/2 inches in diameter
4 star-shaped ornaments, 3 1/2 inches in diameter
3 yards decorative ribbon, 2 1/2 inches wide
Decorative door hanger, if desired

1. Shape wreath into tree (triangle) shape. (If wreath is difficult to shape easily by hand, try this method: Using a wire cutter, divide the circular wired form on the back of the wreath into 3 equal parts. Make one cut each in the inner and center wire form to make bending into shape easier; shape into tree—triangle—shape.)

2. Group dogwood sticks tightly together in a bunch; wrap 1 piece of the florist wire around sticks to secure and twist wire tightly with pliers. Glue dogwood sticks to bottom center of tree to create trunk. Decorate wreath with ornaments using glue gun.

3. Make a bow with ribbon; tie with another piece of florist wire. Attach bow to bottom of tree, just above the trunk. Use decorative door hanger to hang wreath from door. If hanging wreath on wall, make loop with third piece of florist wire and attach to back of wreath.

holiday inspiration

So many ornaments are designed by themes now that creating customized wreaths is a cinch! For the lake home or cabin, pick bears, moose, canoes, pine trees and fishing tackle ornaments. Or for seaside homes, there are shells, lighthouses, boats and fishing nets. Dare to decorate!

JOLLY SNOWMAN WREATH

makes 1 wreath

12-inch round grapevine wreath
18-inch round grapevine wreath
22-inch round grapevine wreath
Four 20-inch pieces florist wire
Wire cutter
Decorative hanger or additional wire
Fleece or knit hat and scarf
Tall rubber gardening boots, ski boots or
     snowmobile boots

1. Wire wreaths together, with 12-inch wreath on top, 18-inch wreath in center and 22-inch wreath on bottom, using 2 pieces of wire between each pair of wreaths. Use wire cutter to trim wire if necessary.

2. Use decorative hanger to hang wreath from door. If hanging wreath on wall, make loop with additional wire and attach to back of wreath. Wreath can be hung outside or inside.

3. Secure hat at an angle on top of 12-inch wreath. Wrap scarf around area where 12- and 18-inch wreaths meet. Place boots on floor below wreath to look like feet.

holiday inspiration

This playful vertical snowman wreath is meant to be hung outdoors but will work just as well inside. Customize his or her look by having fun with the footwear, hat and scarf—how about using snowshoes, skis or rollerblades instead of the boots or a helmet instead of the knit hat! Rest the boots on a decorative holiday doormat and if you don't get snow where you live, just scatter some artificial snow around the boots—oh what fun it is!

Betty Crocker Christmas Cookbook

HOLIDAY GARLAND

makes 1 garland

3 bright-red small apples (such as Rome Beauty or
    Red Rome)

Lemon juice or lemon-lime soda pop

Wire racks

Waxed paper

Spray varnish, if desired

Glue gun and glue sticks

Assorted fresh greenery (fern stems, small evergreen
    or pine branches or leaves), if desired

17 walnuts in shells

14 cinnamon sticks, 3 1/2 inches long (from two
    0.75-oz jars)

8 pinecones, 2 inches long

6 red glitter jingle bells, 3 1/2 inches in diameter

4 pinecones, 4 inches long

2 pinecones, 3 inches long

Purchased artificial garland, about 6 feet long

1. Heat oven to 200°F. Cut each apple length-wise from stem end through core into 4 slices. Dip apples into lemon juice to prevent browning; place on wire racks. Carefully place wire racks on oven rack. Bake 3 hour 30 minutes. Turn off oven; leave apples in oven 8 hours or overnight.

2. Remove wire racks from oven. Place dried apples on waxed paper. Coat each side with 2 light coats of spray varnish, following manufacturer's directions. Attach desired amount of fresh greenery along entire length of garland by twisting one or two garland branches around stems or branches of fresh greenery to secure to garland. Glue dried apples, nuts, jingle bells, pinecones and cinnamon sticks to garland, using glue gun. Let dry.

new twist

Customize your garland!

* String colored dried pasta in holiday shapes to use as a simple garland or to intertwine in purchased green garland.

* String or tie purchased wrapped candies, using brightly colored cording, and intertwine in garland. Candy canes, lollipops and foil-wrapped candies are especially fun choices if you have kids around.

* Tie jingle bells on prestrung beads, using tiny ribbons.

Betty Crocker Christmas Cookbook

Clockwise from top: Leaning Flowers,
Flower Short Cuts, Flower Floaters

new twist

Kick it up a notch by coloring the water with liquid food coloring and mixing in a little glitter!

LEANING FLOWERS

makes 1 arrangement

Square glass vase, 6 to 8 inches tall
1 bunch fresh flowers
Floral scissors
36 inches decorative ribbon, 2 1/2 inches wide,
    ends trimmed

1. Fill vase with 1 1/2 inches water. Trim about 4 inches from flower stems, using floral scissors, so heads of flowers will be about 1 inch above top of vase. Gather flowers to make a bouquet; wrap ribbon around stems twice and tie in bow or knot. Trim ribbon ends.

2. Place flowers in vase, leaning flowers to one side.

FLOWER SHORT CUTS Fill the vase with 4 inches water. Trim about 6 inches from flower stems, using floral scissors, so heads of flowers will be just touching rim of vase. Arrange flowers in vase. Arrange fresh pine, cedar or other holiday greens on edge of vase around flowers.

FLOWER FLOATERS Fill an 3 1/2-inch decorative round glass bowl with 1 inch water. Cut flower head from stem. Float flower on top of holly leaves or other holiday greenery.

Betty Crocker Christmas Cookbook

CRANBERRY KISSING BALL

makes 1 decoration

12 inches 20-gauge wire
1 plastic foam ball, 3 inches in diameter
Round toothpicks
1/2 lb fresh cranberries
1 small bunch (about 5 sprigs) fresh eucalyptus
1 package craft straight pins
1 yard decorative ribbon

1. Wrap wire tightly around diameter of foam ball once. Twist wire at top of ball to secure. Tuck ends into ball.

2. Break toothpicks in half. Push cranberry onto broken end of toothpick; push other end of toothpick into foam ball. Continue until ball is well filled with cranberries.

3. Fill in open spaces on ball with 1 1/2- to 2-inch cuts of eucalyptus, securing with pins.

4. Slip ribbon through wire twist at top; tie ribbon to make loop for hanging ball. The cranberries will stay plump and pretty for about three to four days. To extend its life, hang the ball in a cool spot, such as in an entryway or on a porch.

new twist

Hanging in an entryway, a kissing ball welcomes guests with a romantic touch. Instead of eucalyptus, you may like to add mistletoe or holly for a hint of Christmas past or, if you're not fond of eucalyptus, use popped popcorn to fill in the open spaces between cranberries.

holiday inspiration

Having trouble finding craft straight pins? Look for them in the notions department of sewing and fabric stores.

TWINKLING BEADED VOTIVES

makes 3 votives

3 pieces 26-gauge beading wire, 52 1/2 inches long

Needle-nose pliers

2 packages (0.705 oz each) glass beads, each of different color

Silicone glue*

3 glass votive candleholders (2 1/2 × 2 inches) with votive candles or tea light candles in metal cups

1. Crimp one end of 1 piece of wire with pliers. Thread one color of beads onto wire. When wire is full with beads, crimp opposite end to secure. Repeat with second piece of wire and second color of beads. For third piece of wire, use both colors of beads, alternating colors as desired.

2. Glue one end of beaded wire to a candleholder; hold in place just until glue sets. Wrap beaded wire around candleholder; glue in middle and end to secure. Repeat with remaining beaded wire and candleholders. Add candles.

*Do not use a hot glue gun with glue sticks because the heat of the candles will melt the glue holding the beaded wire or ribbon. Silicone glue, also called adhesive, can withstand higher temperatures and will not melt.

TWISTED BEADED WRAP For each votive, you will need one 52 1/2-inch piece of 28-gauge beading wire and 1 package (3 oz) faceted rochaille beads (6 millimeter). Thread 8 beads onto wire, fold wire in half and twist to make cluster of 8 beads. Skip short space on wire, then repeat process. Continue until end of beading wire. Wrap beaded wire around glass votive candleholder; twist two beaded loops together to hold in place and secure with drop of glue. Continue wrapping, twisting two beaded loops together at midway point to hold in place, until end is reached. Twist end with another beaded loop to hold in place and secure with drop of glue.

RIBBON WRAP For each votive, you will need one 26-inch piece of 1/4- to 3/8-inch-wide decorative ribbon. Glue one end of ribbon to candleholder about 1/4 to 1/2 inch from top; wrap ribbon around votive and glue opposite end to candleholder to secure.

from the heart

CANDLES ARE SO VERY POPULAR and these sparkling beaded votives would really "light up" somebody's Christmas stocking. Make sure to include plenty of tea light or votive candles so they can be enjoyed right away.

Top to bottom: Ribbon Wrap, Twinkling Beaded Votives,
Twisted Bead Wrap

PINES AND CALLAS CENTERPIECE

makes 1 centerpiece

1 square plate, 10 inches in diameter
1 square plate, 8 inches in diameter
7 artificial calla lily flower stems
Wire cutter
Rubber band
52 inches decorative ribbon, 1 3/8 inches wide
2 sprigs artificial pine
Dried princess pine
6 small pinecones

1. Stack square plates. Gather lilies to make a bouquet. Cut stems to same length (about 15 inches), using wire cutter; bind with rubber band. Wrap flower stems with ribbon; tie in a bow, leaving trailing ribbon. Place on top plate.

2. Arrange pine sprigs, princess pine and pinecones on each side of calla stems. Trim ribbon ends as desired.

holiday inspiration

For a pretty and professional touch, trim the ends of the ribbon at an angle, or cut in diagonally from each side to form a $\wedge$ shape.

from the heart

WHAT A TRUE GESTURE FROM THE HEART the Angelic Lighted Centerpiece would be for a dear friend who collects vintage or collectable figurines or ornaments! The whole arrangement could be a composition of antiques or collectables, not just the figurine mentioned in the directions.

Betty Crocker Christmas Cookbook

ANGELIC LIGHTED CENTERPIECE

makes 1 centerpiece

Glitter
1 round plate, 13 inches in diameter
1 large holiday candle or decorative ornament,
    10 inches tall
1 vintage figurine, collectible or ornament
3 Twinkling Beaded Votives (page 312)

Sprinkle glitter on plate; arrange candle,
figurine and votives on plate. Light candles.

GLISTENING FRUIT AND CANDLELIGHT TRAY You
will need three 5-inch pieces of 7/8-inch-wide decorative ribbon; three 5-inch pieces of 5/8-inch-wide
decorative ribbon; 3 tea light or votive candles in
plastic cups; 3 tea light votive or candles in metal
cups; 1 decorative candle stand (10 1/2 inches tall);
1 round metal tray (12 inches in diameter); 1 votive
candle (2 × 2 1/2 inches); beaded or sequined decorative fruit or ornaments; and hot-glue gun with
glue sticks. Glue ribbon around tea light candles in
plastic and metal cups. Place candle stand on
metal tray; add 2-inch votive candle to top of candle stand. Arrange fruit or ornaments around candle stand. Arrange tea light candles around edge of
metal tray.

HOLIDAY FELT PLACE MATS AND NAPKIN RINGS

makes 4 place mats and napkin rings

1/2 yard craft felt (72 inches wide)
Glue stick
16 pieces (13 inch) fiber trim
Holiday stickers
8 pieces (7 inch) fiber trim

1. To make place mats, cut four 17 × 13–inch pieces of felt (remaining felt will be used to make napkin rings). On each place mat, draw 2 parallel lines of glue at each 13-inch side. Place 13-inch pieces of fiber trim on glue; press to secure. Let glue dry. Place holiday stickers on place mats.

2. To make napkin rings, cut four 7 × 2–inch strips from remaining felt. On each felt strip, draw two parallel 7-inch lines of glue down center. Place 7-inch pieces of fiber trim on glue; press to secure. Draw 1/2-inch-wide line of glue on one short end of each felt strip. Bring ends of each felt strip together and overlap to make ring; press together to secure ends. Let glue dry.

METALLIC RICKRACK In addition to the felt and glue stick listed above, you will need four 7-inch pieces, eight 13-inch pieces and eight 17-inch pieces of 5/8-inch-wide metallic rickrack. Cut place mats and napkin rings from felt as directed above. To make place mats, glue rickrack on place mats to create border. To make napkin rings, glue rickrack down center of each felt strip; glue ends together as directed above. Let glue dry.

RIBBON AND GLITTER STICKERS In addition to the felt and glue stick listed above, you will need four 7-inch pieces and eight 17-inch pieces of 3/8-inch-wide decorative ribbon, plus holiday stickers. Cut place mats and napkin rings from felt as directed above. To make place mats, glue ribbon along top and bottom of each place mat. Place holiday stickers at top on center of ribbon. To make napkin rings, glue ribbon down center of each felt strip; glue ends together as directed above. Place holiday sticker on center of ribbon. Let glue dry.

FELT CUTOUTS In addition to the felt and glue stick listed above, you will need four 7-inch pieces, eight 12-inch pieces and eight 16-inch pieces of 5/8-inch-wide decorative ribbon, plus 20 cutout felt shapes in a complementary color and pinking shears. Using pinking shears, cut place mats and napkin rings from felt as directed above. To make place mats, glue ribbon on each place mat to create border. Glue cutout shape on each corner of place mat. To make napkin rings, glue ribbon down center of each felt strip; glue ends together as directed above. Glue cutout shape on top of ribbon on each napkin ring. Let glue dry.

holiday inspiration

Felt is like magic! Do you remember using it for craft projects as a kid? Well, it's great for "adult" projects too! What's the magic? No sewing required—just a pair of scissors, some glue and a little creative energy!

Napkin rings and place mats top to bottom: Holiday Felt,
Ribbon and Glitter Stickers and Felt Cutouts

EMBELLISHED NAPKINS

makes 4 napkins

4 large square fabric napkins, ironed
4 flat ornaments, up to 4 to 5 inches in diameter

1. Lay napkin on a flat surface.*

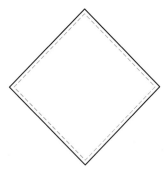

2. Fold napkin in half diagonally into a triangle.

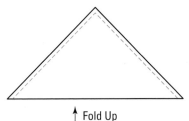

↑ Fold Up

3. Fold long folded side (bottom of triangle) halfway to point of triangle.

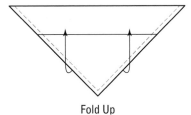

Fold Up

4. Turn napkin over so the widest side is on top.

Turn Napkin Over

5. Fold right and left points up to the point in center, forming one point.

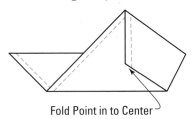

Fold Point in to Center

6. Fold right and left sides in half so the edges meet in the center of the napkin.

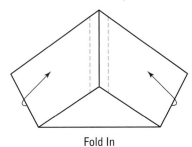

Fold In

7. Pick up at center fold and turn napkin over; napkin will have a pocket on the bottom half and the top half forms a point.

Turn Over

8. Tuck ornament just inside of pocket; lay silverware to sides of plate. Repeat with remaining napkins and ornaments.

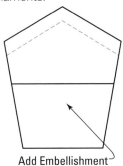

Add Embellishment

*If using patterned napkins, place patterned side down and fold as directed.

holiday inspiration

Learning the knack of napkin art is fun and can dress up a dining table without a big time commitment or cost! It's as easy as a flip of the wrist. Try one of these embellishments instead of the snowflake:

- Snowman or Santa magnet
- Miniature grapevine wreath, up to 4 inches in diameter
- Miniature pine wreath, up to 4 inches in diameter
- Individual wooden or magnetic letters
- Fresh or artificial flowers
- Fresh herbs

Good-quality, heavy paper napkins can be used instead of fabric napkins for casual occasions or for a kids' table.

Your napkins don't need to match. It can be even more fun to use a couple of coordinating colors or patterns and alternate them on the table.

HOLIDAY CANDY TRAINS

makes 4 candy trains

see photo on page 276, bottom

Glue gun and glue sticks

4 sixteen-inch lengths 3/8-inch-wide red or
    green ribbon

4 packages chewing gum (5 sticks each)

8 boxes (1 to 1.5 oz each) candy

12 foil-wrapped rectangular chocolate mints,
    unwrapped

40 hard peppermint candies

4 foil-wrapped rolls (about 0.9 oz each)
    ring-shaped hard candies

1. For cars of each train, glue end of 1 ribbon onto wide side of 1 gum package, 1 candy box, 3 stacked mints and 1 more candy box, spacing cars about 1/2 inch apart. For wheels, glue 4 peppermint candies onto sides of gum package and 2 candies onto sides of candy boxes and stacked mints.

2. For engine, glue roll of ring-shaped candies onto top of gum package. Glue 2 foil-wrapped candies onto top of engine.

3. Glue additional candies onto tops of train cars as desired.

4. Repeat to make remaining 3 trains.

holiday inspiration

Choo-choo! Holiday Candy Trains can brighten as well as add fun to any buffet or table arrangement. In a pinch, clear tape can be used instead of glue.

STARRY ICE BEVERAGE COOLER

makes 1 beverage cooler

1/2-gallon paperboard milk carton

1-liter clear plastic soft drink bottle

Ice cubes

Lemon peel, cut into star shapes

Cranberries

Fresh herb sprigs, such as rosemary or thyme

Water

1. Open milk carton completely at top; wash inside. Wash plastic bottle inside and out; remove any labels. Place plastic bottle in center of milk carton. Fill milk carton with ice cubes.

2. Arrange lemon peel, cranberries and herbs among ice cubes toward sides of milk carton. Tape top of bottle to milk carton to keep it from floating. Fill milk carton with water (do not fill bottle).

3. Freeze about 24 hours or until firm. Peel off milk carton. To use, place beverage cooler in deep tray. Fill bottle with beverage, using a funnel.

holiday inspiration

- Want to be the star of the holiday party circuit? You can bet nobody else will have this beautiful, icy beverage cooler—and it's very easy to make! Fill the cooler with your favorite white wine or fruit punch recipe; then get set for the "How did you do that?" comments.

- Use a cloth napkin or towel to hold the beverage cooler when you pour to catch drips from the melting ice.

holiday inspiration

The possibilities for creating these cottages are endless. How about making miniature cottages? Use whole pecan halves or square-shaped cereal for the "shingles" instead of the bran cereal shreds. Once your cottages are made, complete the snowy outdoor scene by adding decorated trees! To make trees, use sugar-style ice-cream cones with pointed ends. Stir desired amount of green food color into remaining frosting on plate. Insert one or two fingers into cone to hold while frosting the outside. Decorate trees as desired using assorted decorating decors. Arrange trees around cottage.

Kids may want to use zany, brightly colored cereals and candies or even tint the frosting with food color before using it as the "glue" that sticks the decorations to the cottage. Let their creativity shine!

CHRISTMAS COTTAGE

makes 1 cottage

One 3 × 5–inch cottage

7 whole graham crackers

1 container (1 lb) creamy white frosting

1 cup sliced almonds

1 cup bran cereal shreds

1 chocolate graham cracker square

Royal Icing (page 114)

1 red jelly bean or other small red candy

16 yellow gumdrops

Assorted decorating candies and decors (such as red cinnamon candy, jelly beans, hard peppermint candies, holiday shot, nonpareils, miniature theme shapes such as stars, or colored sugars)

Miniature marshmallows, white popcorn, coconut, cotton candy or decorator sugar crystals

1. With serrated knife, use gentle sawing motion to cut a ∧ shape from one short end of a whole cracker to form peaked side of cottage (see illustration **a** below). Repeat with another whole cracker for the other end of the cottage; set aside.

2. Spread frosting onto a flat plate. Spread almonds and cereal onto separate flat plates.

3. Dip all edges of one whole cracker into frosting, then lay it flat on a piece of waxed paper; this will be the floor of the cottage. Dip edges and one flat side of the two ∧-shaped crackers into frosting; lightly press frosted side of each cracker into almonds to cover.

4. Attach ∧ shaped crackers, vertically, on each short end of the cottage floor with almonds facing outward, forming the peaks for the front and back of the cottage. Dip one flat side of two whole crackers into frosting; attach horizontally with frosting facing outward, on each long side of the cottage floor, forming the sides of the cottage (see illustration **b** below).

5. For roof, dip edges and one flat side of each remaining whole cracker into frosting; lightly press frosted side of each cracker into cereal to cover. Attach pieces, with cereal facing outward, to form roof; gently press into place (see illustration **c** below).

6. For door, separate chocolate graham cracker square in half at perforation; reserve one half for another use. Frost one side of the remaining chocolate graham cracker with frosting, attach by pressing lightly onto center of one almond-coated cracker. Attach jelly bean or red cinnamon candy with frosting to door for doorknob. Using Royal Icing, pipe two 4-paned windows on each side of cottage; attach one yellow gumdrop with frosting into center of each window pane to resemble lights. If desired, pipe Royal Icing along cottage roof lines to form icicles. Decorate cottage as desired using assorted decorating decors. Arrange cottage on decorative flat plate, platter or tabletop; sprinkle surface of plate with miniature marshmallows to look like snow. Let cottage stand uncovered 30 minutes for frosting to set.

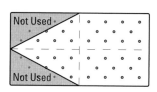

a. Form the peaked sides.

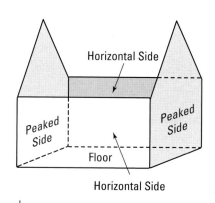

b. Form the front and back.

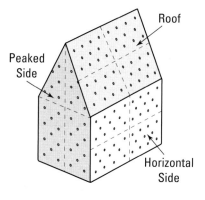

c. Form the roof.

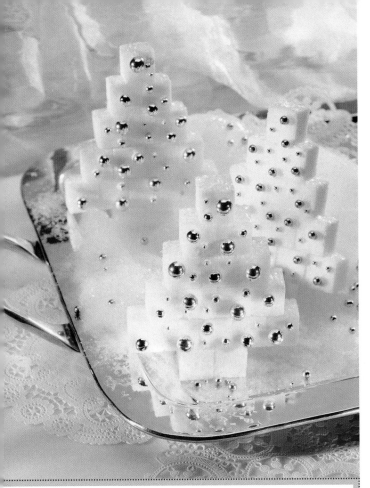

SUGAR-CUBE TREES

makes 7 sugar-cube trees

119 sugar cubes (about one 1-lb box)
Glue gun and glue sticks or vanilla creamy
  frosting (from 1-lb container)
Silver or colored dragées (nonedible; for
  decoration only)

1. Line cookie sheet with waxed paper. For each tree, attach 5 sugar cubes in a row, using glue or frosting, and make 1 row of 4 cubes, 1 row of 3 cubes and 1 row of 2 cubes. Attach rows in descending order, centering shorter rows on longer rows, in Christmas tree shape.

2. For tree trunk, attach 2 cubes below center of 5-cube row. For tree top, attach 1 cube onto center of 2-cube row. Let dry on cookie sheet.

3. Decorate trees by attaching dragées with glue or frosting. Arrange trees upright on table for centerpiece or place cards. Sugar-Cube Trees are not edible; for decoration only.

holiday inspiration

Here are a few ideas to make your Sugar-Cube Trees extra special:

- To make a snow-sparkling tree, brush assembled trees with just enough light corn syrup to cover and sprinkle with white decorator sugar crystals.

- Personalize trees by piping on decorating icing from a tube. Guests can take trees home as a Christmas party memento.

- Make a winter "wonderland-scape." Drape cotton batting over table; add trees at different heights. String miniature battery-powered lights around trees.

MINIATURE CANDY TOPIARY

makes 1 topiary

Scissors with pointed tips

1 ball shape (1 1/2 to 2 1/2 inches in diameter) green or white floral foam

1 package (125-count) round toothpicks

Assorted soft fruit snacks and candies (spearmint leaves, red and green nonpareil buttons, fruit shapes, gumdrops or gummies)

1 plain or striped candy cane stick, 5 to 7 1/2 inches long

1 large apple or orange

Decorative cup or small bowl

1. Using one point of scissors, carefully make a hole in bottom of foam ball about two-thirds of the way into the center of the ball so the candy cane stick can be inserted for the topiary trunk.

2. Break toothpicks in half as needed. Insert toothpicks in random order on ball to cover surface until they securely in place without covering hole for candy cane stick. Push each piece of candy onto toothpick half. Number of candies needed will depend on size of foam ball and type of candies being used. Insert candy cane stick into opening.

3. Cut about 1/4-inch slice from bottom of apple so it stands flat. Using one point of scissors, carefully make a hole in the top of the apple about two-thirds of the way into the center of the apple so the candy cane stick can be inserted for the topiary trunk.

4. Place candy cane stick into opening in apple; place on plate.

new twist

- A large orange or pear can be substituted for the apple for a different look.

- For a candy-filled ice-cream cone base, make the topiary top using a 1 1/2-inch-diameter foam ball so topiary won't be top-heavy. Carefully insert one end of a candy cane stick into an unwrapped chocolate-covered caramel; place in flat-bottomed ice-cream cone. Fill cone up to the top with various small hard candies to weight it down. Place on decorative plate.

GINGERBREAD VILLAGE

makes One 4-building village

1/2 cup packed brown sugar
1/4 cup shortening
3/4 cup full-flavor molasses
1/3 cup cold water
3 1/2 cups all-purpose flour
1 teaspoon baking soda
1 teaspoon ground ginger
1/2 teaspoon salt
1/2 teaspoon ground allspice
1/2 teaspoon ground cloves
1/2 teaspoon ground cinnamon
Assorted candies, nuts, cookies, crackers and cereal
Gingerbread Frosting (at right)
or
Royal Icing (page 114)

1. Heat oven to 350°F. Grease bottoms and sides of 9-inch square pan and 15 × 10 × 1–inch pan with shortening. In large bowl, mix brown sugar, shortening and molasses. Stir in cold water. Stir in remaining ingredients except candies and frosting.

2. Press one-third of dough into square pan. Press remaining dough into rectangular pan. Bake 1 pan at a time about 15 minutes or until no indentation remains when touched in center. Cool 5 minutes. Turn upside down onto large cutting surface. Immediately cut rectangle into fourths and then into buildings (see illustration **a** below). Cut square into braces as shown (see illustration **b** below). Cool completely.

3. Make Gingerbread Frosting or Royal Icing. Decorate fronts of buildings as desired, using frosting and assorted candies, nuts, cookies, crackers and cereal. Use frosting to attach braces to backs of buildings. Let stand 30 minutes or until frosting is completely set. Complete by decorating as desired.

holiday inspiration

Impress everyone by making your Gingerbread Village the centerpiece on your dining room table or buffet table, or make it the focal point of your fireplace mantle.

GINGERBREAD FROSTING

2 cups powdered sugar
1/3 cup shortening
2 tablespoons light corn syrup
5 to 6 teaspoons milk

In medium bowl, beat all ingredients with spoon until smooth and spreadable.

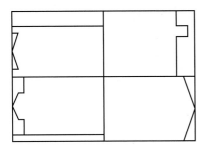

a. Cut jelly roll into fourths and then into buildings.

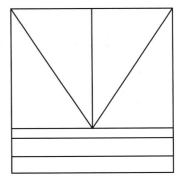

b. Cut square into braces.

GINGERBREAD COOKIE TREE

makes 1 decorative cookie tree

Three recipes of dough from:

Gingerbread Village (page 326)

9 cookie cutters, ranging from 1 3/4 inches to
   8 1/2 inches in diameter (increasing by 3/4 inch
   from one size to the next)

Gingerbread Frosting (page 326)

or

Royal Icing (page 114)

Colored glitter sugars

Silver or colored dragées (nonedible; for decoration
   only), if desired

Powdered sugar

1. Prepare dough, 1 recipe at a time. Cover; refrigerate about 2 hours or until firm.

2. Heat oven to 350°F. Lightly grease cookie sheet with shortening. Roll 1 recipe of dough at a time 1/4 inch thick on lightly floured cloth-covered surface. Cut 3 cookies each with the 3 largest sizes of floured cookie cutters to make 9 cookies. Cut 2 cookies each with the remaining sizes of floured cookie cutters to make 12 cookies. Place about 2 inches apart on cookie sheet. Bake large cookies 12 to 14 minutes, small cookies 10 to 12 minutes, or until no indentation remains when touched. Cool slightly; remove from cookie sheet to wire rack. Cool completely.

3. Make Gingerbread Frosting or Royal Icing. On serving plate, assemble tree by stacking unfrosted cookies, starting with largest cookies and stacking in descending sizes, attaching each with a small dab of frosting in center. Let tree stand about 30 minutes or until frosting is completely set, or hold cookies in place with bamboo skewers if necessary. Use remaining frosting to pipe "snow" on the tree, using decorating bag or resealable food-storage plastic bag with small tip of corner cut off to allow drizzling. Decorate with glitter sugar and dragées. Or, dust the points of the tree with powdered sugar. Tree is not edible; for decoration only.

new twist

How about a Miniature Cookie Tree to complete the landscape of your village? Make the Gingerbread Cookie Tree as directed, but use just the 5 smallest sizes of cookie cutters to cut out the cookies. Decorate as desired.

• For a magical touch, immediately after frosting the tree, sprinkle with decorator sugar crystals to make it glisten like snow. Place a single cookie made from the 2-inch cookie cutter at top of tree. Paint with gold luster dust mixed with a little lemon extract.

• If you want to make this an edible centerpiece, use candy decorations instead of the dragées and decorate the treetop star cookie with frosting instead of luster dust.

SANTA'S CANDY SLEIGHS

makes 4 sleighs

Glue gun and glue sticks

8 candy canes, 6 inches long

4 bars (13 oz each) chocolate-covered peanut, caramel and nougat candy

4 boxes (1.5 oz each) raisins

4 foil-covered peanut butter or chocolate Santas (1 oz each)

Assorted foil-wrapped candies and hard peppermint candies

1. For each sleigh, pipe glue along sides of 2 candy canes (in wrappers); attach to either side of candy bar to make sleigh runners.

2. Glue raisin box to top of candy bar. Glue Santa to front of raisin box and on top of candy bar so it resembles Santa in the sleigh. Glue additional assorted candies onto top of raisin box, if desired.

from the heart

OH WHAT FUN IT IS TO MAKE A SANTA'S CANDY SLEIGH! Personalize sleighs for gift giving by adding tiny gift boxes with a name written with a metallic pen.

STRING 'N EAT NECKLACES

prep 45 min *total time* 45 min *makes* 4 necklaces

4 pieces (about 36 inches each) red string licorice

1/3 cup Cheerios cereal

1 roll (1.5 oz) brightly colored ring-shaped gummy candy

1 package (1.25 oz) pastel-colored tube-shaped licorice candies

1/2 cup miniature marshmallows

1 tablespoon all-purpose flour

1. Onto each piece of string licorice, string an arrangement of the cereal, candies and marshmallows (to prevent stickiness, dip 1 end of the string licorice into flour before poking it through each marshmallow).

2. When each licorice string is 3/4 full, tie the ends of the licorice together into a double knot to make a necklace. If desired, wrap plastic wrap around each necklace to keep it clean.

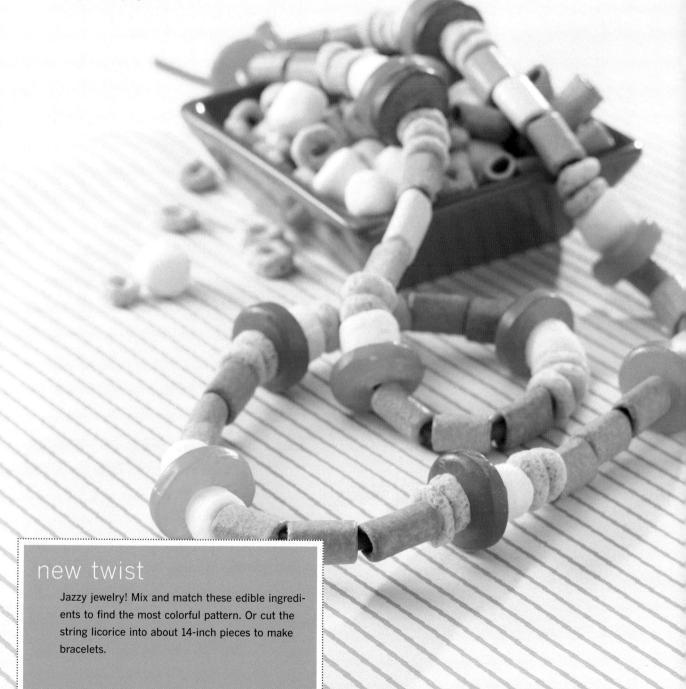

new twist

Jazzy jewelry! Mix and match these edible ingredients to find the most colorful pattern. Or cut the string licorice into about 14-inch pieces to make bracelets.

POINSETTIA CANDY ORNAMENTS

makes 4 ornaments

4 squares foil (8 inch)

20 red ring-shaped hard candies (from 6.5-oz bag)

8 green ring-shaped hard candies (from 6.5-oz bag)

2 plastic drinking straws, cut into 4-inch pieces

Gold dragees (nonedible; for decoration only) or yellow nonpareil candy decors

Toothpicks

4 pieces 1/8-inch-wide ribbon or monofilament line (fishing line), 6 to 8 inches long

1. Heat oven to 325°F; place 1 square of foil on cookie sheet. Because of the variables in how different colors of candies melt and the need to work quickly to complete the ornament after removing it from the oven, baking more than one ornament at a time is not recommended.

2. See illustration **a**. Unwrap only the red candies. On foil, arrange 5 red candies in circle, leaving an opening about 1/2 inch in diameter in the center. With wrappers on, cut 6 green candies in half and 1 green candy into quarters with scissors or knife; remove wrappers.* For leaves, arrange 3 green halves, rounded side out, on 3 sides of the red candies, making sure cut sides touch red candies. Place 1 green quarter of candy in center of red candies. Very carefully transfer cookie sheet to oven, baking only one ornament at a time. (Candies must be fresh in order to melt properly; if they aren't, they will not melt.)

3. Bake 3 to 6 minutes, watching closely for candy to melt (melting time will depend on the candy and how much you want the ornament to melt).** Remove from oven; immediately insert end of drinking straw 1/2 inch from top of ornament to create opening for hanging; sprinkle ornament lightly with candy decors. Rotate straw a quarter turn after 30 seconds and again after 1 minute; remove straw (this prevents the straw from sticking to the candy, which could cause the ornament to break when removed).

new twist

- Make Sun Catchers! Just hang the ornaments on a window with one of those suction cup type hangers available in hardware stores or in the hardware department of large discount stores.

- Make a sweet treat of Christmas Candy Lollipops. Insert paper candy or cookie stick into bottom of any shape of ornament immediately after removing it from the oven (omit straw). Cool completely before removing from foil.

Betty Crocker Christmas Cookbook

4. Working quickly, form flower petal points by drawing the tip of a toothpick through each candy to form a point. If the candy has cooled too much, return the cookie sheet to the oven and heat 1 to 2 minutes longer and try again. Allow ornament to cool completely on cookie sheet; gently remove foil. Thread ribbon through the hole made with the straw to hang the ornament (see illustration **b**).

*Cutting candies with the wrapper on prevents shattering.

**Due to the heat of melted candy, ornaments continue to melt slightly once out of the oven until the temperature of the candy drops. Also, smaller pieces and outside pieces melt more quickly.

SANTA ORNAMENTS To make 4 ornaments, you will need 4 red, 4 orange and 16 white ring-shaped hard candies. Use small round candies for the eyes and nose. On foil, arrange 3 white candies in a semicircle, then add 1 orange candy in center for face. Cut 1 white candy in half and arrange with curved sides out above orange candy. Arrange 1 red candy at top for hat. Continue as directed in Step 3—except omit candy decors and instead sprinkle coconut on ornament for "beard," pressing lightly with back of spoon. Add candies for eyes and nose, pressing lightly. Cool as directed in Step 4 (see illustration **c**).

TREE ORNAMENTS To make 4 ornaments, you will need 24 green and 4 rectangular hard peppermint candies. On foil, arrange green candies to make 1 row of 3 candies, 1 row of 2 candies and 1 row of 1 candy. Add 1 peppermint candy at center of bottom row for trunk. Continue as directed in Step 3—except omit candy decors and instead sprinkle tree with desired candy decorations. Cool as directed in Step 4 (see illustration **d**).

WREATH ORNAMENTS To make 4 ornaments, you will need 24 green and 8 red ring-shaped hard candies (cut in half). On foil, arrange 6 green candies in a circle, then add 4 red candy halves on either side of one green candy to create bow. Continue as directed in Step 3—except omit candy decors and instead sprinkle wreath with edible green glitter and desired candy decorations. Cool as directed in Step 4.

a. Form the Poinsettia ornament.

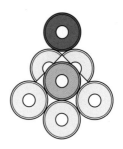

b. Form the Santa ornament.

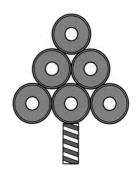

c. Form the Tree ornament.

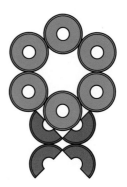

d. Form the Wreath ornament.

Clockwise from top: Beaded "Icicles" Wrap, Tinsel Star Topper, Beaded Initial

BEADED "ICICLES" WRAP

makes 1 icicle wrap

1 package faceted beads (6 millimeter, 480 pieces)
2 yards 28-gauge beading wire
Gift-wrapped package

1. Thread beads, a few at a time, onto wire. At every half-inch or inch of wire, grasp one bead, fold the wire in half, then twist the wire to create a hanging icicle with a bead at the end. Repeat until all wire is used, making icicles of varying lengths.

2. Wrap beaded wire around package. Twist ends together to secure.

BEADED INITIAL You will need 1 yard of 24-gauge beading wire, 1 package (3 oz) rochaille beads and wired cording. Crimp one end of wire with needle-nose pliers. Thread beads onto wire until filled. Crimp opposite end of wire to secure beads. Shape beaded wire into desired initial. Wrap wired cording around package; add initial and twist to secure.

TINSEL STAR TOPPER You will need 3 red velvet or tinsel stems (from a package of 12 stems); stems will be stocked with the chenille stems (pipe cleaners). Bend one stem into 11 equal parts; shape into star. Using 11th bend, twist to secure and create loop. Wrap second stem around star to create shooting star effect with two tails. Wrap third stem around base of star, twist and wrap around package.

FLOWER BUD Glue artificial flower bud to top of wrapped package, using hot-glue gun with glue sticks.

from the heart

WE ALL KNOW SOMEONE WHO WRAPS THE MOST BEAUTIFUL PACKAGES—so beautiful you don't want to open them! Why not give them a gift of these out-of-the-ordinary gift wrap adornments?

P B AND J BIRD FEEDER TREAT

makes 1 bird feeder treat

4 unsalted rice cakes, about 3 inches in diameter
About 1/4 cup peanut butter
Birdseed
About 3 tablespoons jelly or peanut butter
1 length of twine or yarn, 2 feet long
Dried cranberries (from 6-oz package) or orange slice
1 length of floral wire, 1 foot long
Ribbon, 6 to 12 inches long, if desired

1. Poke a hole in the middle of each rice cake, using a skewer. Spread peanut butter over 2 rice cakes. Top with other 2 rice cakes to make 2 sandwiches.

2. Spread birdseed on cookie sheet. Spread jelly on edges of each sandwich; roll in birdseed until edges are completely covered.

3. Tie a double knot about 6 inches from one end of twine. Thread sandwich, through center hole, on other end of twine. Tie another double knot in twine about 6 inches from sandwich. Thread on second sandwich. Tie a loop in top end of twine to allow bird feeder to hang.

4. Thread cranberries on floral wire, leaving 1 inch of bare wire on each end. Twist ends together to form a circle; form into a heart shape. Tie cranberry heart or orange slice to bottom end of twine. Tie ribbon around twine into bow.

new twist

Trim a tree in your yard with edible decorations to help the birds celebrate the season:

- Spread peanut butter on pinecones, roll in birdseed and nestle in branches.

- Slice oranges, and hang from branches with brightly colored waterproof ribbon.

- Thread popcorn and cranberries onto string to hang from branches.

helpful nutrition and cooking information

nutrition guidelines

We provide nutrition information for each recipe that includes calories, fat, cholesterol, sodium, carbohydrate, fiber and protein. Individual food choices can be based on this information.

RECOMMENDED INTAKE FOR A DAILY DIET OF 2,000 CALORIES AS SET BY THE FOOD AND DRUG ADMINISTRATION

Total Fat	Less than 65g
Saturated Fat	Less than 20g
Cholesterol	Less than 300mg
Sodium	Less than 2,400mg
Total Carbohydrate	300g
Dietary Fiber	25g

CRITERIA USED FOR CALCULATING NUTRITION INFORMATION

- The first ingredient was used wherever a choice is given (such as 1/3 cup sour cream or plain yogurt).

- The first ingredient amount was used wherever a range is given (such as 3- to 3 1/2–pound cut-up broiler-fryer chicken).

- The first serving number was used wherever a range is given (such as 4 to 6 servings).

- "If desired" ingredients and recipe variations were not included (such as sprinkle with brown sugar, if desired).

- Only the amount of a marinade or frying oil that is estimated to be absorbed by the food during preparation or cooking was calculated.

INGREDIENTS USED IN RECIPE TESTING AND NUTRITION CALCULATIONS

- Ingredients used for testing represent those that the majority of consumers use in their homes: large eggs, 2% milk, 80%-lean ground beef, canned ready-to-use chicken broth and vegetable oil spread containing not less than 65 percent fat.

- Fat-free, low-fat or low-sodium products were not used, unless otherwise indicated.

- Solid vegetable shortening (not butter, margarine, nonstick cooking sprays or vegetable oil spread as they can cause sticking problems) was used to grease pans, unless otherwise indicated.

EQUIPMENT USED IN RECIPE TESTING

We use equipment for testing that the majority of consumers use in their homes. If a specific piece of equipment (such as a wire whisk) is necessary for recipe success, it is listed in the recipe.

- Cookware and bakeware without nonstick coatings were used, unless otherwise indicated.

- No dark-colored, black or insulated bakeware was used.

- When a pan is specified in a recipe, a metal pan was used; a baking dish or pie plate means ovenproof glass was used.

- An electric hand mixer was used for mixing only when mixer speeds are specified in the recipe directions. When a mixer speed is not given, a spoon or fork was used.

BettyCrocker.com

cooking terms glossary

BEAT Mix ingredients vigorously with spoon, fork, wire whisk, hand beater or electric mixer until smooth and uniform.

BOIL Heat liquid until bubbles rise continuously and break on the surface and steam is given off. For rolling boil, the bubbles form rapidly.

CHOP Cut into coarse or fine irregular pieces with a knife, food chopper, blender or food processor.

CUBE Cut into squares 1/2 inch or larger.

DICE Cut into squares smaller than 1/2 inch.

GRATE Cut into tiny particles using small rough holes of grater (citrus peel or chocolate).

GREASE Rub the inside surface of a pan with shortening, using pastry brush, piece of waxed paper or paper towel, to prevent food from sticking during baking (as for some casseroles).

JULIENNE Cut into thin, matchlike strips, using knife or food processor (vegetables, fruits, meats).

MIX Combine ingredients in any way that distributes them evenly.

SAUTÉ Cook foods in hot oil or margarine over medium-high heat with frequent tossing and turning motion.

SHRED Cut into long thin pieces by rubbing food across the holes of a shredder, as for cheese, or by using a knife to slice very thinly, as for cabbage.

SIMMER Cook in liquid just below the boiling point on top of the stove; usually after reducing heat from a boil. Bubbles will rise slowly and break just below the surface.

STIR Mix ingredients until uniform consistency. Stir once in a while for stirring occasionally, often for stirring frequently and continuously for stirring constantly.

TOSS Tumble ingredients (such as green salad) lightly with a lifting motion, usually to coat evenly or mix with another food.

metric conversion guide

VOLUME

U.S. Units	Canadian Metric	Australian Metric
1/4 teaspoon	1 mL	1 ml
1/2 teaspoon	2 mL	2 ml
1 teaspoon	5 mL	5 ml
1 tablespoon	15 mL	20 ml
1/4 cup	50 mL	60 ml
1/3 cup	75 mL	80 ml
1/2 cup	125 mL	125 ml
2/3 cup	150 mL	170 ml
3/4 cup	175 mL	190 ml
1 cup	250 mL	250 ml
1 quart	1 liter	1 liter
1 1/2 quarts	1.5 liters	1.5 liters
2 quarts	2 liters	2 liters
2 1/2 quarts	2.5 liters	2.5 liters
3 quarts	3 liters	3 liters
4 quarts	4 liters	4 liters

WEIGHT

U.S. Units	Canadian Metric	Australian Metric
1 ounce	30 grams	30 grams
2 ounces	55 grams	60 grams
3 ounces	85 grams	90 grams
4 ounces (1/4 pound)	115 grams	125 grams
8 ounces (1/2 pound)	225 grams	225 grams
16 ounces (1 pound)	455 grams	500 grams
1 pound	455 grams	1/2 kilogram

MEASUREMENTS

Inches	Centimeters
1	2.5
2	5.0
3	7.5
4	10.0
5	12.5
6	15.0
7	17.5
8	20.5
9	23.0
10	25.5
11	28.0
12	30.5
13	33.0

TEMPERATURES

Fahrenheit	Celsius
32°	0°
212°	100°
250°	120°
275°	140°
300°	150°
325°	160°
350°	180°
375°	190°
400°	200°
425°	220°
450°	230°
475°	240°
500°	260°

Note: The recipes in this cookbook have not been developed or tested using metric measures. When converting recipes to metric, some variations in quality may be noted.

index

Note: *italicized* page references indicate photographs and illustrations

A

B

continues

continues

BettyCrocker.com

continues

BettyCrocker.com

Complete your cookbook library
with these Betty Crocker titles

Betty Crocker Baking for Today

Betty Crocker Basics

Betty Crocker's Best Bread Machine Cookbook

Betty Crocker's Best Chicken Cookbook

Betty Crocker's Best Christmas Cookbook

Betty Crocker's Best of Baking

Betty Crocker's Best of Healthy and
Hearty Cooking

Betty Crocker's Best-Loved Recipes

Betty Crocker's Bisquick® Cookbook

Betty Crocker Bisquick II Cookbook

Betty Crocker Bisquick Impossibly Easy Pies

Betty Crocker Celebrate!

Betty Crocker's Complete Thanksgiving Cookbook

Betty Crocker's Cook Book for Boys and Girls

Betty Crocker's Cook It Quick

Betty Crocker Cookbook, 10th Edition—
The **BIG RED** *Cookbook*®

Betty Crocker's Cookbook, Bridal Edition

Betty Crocker's Cookie Book

Betty Crocker's Cooking Basics

Betty Crocker's Cooking for Two

Betty Crocker's Cooky Book, Facsimile Edition

Betty Crocker Decorating Cakes and Cupcakes

Betty Crocker's Diabetes Cookbook

Betty Crocker Dinner Made Easy with
Rotisserie Chicken

Betty Crocker Easy Everyday Vegetarian

Betty Crocker Easy Family Dinners

Betty Crocker's Easy Slow Cooker Dinners

Betty Crocker's Eat and Lose Weight

Betty Crocker's Entertaining Basics

Betty Crocker's Flavors of Home

Betty Crocker 4-Ingredient Dinners

Betty Crocker Grilling Made Easy

Betty Crocker Healthy Heart Cookbook

Betty Crocker's Healthy New Choices

Betty Crocker's Indian Home Cooking

Betty Crocker's Italian Cooking

Betty Crocker's Kids Cook!

Betty Crocker's Kitchen Library

Betty Crocker's Living with Cancer Cookbook

Betty Crocker Low-Carb Lifestyle Cookbook

Betty Crocker's Low-Fat, Low-Cholesterol
Cooking Today

Betty Crocker More Slow Cooker Recipes

Betty Crocker's New Cake Decorating

Betty Crocker's New Chinese Cookbook

Betty Crocker One-Dish Meals

Betty Crocker's A Passion for Pasta

Betty Crocker's Picture Cook Book,
Facsimile Edition

Betty Crocker's Quick & Easy Cookbook

Betty Crocker's Slow Cooker Cookbook

Betty Crocker's Ultimate Cake Mix Cookbook

Betty Crocker's Vegetarian

Betty Crocker Why It Works

Betty Crocker Win at Weight Loss Cookbook

Cocina Betty Crocker

BettyCrocker.com